SCHOLASTIC

100
2014 CURRICULUM
COMPUTING LESSONS

WITHDRAWN

2 0 JUN 2023

Recommended system requirements:

- Windows: XP (Service Pack 3), Vista (Service Pack 2), Windows 7 or Windows 8 with 2.33GHz processor
- Mac: OS 10.6 to 10.8 with Intel Core™ Duo processor
- 1GB RAM (recommended)
- 1024 x 768 Screen resolution
- CD-ROM drive (24x speed recommended)
- 16-bit sound card
- Adobe Reader (version 9 recommended for Mac users)
- Broadband internet connections (for installation and updates)

For all technical support queries, please phone Scholastic Customer Services on 0845 6039091.

SCHOLASTIC

Book End, Range Road, Witney, Oxfordshire, OX29 0YD
www.scholastic.co.uk

© 2014, Scholastic Ltd

1 2 3 4 5 6 7 8 9   4 5 6 7 8 9 0 1 2 3

British Library Cataloguing-in-Publication Data
A catalogue record for this book is available from the
British Library.

ISBN 978-1407-12858-0
Printed by Bell & Bain Ltd, Glasgow

Due to the nature of the web we cannot guarantee
the content or links of any site mentioned. We strongly
recommend that teachers check websites before using
them in the classroom.

Extracts from *The National Curriculum in England,
Computing Programme of Study* © Crown Copyright.
Reproduced under the terms of the Open Government
Licence (OGL). http://www.nationalarchives.gov.uk/doc/
open-government-licence/open-government-licence.htm

Authors
Zoe Ross and Steve Bunce

Editorial team
Mark Walker, Jenny Wilcox, Kim Vernon, Lucy Tritton,
Sarah Sodhi, Suzanne Adams

Cover Design
Andrea Lewis

Design
Sarah Garbett @ Sg Creative Services

CD-ROM development
Hannah Barnett, Phil Crothers, MWA Technologies
Private Ltd

Illustrations
Tomek.gr

Acknowledgements
The publishers gratefully acknowledge permission
to reproduce the following copyright material:

The Lifelong Kindergarten Group For the use of
screenshots from the 'Scratch' program. Scratch
is developed by the Lifelong Kindergarten Group at
the MIT Media Lab. See http://scratch.mit.edu

Carnegie Mellon University for the use of
screenshots from the 'Alice' program.

Every effort has been made to trace copyright
holders for the works reproduced in this book,
and the publishers apologise for any inadvertent
omissions.

Contents

Introduction

About the series

The *100 Computing Lessons* series is designed to meet the requirements of the 2014 Curriculum, Computing Programmes of Study. There are three books in the series, Years 1–2, 3–4 and 5–6, and each book contains lesson plans, resources and ideas matched to the new curriculum. It can be a complex task to ensure that a progressive and appropriate curriculum is followed in all year groups; this series has been carefully structured to ensure that a progressive and appropriate curriculum is followed throughout.

About the new curriculum

Computing is a subject full of opportunities for children to develop their thinking, with practical programming skills, focused on real world examples. The new 'Computing' curriculum replaces the old 'ICT' curriculum.

The National Curriculum for Computing aims to ensure that all pupils:

- *can understand and apply the fundamental principles and concepts of computer science, including abstraction, logic, algorithms and data representation*
- *can analyse problems in computational terms, and have repeated practical experience of writing computer programs in order to solve such problems*
- *can evaluate and apply information technology, including new or unfamiliar technologies, analytically to solve problems*
- *are responsible, competent, confident and creative users of information and communication technology.*

The National Curriculum Programme of Study for Computing contains guidance for Key Stages 1 and 2. The subject focuses on computational thinking with an emphasis on programming. In addition, there are other areas of computing which have equal importance. In this series, the National Curriculum has been divided into four key subject areas:

- Algorithms and programming
- Data and information
- How computers work
- Communication and e-safety

The 'Algorithms and programming' parts of the Programme of Study have been combined into one block, as they are closely related and there is a progression over the key stages. Each year there are two 'Algorithms and programming' blocks and one each for 'Data and information', 'How computers work', 'Communication' and 'E-safety'.

Terminology

In this guide, the main terms used are:

Subject areas: the area of the subject, for computing, we will use 'Algorithms and programming', 'Data and information', 'How computers work' and 'Communication and e-safety'.

Objectives: by the end of Key Stage 1 and Key Stage 2, children are expected to know, apply and understand the matters, skills and processes detailed in the relevant programme of study.

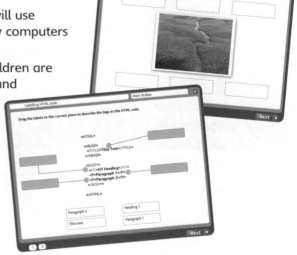

■ SCHOLASTIC

About the book

This book is divided into twelve chapters; six for each year group. Each chapter contains a half-term's work and is based around a topic or theme. Each chapter follows the same structure:

Chapter introduction

At the start of each chapter there is a summary of what is covered. This includes:

- **Introduction:** A description of what is covered in the chapter.
- **Expected prior learning:** What the children are expected to know before starting the work in the chapter.
- **Chapter at a glance:** This is a table that summarises the content of each lesson, including: the curriculum objectives, lesson objectives, a summary of the activities and the outcome.
- **Overview of progression:** A brief explanation of how the children progress through the chapter.
- **Creative context:** How the chapter could link to other curriculum areas.
- **Background knowledge:** A section explaining grammatical terms and suchlike to enhance your subject knowledge, where required.

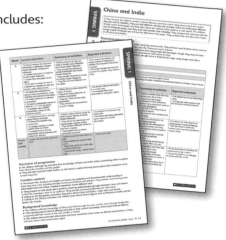

Lessons

Each chapter contains six weeks' of lessons. At the start of each week there is an introduction about what is covered. The lesson plans then include the relevant combination of headings from below.

- **Curriculum objectives:** The relevant objectives from the Programme of Study.
- **Lesson objectives:** Objectives that are based upon the Curriculum objectives, but are more specific broken-down steps to achieve them.
- **Expected outcomes:** What you should expect all, most and some children to know by the end of the lesson.
- **Resources:** What you require to teach the lesson.
- **Introduction:** A short and engaging activity to begin the lesson.
- **Whole-class work:** Working together as a class.
- **Group/Paired/Independent work:** Children working independently of the teacher in pairs, groups or alone.
- **Differentiation:** Ideas for how to support children who are struggling with a concept or how to extend those children who understand a concept without taking them onto new work.
- **Review:** A chance to review the children's learning and ensure the outcomes of the lesson have been achieved.

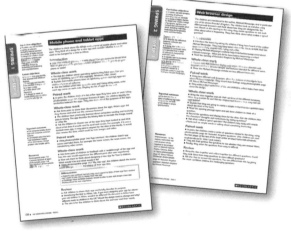

Assess and review

At the end of each chapter are activities for assessing and reviewing the children's understanding. These can be conducted during the course of the chapter's work or saved until the end of the chapter or done at a later date. They are set out the same as lesson plans with an underlying assessment focus.

Photocopiable pages

At the end of each chapter are some photocopiable pages that will have been referred to in the lesson plans. These sheets are for the children to use. There is generally a title, an instruction, an activity and an 'I can' statement at the bottom. The children should be encouraged to complete the 'I can' statements by colouring in the traffic lights to say how they think they have done (red – not very well, amber – ok, green – very well).

These sheets are also provided on the CD-ROM alongside additional pages as referenced in the lessons (see page 7 About the CD-ROM).

Tablet appendix

At the end of the book are 16 additional lessons which have been written with a specific focus on tablet computers and other touch-screen devices.

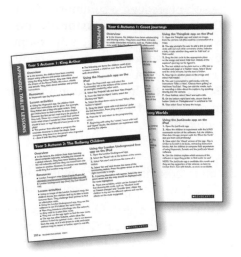

■SCHOLASTIC

About the CD-ROM

The CD-ROM contains:

- Printable versions of the photocopiable sheets from the book and additional photocopiable sheets as referenced in the lesson plans.
- Interactive activities for children to complete or to use on the whiteboard.
- Media resources to display.
- Printable versions of the lesson plans.
- Digital versions of the lesson plans with the relevant resources linked to them.

Getting started

- Put the CD-ROM into your CD-ROM drive.
  - For Windows users, the install wizard should autorun, if it fails to do so then navigate to your CD-ROM drive. Then follow the installation process.
  - For Mac users, copy the disk image file to your hard drive. After it has finished copying double-click it to mount the disk image. Navigate to the mounted disk image and run the installer. After installation the disk image can be unmounted and the DMG can be deleted from the hard drive.
- To complete the installation of the program you need to open the program and click 'Update' in the pop-up. Please note – this CD-ROM is web-enabled and the content will be downloaded from the internet to your hard-drive to populate the CD-ROM with the relevant resources. This only needs to be done on first use, after this you will be able to use the CD-ROM without an internet connection. If at any point any content is updated you will receive another pop-up upon start up with an internet connection.

Navigating the CD-ROM

There are two options to navigate the CD-ROM either as a Child or as a Teacher.

Child

- Click on the 'Child' button on the first menu screen.
- In the second menu click on the relevant class (please note only the books installed on the machine or network will be accessible. You can also rename year groups to match your school's naming conventions via the Teacher > Settings > Rename books area).
- A list of interactive activities will be displayed, children need to locate the correct one and click 'Go' to launch it.
- There is the opportunity to print or save a PDF of the activity at the end.

Teacher

- Click on the Teacher button on the first menu screen and you will be taken to a screen showing which of the *100 Computing* books you have purchased. From here, you can also access information about getting started and the credits.
- To enter the product click 'Next' in the bottom right.
- You then need to enter a password (the password is: login).
  - On first use: Enter as a Guest by clicking on the 'Guest' button.
  - If desired, create a profile for yourself by adding your name to the list of users. Profiles allow you to save favourites and to specify which year group(s) you wish to be able to view.
  - Go to 'Settings' to create a profile for yourself – click 'Add user' and enter your name. Then choose the year groups you wish to have access to (you can return to this screen to change this at any time). Click on 'Login' at the top of the screen to re-enter the disk under your new profile.
- On subsequent uses you can choose your name from the drop-down list. The 'Guest' option will always be available if you, or a colleague, wish to use this.
- You can search the CD-ROM using the tools or save favourites.

For more information about how to use the CD-ROM, please refer to the help file which can be found in the teacher area of the CD-ROM. It is a red button with a question mark on it on the right-hand side of the screen just underneath the 'Settings' tab.

King Arthur

This chapter uses a King Arthur theme to deepen and extend the children's knowledge and understanding of algorithms, programming and computational thinking as they begin by problem solving and codebreaking. They then create algorithms for drawing geometrical shapes before coding these into Scratch and developing their understanding further by creating patterns and a simple shapes-based quiz.

Expected prior learning

● The children have already been introduced to algorithms, programming, logical thinking and problem solving in earlier years. They have also previously used Scratch and will be developing their ability to apply their knowledge, skills and understanding to different situations, puzzles and languages in this chapter. They will need some understanding of the story of King Arthur to get the most out of the activities.

Chapter at a glance

Subject area
• Algorithms and programming

National Curriculum objective
• To design, write and debug programs that accomplish specific goals, including controlling or simulating physical systems; solve problems by decomposing them into smaller parts. To use sequence and repetition in programs; work with variables and various forms of input and output. To use logical reasoning to explain how some simple algorithms work and to detect and correct errors in algorithms and programs.

Week	Lesson objectives	Summary of activities	Expected outcomes
1	• To develop problem solving skills by solving different puzzles. • To decompose larger problems into smaller ones. • To use logical reasoning to recognise and extend image and number patterns.	• Children understand that there are different ways to solve number and logic puzzles. • They solve number and logic puzzles.	• Can use logical reasoning to solve a variety of puzzles. • Can recognise and extend patterns.
2	• To use logical reasoning to solve code problems. • To be able to use decomposition to break larger code problems into smaller ones. • To understand techniques that can be used to design and break codes. • To create own codes for others to solve.	• Children understand that there are different types of code. • They break codes and write coded replies.	• Can use logical reasoning and decomposition to break codes. • Can develop own codebreaking activities for peers.
3	• To decompose the task of drawing a shape into sub-tasks. • To write algorithms for drawing simple shapes. • To use loops (repetition) to design efficient algorithms. • To test and debug their algorithms as necessary. • To explain how they have used loops to make their algorithm efficient.	• Children write algorithms to draw different geometrical shapes. • They recognise and understand patterns in the algorithms.	• Can create algorithms to draw simple shapes. • Can use sequences of loops (repetition) to create efficient algorithms.
4	• To use a program to implement their designed algorithms. • To work collaboratively to debug their algorithms as necessary. • To explain how the program is executing their algorithm and using loops efficiently.	• Children write programs in Scratch to execute their shape algorithms. • They create shape patterns in Scratch.	• Can write a program to execute their algorithm to draw simple shapes. • Can explain how their program is using loops.

■SCHOLASTIC

Week	Lesson objectives	Summary of activities	Expected outcomes
5	• To know that comments can be added to a program. • To annotate a program with simple comments. • To work collaboratively to ensure comments are clear and unambiguous. • To be able to explain why comments are useful when writing programs.	• Children plan and create a simple shapes quiz. • They use input, output and broadcasts. • They use effective comments to explain their code.	• Can understand why comments are used in computer programs. • Can annotate a program with simple comments.
6	• To understand how and why conditions and two-way selection are used in algorithms and programs. • To design, write and test a program that uses conditions and two-way selection. • To debug their program as necessary. • To annotate their program with simple comments. • To explain how their program uses conditions and two-way selection.	• Children understand two-way selection and conditions. • They add two-way selection to the shapes quiz and use comments to explain the code. • They complete, test and debug the shapes quiz.	• Can understand the use of conditions and two-way selection when writing simple algorithms and programs. • Can use conditions and two-way selection in algorithms and programs.
Assess and review	• Assess and review the half term's work.	• Understanding what a portfolio is and deciding what should go into their portfolio. • Creating an effective portfolio of the work they have completed in this chapter, including images and helpful explanation text.	• Assess and review.

Overview of progression

• In this chapter, the children build upon their prior knowledge and understanding of algorithms and programming using Scratch. They begin by using problem solving, logical thinking and decomposition skills to solve puzzles and problems before writing algorithms to create different geometrical shapes. They then implement their algorithms using Scratch, making use of repetition, inputs and outputs, two-way selection and conditions and comments. Finally, they are asked to present their work in a portfolio.

Creative context

• These lessons have strong links to the mathematics curriculum as children use logical thinking and problem-solving techniques in the first two lessons. Subsequent lessons are based on geometry, further developing the children's understanding of shape and angle. The lessons should also draw upon the children's learning in English as they are required to plan their work, write comments on their programs and create a portfolio of their work as an assessment task.

Background knowledge

• From the work they have already completed, the children will know about problem solving, logical thinking and planning and writing programs in Scratch.
• From assessing the children's understanding in previous units, you will need to assess the children's capability in writing algorithms and translating these into programming code within Scratch and provide additional support as necessary.
• It is important that you are a relatively able user of Scratch for this chapter. There are many tutorials on the Scratch website, which introduce the programming language. By working through some of the tutorials, prior to the lesson, you should feel comfortable with Scratch. Encourage the children to share their learning, which will increase the body of knowledge within the class.
• The lessons in this chapter assume the use of Scratch 1.4, although other versions, including the online version, could be used.

Curriculum objectives
● To design, write and debug programs that accomplish specific goals, including controlling or simulating physical systems; solve problems by decomposing them into smaller parts. To use sequence and repetition in programs; work with variables and various forms of input and output. To use logical reasoning to explain how some simple algorithms work and to detect and correct errors in algorithms and programs.

Lesson objectives
● To develop problem solving skills by solving different puzzles.
● To decompose larger problems into smaller ones.
● To use logical reasoning to recognise and extend image and number patterns.

Expected outcomes
● Can use logical reasoning to solve a variety of puzzles.
● Can recognise and extend patterns.

Resources
Photocopiable page 17 'King Arthur number puzzles'; photocopiable page 18 'King Arthur logic puzzles'; rough paper if required for logic puzzles

Puzzle solving

In this lesson, the children use their problem-solving, logical reasoning, decomposition and pattern-recognition skills to solve a variety of different puzzles relating to the King Arthur theme. Such skills, together with tenacity and creativity, are important when developing computational thinking.

Introduction
● Display the first puzzle from photocopiable page 17 'King Arthur number puzzles' on the whiteboard as children arrive in the classroom.
● Can they solve it?

Whole-class work
● Explain that in this lesson they will be acting as King Arthur and his knights and will develop their problem-solving, decomposition, logical thinking and pattern-recognition skills.
● Explain that these skills all help with computational thinking, or understanding how we can program computers. Explain that you are going to start with number puzzles.
● Give out the photocopiable page 17 'King Arthur number puzzles'. If you wish, you could go through the next puzzle as a class, asking the children to share their solution and discuss how they went about solving it.

Paired/group work
● The children work through the photocopiable sheet in pairs or small groups.
● The patterns shown are: 1a) add 7 each time; 1b) add 8, 9, 10, and so on; 1c) add the previous two numbers together; 1d) multiply by the previous number; 1e) minus 0, 1, 2, and so on; 2a) add 2, 4, 6, and so on; 2b) add the previous two numbers together 2c) going backwards minus 5, 4, 3, and so on; 2d) minus 1, 2, 3, and so on.

Whole-class work
● As a class go through the solutions to the number puzzles.
● The children should self- or peer-assess their work.
● Asking children to share, not only their solutions, but also how they solved the problems, can be helpful to others and helpful to you in assessing their understanding and addressing any misunderstandings.
● Give out photocopiable page 18 'King Arthur logic puzzles' and explain the requirements of the task.
● Encourage them to use the table provided and to work through each statement carefully. Ensure that they have rough paper to work on if needed too.

Paired/group work
● The children work through the photocopiable sheet in pairs or small groups.

Differentiation
● Support: Less confident learners may benefit from mixed-ability pairings and may need adult support in the number and logic puzzle tasks. Encourage them to take a systematic approach and work through puzzles step by step if they feel overwhelmed.
● Challenge: More confident learners will be able to work through the puzzles with ease. Encourage them to think of their own puzzles to share with their peers.

Review
● Encourage the children to share their answers to the logic puzzles and discuss how they found the answers. Ask: *How did using a table help you? Did anybody use any other methods to help you solve the puzzle?*
● Ask the children to consider how the skills they have developed while working on the tasks could help them when working with computers. This is a challenging question and you may need scaffolding questions such as: *When do you think you use problem solving when you are working with computers?*

Curriculum objectives
● To design, write and debug programs that accomplish specific goals, including controlling or simulating physical systems; solve problems by decomposing them into smaller parts. To use sequence and repetition in programs; work with variables and various forms of input and output. To use logical reasoning to explain how some simple algorithms work and to detect and correct errors in algorithms and programs.

Lesson objectives
● To use logical reasoning to solve code problems.
● To be able to use decomposition to break larger code problems into smaller ones.
● To understand techniques that can be used to design and break codes.
● To create own codes for others to solve.

Expected outcomes
● Can use logical reasoning and decomposition to break codes.
● Can develop own codebreaking activities for peers.

Resources
Media resource 'Your mission' on the CD-ROM; photocopiable page 19 'Code Cracking (1)'; photocopiable page 20 'Code Cracking (2)'; photocopiable page 21 'My codes'; photocopiable page 'Answers to code cracking' from the CD-ROM

Codebreaking

In this lesson, the children undertake a number of code breaking activities in order to develop their computational thinking skills further. They act as King Arthur's Knights of the Round Table and endeavour to break codes being sent to them by the captured King Arthur. In doing so, they work collaboratively to think creatively and logically, recognise patterns and crack the codes.

Introduction
● Remind the children that in the last lesson they solved a number of different problems using their computational thinking skills. Recap these skills.
● Explain that in this lesson they are going to be developing these skills further and that they will be working on a very important mission!
● Display the media resource 'Your mission' on the whiteboard.
● Can they crack the code to get the message that King Arthur has sent?

Whole-class work
● Once they have solved the first code, explain that in this lesson they will be unscrambling coded messages and designing their own coded message.
● Ask the children to share their knowledge of the different types of codes there are (for example, these could be images, numbers, letters).
● Give out photocopiable pages 19 and 20 'Code cracking (1)' and 'Code cracking (2)' and explain to the children that their task is to crack the codes and help the knights to rescue King Arthur.
● You may wish to crack one code as a class, discussing how the code can be cracked. Alternatively, you can give the two different codes to different groups.

Paired work
● The children should work through the photocopiable sheets, working collaboratively with other pairs should they get stuck.
● Use your professional judgement to determine if the children need hints to help them get started.

Whole-class work
● Go through the codes they have solved and ask the children to share how they went about cracking the codes. Use the photocopiable page 'Answers to code cracking' from the CD-ROM to check answers.
● Give out photocopiable page 21 'My codes' and show the second screen of the media resource 'Your mission', which explains that they must come up with their own codes to communicate with King Arthur and the other knights.
● Discuss as a class what constitutes a 'good' code (not too hard to crack, but not too easy to break, perhaps including images, numbers and so on).

Paired work
● Give out the photocopiable page 21 'My codes' to each child and ask them to come up with their own code. They write a coded message to their partner in the space given and fold the paper in half so only the message is shown, before swapping messages with their partner who tries to decipher their code.

Differentiation
● Support: Less confident learners may benefit from mixed-ability pairings or further adult support in understanding their codes and creating their own. They should be encouraged to focus on simple codes that are similar to the examples given.
● Challenge: More confident learners will be able to create and break more complex codes. You could pair more confident learners together to facilitate this.

Review
● As a class, discuss how they created and cracked each other's codes.
● Ask the children, in pairs, to come up with three top tips for cracking codes and three top tips for creating codes, and share some of these with the class.

Curriculum objectives

● To design, write and debug programs that accomplish specific goals, including controlling or simulating physical systems; solve problems by decomposing them into smaller parts. To use sequence and repetition in programs; work with variables and various forms of input and output. To use logical reasoning to explain how some simple algorithms work and to detect and correct errors in algorithms and programs.

Lesson objectives

● To decompose the task of drawing a shape into sub-tasks.
● To write algorithms for drawing simple shapes.
● To use loops (repetition) to design efficient algorithms.
● To test and debug their algorithms as necessary.
● To explain how they have used loops to make their algorithm efficient.

Expected outcomes

● Can create algorithms to draw simple shapes.
● Can use sequences of loops (repetition) to create efficient algorithms.

Resources

Media resource 'Shapes' on the CD-ROM; photocopiable page 22 'Shape algorithms'

Shape algorithms

In this lesson, the children are challenged to apply the logical thinking and problem-solving skills they have been developing in previous lessons as they are tasked with writing, testing and debugging algorithms to create different shapes, using iteration where appropriate to make their algorithms efficient.

Introduction

● Remind the children that they have been developing their computational thinking skills and that they will be using these skills to write algorithms to draw different shapes in today's lesson.
● Display media resource 'Shapes' on the CD-ROM on the whiteboard and ask the children to name the shapes.

Whole-class work

● Using the media resource that shows the steps for drawing the shapes on each subsequent page, discuss as a class the algorithm for drawing the first shape (or if needed for clarification of the task, the second shape).
● You can use volunteers to help you do this. Ensure that you highlight the need for 'pen down'.
● Explain to the children that they can use shorthand to do this (for example, F10 = forward 10, TR90 = turn right 90 degrees).
● Give out the photocopiable page 22 'Shape algorithms' and go through the shapes with the children, helping them by highlighting the angles that are shown.
● Ask questions to see whether the children can spot that each shape requires a 360 degree turn in total and discuss this with them. Highlight to them how they can work out how many degrees to turn by looking at the number of turns needed (for example, four turns are needed for a square = 360/4 = 90 degrees; six turns are needed for a hexagon = 360/6 = 60 degrees).
● Remind them to use 'repeat' to ensure that their algorithm is as efficient as possible.

Independent/paired work

● Ask the children to complete their worksheet, writing algorithms for each of the shapes.
● Encourage them to test out their algorithms on blank paper before writing their final algorithm.
● Giving instructions to each other will help them complete their algorithms accurately.
● When they complete their work, they should compare their algorithms with others and discuss any differences, debugging their algorithms as necessary.

Differentiation

● Support: Less confident learners may need further support to help them to complete their algorithms. They should focus on the simpler shapes.
● Challenge: More confident learners should be able to come up with their own shapes and associated algorithms.

Review

● Use the media resource 'Shapes' to go through the algorithms.
● Ask the children to self-assess their work as you discuss it as a class. You can also assess their progress by their responses to the discussions and their algorithms.

Shape programs

In this lesson, children will use Scratch to implement their algorithms, making use of the Scratch 'pen' scripts. They will code their shapes and understand how to use loops to make their code more efficient.

Curriculum objectives
● To design, write and debug programs that accomplish specific goals, including controlling or simulating physical systems; solve problems by decomposing them into smaller parts. To use sequence and repetition in programs; work with variables and various forms of input and output. To use logical reasoning to explain how some simple algorithms work and to detect and correct errors in algorithms and programs.

Lesson objectives
● To use a program to implement their designed algorithms.
● To work collaboratively to debug their algorithms as necessary.
● To explain how the program is executing their algorithm and using loops efficiently.

Expected outcomes
● Can write a program to execute their algorithm to draw simple shapes.
● Can explain how their program is using loops.

Resources
Completed photocopiable page 22 'Shape algorithms' from previous lesson; Scratch; media resource 'Shapes' on the CD-ROM; Scratch sample files 'Shapes' and 'Shape circles' (opened from the Quick links section of the CD-ROM)

Introduction
● Recap last week's work with the children, reminding them how they wrote algorithms for different shapes.
● Explain that this week they will be implementing their algorithms using Scratch's inbuilt pen tool.
● If any of the children have already discovered the pen tool in earlier work, encourage them to share what they know with the class.

Whole-class work
● Show the Scratch interface on the whiteboard and, using volunteers if you wish, as a class create a program to draw a square using the children's knowledge and understanding of how to create a square algorithm from last week's work.
● Highlight how the algorithm works to put the pen down, so the sprite will draw a square, and also highlight the use of repeats, turns and moves.
● Depending on your class's confidence, you could show them the sample Scratch file 'Shapes' (opened from the Quick links section of the CD-ROM), which shows code for creating all the shapes. Although you may feel this would be better shown at the start of the next whole-class work section as outlined below, letting the children try to work things out for themselves initially.

Independent/paired work
● The children should use their completed photocopiable page 22 'Shape algorithms' from the last lesson to program their shapes into Scratch.
● They can either create all the shapes in one program, or create one program for each shape. They should save all their shape programs.

Whole-class work
● Go through the scripts as a class, using the sample Scratch file 'Shapes' to help you if you wish and dealing with any misunderstandings. The children can self-assess their work.
● Discuss with them how they could create circular patterns with the shapes and create an algorithm as a class. You can show them the Scratch file 'Shape circles' to show them what you mean, only showing them the code after they have worked it out.

Independent/paired work
● The children should try to create their own circular, and other, patterns in Scratch.
● Encourage them to be as creative as possible.

Differentiation
● Support: Less confident learners may need additional support when programming their algorithms and should be encouraged to focus on simple shapes.
● Challenge: More confident learners can be encouraged to write programs to create their own shapes and patterns.

Review
● Review a selection of the children's work on the board, asking some of the children to share their work and how they created their patterns.
● Discuss as a class how using loops (repeats) in the programs makes them more efficient.

Curriculum objectives
● To design, write and debug programs that accomplish specific goals, including controlling or simulating physical systems; solve problems by decomposing them into smaller parts. To use sequence and repetition in programs; work with variables and various forms of input and output. To use logical reasoning to explain how some simple algorithms work and to detect and correct errors in algorithms and programs.

Lesson objectives
● To know that comments can be added to a program.
● To annotate a program with simple comments.
● To work collaboratively to ensure comments are clear and unambiguous.
● To be able to explain why comments are useful when writing programs.

Expected outcomes
● Can understand why comments are used in computer programs.
● Can annotate a program with simple comments.

Resources
Saved Scratch files from the previous lesson; Scratch sample file 'Merlin's shapes' (opened from the Quick links section of the CD-ROM); photocopiable page 23 'Merlin's shapes quiz plan'

Planning a shape quiz

In this lesson, the children use the skills they have acquired so far in this chapter, together with those from their work on Scratch in earlier years, particularly Year 4 Summer 2, to create a simple shape quiz for children from a younger year group. The children will plan their quiz and the algorithms they need before starting to program their quiz in Scratch over the next two lessons, using comments to explain their code.

Introduction
● Recap last week's work with the children, reminding them that they wrote programs to create different shapes and patterns.
● Explain that, over the course of the next two lessons, they are going to be creating a shape quiz, bringing together their learning from the previous lessons in this chapter.

Whole-class work
● Show them the Scratch sample file 'Merlin's shapes' (opened from the Quick links section of the CD-ROM) and work through it as a class, discussing how it works and how the code uses the player's input to draw the shapes.
● Highlight the use of 'broadcast' and 'when I receive' and discuss how the use of comments helps to show what the code is doing.
● Explain that in the sample the additional rectangle and pentagon shapes are used. You may wish to discuss the algorithms for these as a class.
● Encourage the children to be as creative as possible with their own quiz, improving on the sample one where possible.

Independent/paired work
● Give the children photocopiable page 23 'Merlin's shapes quiz plan' and ask them to do a quick text plan of the algorithms they will need for their quiz, using their saved shapes Scratch file from last week to help them.
● After they have done so, and you may wish to check their algorithms, they start to work on their program in Scratch.
● Ask the children to focus on getting their input boxes and shapes working and tell them you will deal with the sounds (and 'if' statements) next lesson.
● Ask them to add comments to their code as they write it, to explain what they are doing and why.

Differentiation
● Support: Less confident learners may need additional support with understanding the code and underlying algorithms behind the quiz. You could give them a simplified version of the sample file to work with.
● Challenge: More confident learners will be able to work confidently and improve on the sample quiz. Encourage them to add detailed and useful comments to their code.

Review
● Ask the children to review the work they have completed this lesson and assess the work they need to complete in order to finish their quiz next lesson. They could write a task list.
● Ask the children to share with a partner why it is important to use comments in a program and ask two or three pairs to share their thoughts with the class.

Curriculum objectives
● To design, write and debug programs that accomplish specific goals, including controlling or simulating physical systems; solve problems by decomposing them into smaller parts. To use sequence and repetition in programs; work with variables and various forms of input and output. To use logical reasoning to explain how some simple algorithms work and to detect and correct errors in algorithms and programs.

Lesson objectives
● To understand how and why conditions and two-way selection are used in algorithms and programs.
● To design, write and test a program that uses conditions and two-way selection.
● To debug their program as necessary.
● To annotate their program with simple comments.
● To explain how their program uses conditions and two-way selection.

Expected outcomes
● Can understand the use of conditions and two-way selection when writing simple algorithms and programs.
● Can use conditions and two-way selection in algorithms and programs.

Resources
Completed photocopiable page 23 'Merlin's shapes quiz plan' from previous lesson; sample Scratch file 'Merlin's shapes' (opened from the Quick links section of the CD-ROM)

Shapes quiz conditions and selection

In this lesson, the children will be using selection and conditions in their quiz. They will write at least one algorithm to include selection and conditions and then code this into their quiz, adding comments to their program to demonstrate their understanding. They will also complete their quiz and work collaboratively to test and debug their quiz as necessary.

Introduction
● Give out photocopiable page 23 'Merlin's shapes quiz plan' from last week.
● Remind the children of the work they were doing last week in their shapes quiz and ask them to look at their task list, if they completed one, to recap what they need to complete during this lesson to complete their quiz.
● Ask a few of the children to share what they need to do with you.
● Explain that you are going to discuss one extra element you would like them to include in their quiz.

Whole-class work
● Show the children the sample Scratch file 'Merlin's shapes' again and highlight to them the use of sound.
● Explain that this is a selection statement and discuss how it is working (the condition of 'answer = circle' is being tested to see if it's true or false). You could use everyday examples such as, *If it's raining, I'll wear my raincoat, otherwise I'll wear my jumper.*

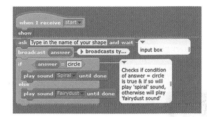

● Ask the children to work in pairs to come up with other everyday examples and share a few of these as a class.
● Ask the children to come up with ways (other than the one given in the sample Scratch file) that they could use a two-way selection statement. They should write this on their photocopiable sheet along with the rest of their algorithms and add it to their task list.
● Explain you would like them to include at least one two-way selection statement and add clear comments to show their understanding of how it is working.

Independent/paired work
● The children work through their task sheet, completing their shapes quiz, including at least one two-way selection statement as appropriate.
● Once finished, they swap with a partner or other pair and test each other's quizzes, working collaboratively to debug their work as appropriate.

Differentiation
● Support: Less confident learners may benefit from support with understanding and using two-way selection. If this is too difficult a concept for them, encourage them to focus on finishing a simple version of the quiz.
● Challenge: More confident learners should be able to include two-way selection with confidence and add suitable comments to their work to demonstrate their understanding of the concept. Encourage them to refine their code and quiz and help others to debug their work as appropriate.

Review
● Select some of the quizzes to review as a class (saving their work in a shared area will be helpful for this as will be noting which children have included aspects in their quiz that will be interesting to show). Ask the children to talk through their quizzes as they are shown to explain how they have made use of two-way selection, comments and other interesting elements.
● Assess the children's understanding by reviewing their quiz, their comments and contribution to class discussions.

Curriculum objectives
● To design, write and debug programs that accomplish specific goals, including controlling or simulating physical systems; solve problems by decomposing them into smaller parts. To use sequence and repetition in programs; work with variables and various forms of input and output. To use logical reasoning to explain how some simple algorithms work and to detect and correct errors in algorithms and programs.

Lesson objectives
● To demonstrate their understanding of the algorithms and programs they have created in a coherent way.
● To present work in a logical and visually pleasing way.
● To understand what a portfolio is and why it is a useful way of presenting work.

Expected outcomes
● Can present their work in a logical and easy to read way.
● Can explain the code they have written simply and effectively in order to demonstrate their understanding.

Resources
Media resource 'Example portfolio' on the CD-ROM; suitable presentation software for portfolio creation

King Arthur: Assess and review

In this lesson, the children are asked to demonstrate their learning from the chapter by creating a portfolio of the work they have completed during this chapter (particularly their algorithms and programming work from lessons 3–6). In this way, children consolidate their learning and are introduced to the idea of producing a portfolio of work. Use this portfolio to assess their knowledge, understanding and progress, and plan future work on this topic accordingly.

Introduction
● Discuss with the children what they have learned during this chapter.
● Explain that one way of showing what they have learned is by putting together a portfolio of their work. Discuss what a portfolio is and why they think it is useful.
● Explain that in today's lesson they will be choosing their best work and displaying it in a portfolio.
● Discuss what they could include in their portfolio of work for this chapter.

Whole-class work
● You can show children the media resource 'Example portfolio' on the CD-ROM as a guide, asking what they think is effective and what else they think should be included.
● Highlight the use of text to explain the image shown and discuss what makes good explanatory text.
● Depending on the children's confidence with using presentation software, you may wish to recap some of the skills they need, including adding images and text. Show them how to save a picture of their scripts in Scratch (right-click on the grey area in the scripts column, select 'save picture of scripts') and take screenshots of their work.

Independent work
● Ask the children to create their portfolio and save it in a shared area for you to access and assess.

Differentiation
● Support: Less confident learners may need further support in understanding how to create their portfolio and discuss their work. Encourage them to create a portfolio of images and simple explanations.
● Challenge: More confident learners should be able to create a portfolio of a high standard with ease. They can be encouraged to write detailed and evaluative explanations of their work.

Review
● Ask the children to consider and share what they have learned about creating a portfolio of their work. If you wish, you could show some of the portfolios they have created.
● Assess the children's work by looking through their portfolios and considering their work during this chapter as a whole.

King Arthur number puzzles

■ King Arthur is looking for another knight.
■ He has set a series of number puzzles to find out who could be clever enough to be one of his knights. Could it be you?

1. What numbers comes next in these sequences?

a) 2   9   16   23   30   _   _

b) 8   16   25   35   46   _   _

c) 2   6   8   14   22   _   _

d) 1   5   5   25   125   _   _

e) 13   13   12   10   7   _   _

2. Can you find the missing numbers?

a) 1   3   _   13   21   _   _

b) 2   4   6   10   _   26   _

c) 25   20   16   13   _   10   _

d) 11   10   8   _   1   _   −10

I can solve number puzzles.

How did you do?

King Arthur logic puzzles

■ King Arthur now wants to know whether you can solve these logic puzzles he has set you. Think carefully and work systematically to find the answers.

Four of the Knights of the Round Table want to have a secret meeting next week and need to decide on the best day according to their diaries.

Sir Lancelot can only meet on Monday, Wednesday or Friday.

King Arthur cannot meet on Tuesday, Wednesday or Saturday.

Sir Galahad is busy on Monday and Thursday.

Sir Percival can meet on Monday, Tuesday and Friday.

They are meeting with the rest of the knights on Sunday.

■ Use this table to help you answer the questions below.

	Monday	Tuesday	Wednesday	Thursday	Friday	Saturday	Sunday
King Arthur							
Sir Lancelot							
Sir Galahad							
Sir Percival							

What day(s) would be best for the knights to meet? _____

Why? _____

I can solve logic puzzles.

How did you do?

PHOTOCOPIABLE

Code cracking (1)

King Arthur needs your help!

He has written you coded messages to decipher.

Can you crack the codes below and help the knights to rescue King Arthur?

■ Use this table to help you:

A	B	C	D	E	F	G	H	I	J	K	L	M
			A									

N	O	P	Q	R	S	T	U	V	W	X	Y	Z

1. WKH VDARQV KDYH FDSWXUHG PH

_____

2. L DP LQ D WDOO WRZHU

_____

3. L KDYH QR IRRG

_____

4. FRPH TXLFNOB!

_____

I can crack coded messages.

How did you do?

Code cracking (2)

King Arthur needs your help! He has written you coded messages you need to decipher.

Can you crack the codes below and help the knights to rescue King Arthur?

■ Use this table to help you:

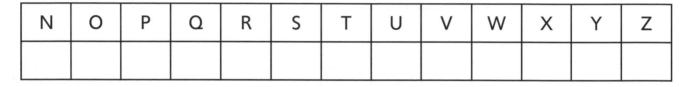

A	B	C	D	E	F	G	H	I	J	K	L	M

N	O	P	Q	R	S	T	U	V	W	X	Y	Z

I. FCJN KC!

_____

2. G LCCB UYRCP

_____

3. RFC QYVMLQ YPC EMGLE RM IGJJ KC

_____

4. G YK GL RFC BSLECML

_____

I can crack coded messages.

How did you do?

My codes

- In the space below, develop your own code to send a message to King Arthur and his knights.

- Fold along here when your teacher tells you.

- -

- Use your code to write a message to King Arthur or another knight in the space below.

I can create codes for others to break and write coded messages to others.

How did you do?

Shape algorithms

■ Write algorithms for drawing these shapes.

Algorithms

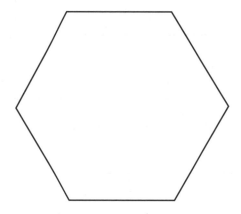

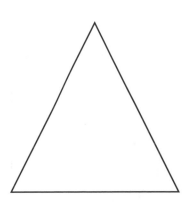

I can write algorithms to draw shapes.

How did you do?

PHOTOCOPIABLE

SCHOLASTIC
www.scholastic.co.uk

Name: _____ Date: _____

Merlin's shape quiz plan

■ Use the space below to plan what needs to happen step by step.

I can create algorithms for my shape quiz.

How did you do?

The Railway Children

This chapter engages the children in the theme of the story *The Railway Children*, which was published in 1906. The children learn more about the World Wide Web and the internet. They understand that the internet is a massive network of computers sharing information and following a common way of communicating, called a protocol.

As the children develop their understanding of how computers work, they learn about how data are transported on the internet as ones and zeros in packets. These packets are delivered to different computer addresses called 'IP addresses'.

The Railway Children was published in Edwardian times but explores the Victorian theme of technological innovation. The children consider how technology has changed with time and whether all new technology is beneficial.

Expected prior learning

- The children will have learned about different networks such as wired, wireless and mobile networks.
- They will have used the World Wide Web to search for information and viewed websites.
- They will have collaborated online, using web tools and sent and received emails.

Chapter at a glance

Subject area
• How computers work

National Curriculum objective
• To understand computer networks including the internet; how they can provide multiple services, such as the World Wide Web; and the opportunities they offer for communication and collaboration. • To use technology safely, respectfully and responsibly.

Week	Lesson objectives	Summary of activities	Expected outcomes
1	• To describe the internet in terms of a global network. • To describe the World Wide Web and how users connect. • To explain the difference between the World Wide Web and the internet. • To use analogies to describe networks, including the internet.	• Children are introduced to the story *The Railway Children*. • They look at train maps and work out routes. • They recognise the analogy between the railway as a network of stations and the internet as a network of servers.	• Can explain what the World Wide Web and the internet are and explain the difference. • Can use analogies of train tracks and trains to describe the internet.
2	• To send and receive messages using paper. • To send and receive messages using online tools. • To compare sending and receiving messages using physical methods and online tools. • To use an analogy to describe how data can be broken into packets of data (for example, the paper chase sequence in *The Railway Children*).	• Children understand how the railway and a canal network were built to move people and goods around the country. • They understand that the internet moves information around the world. • They read about the paper chase incident in the story. • They play a game sending paper messages around the classroom. • They send online messages to each other.	• Can send and receive messages using different methods. • Can use the paper chase analogy (for example in *The Railway Children*) to show how web pages can be broken into smaller packets of data.
3	• To describe how packets of data can be transported on the internet. • To describe how data can be transported using a protocol to organise them. • To create a simple model to describe how web pages are formed from packets.	• Children learn more about how packets of information are delivered by the internet. • They understand that in order to make sense of packets of data a protocol is used to order them. • They look at a simple model of a web page to see how it is broken into pieces (packets of information) and reconstructed.	• Can describe how data are transported on the internet, including packets and the notion of a protocol. • Can create a simple model to describe how the web pages are formed from packets.

Week	Lesson objectives	Summary of activities	Expected outcomes
4	• To use the binary number system to count to ten. • To know that computers use binary code to communicate. • To describe how the telegraph was used in the railway system to send messages via Morse code and how computers can send messages using binary code.	• Children understand that web pages are broken down into packets of data and this data is sent as binary code (ones and zeros). • They learn how to count in binary and send messages to each other. • They learn how the telegraph system worked to send messages, using 'on' and 'off'.	• Can use the binary number system to count to ten. • Can explain that computers communicate using binary code.
5	• To know that a byte is a collection of digital information. • To explain that large volumes of data can be given a prefix, such as, kilobytes, megabytes, gigabytes and larger. • To recognise examples of kilobytes, megabytes, gigabytes, in everyday life.	• Children learn how websites have addresses in the same way as houses, and that the characters in the story live at Three Chimneys. • They look at the size of data in websites and how this is expressed, for example, kilobytes, megabytes, gigabytes, terabytes.	• Can know that a byte is a unit of digital information. • Can explain that large volumes of data can be described using terms, such as, kilobytes, megabytes, gigabytes. • Can identify examples of digital information in everyday life.
6	• To retell a story and describe how the development of technology has benefitted everyday life (for example, the technological improvements featured in The Railway Children and since that period). • To discuss how technology in modern life can affect our health in both positive and negative ways. • To use technology safely and responsibly.	• Children study the plot of The Railway Children and, if it was set today, how it would be different. • They consider how the internet, GPS and mobile phones would change things. • Children plan a modern-day version of the story. • They consider how technology can benefit us and also be detrimental. • They consider how to use technology safely and responsibly.	• Can discuss the health and safety aspects of using technology.
Assess and review	• Assess and review the half term's work.	• Children review how the railway is a network of train lines taking people from one place to another. • They use binary codes to send each other messages. • They explore the difference between the World Wide Web and the internet.	• Assess and review.

Overview of progression

● The children know about searching online for information and will probably have heard the expression 'search the internet'. In this chapter, they learn that the internet is the network of computers. This progresses their learning about networks.
● They learn that the World Wide Web is the service on the internet, sharing information via websites.
● They develop their understanding of the sizes of amounts of data, through recognising everyday use of kilobytes (KB), megabytes (MB) and gigabytes (GB) and even terabytes (TB).

Creative context

● The lessons link closely to the English curriculum. Through studying the text of The Railway Children by Edith Nesbit, the children describe settings, characters and atmosphere and integrate dialogue to convey character and advance the action. They provide reasoned justifications for their views.
● Linking to maths, the children look at binary numbers and convert them to the decimal system. They look at large number prefixes such as 'kilo', 'mega', 'giga' and even 'tera'. The children also solve word problems.

Background knowledge

● The children will have used computers to access information on the internet. However, they may not have considered how computers transfer data or how they put a web page together.
● They discuss places where they see kilobytes, megabytes, gigabytes and terabytes.
● They look at changes from the Edwardian period to today, thinking how technology has changed our lives, improving communication, but also affecting our health and social lives.

Curriculum objectives
● To understand computer networks including the internet; how they can provide multiple services, such as the World Wide Web; and the opportunities they offer for communication and collaboration.
● To use technology safely, respectfully and responsibly.

Objectives
● To describe the internet in terms of a global network.
● To describe the World Wide Web and how users connect.
● To explain the difference between the World Wide Web and the internet.
● To use analogies to describe networks, including the internet (for example, using train track networks).

Expected outcomes
● Can explain what the World Wide Web and the internet are and explain the difference.
● Can use analogies of train tracks and trains to describe the internet.

Resources
Photocopiable page 33 'Train routes'; *The Railway Children* by Edith Nesbit

Rail maps and internet maps

Using the theme of *The Railway Children*, the children look at rail maps to see how stations are connected and make analogies with computer networks, including a global network, the internet.

Introduction

● Read the introduction to the story. The text can be found online at Project Gutenburg (www.gutenberg.org/ebooks/1874). It appears in different formats, as a electronic book format (epub) or Kindle version, as plain text (txt) or online as an HTML page (www.gutenberg.org/files/1874/1874-h/1874-h. htm).
● Project Gutenburg aims to share books electronically, so that everyone can access them (http://en.wikipedia.org/wiki/Project_Gutenberg). Ask: *How can you read books online?*
● Explain that in the lessons they will be thinking about networks and the World Wide Web and about how the information in the books is transferred.

Whole-class work

● Explain that the railway is a network of train lines taking people from one place to another.
● Share railway websites, to see maps of rail networks, for example, the National Rail map (www.nationalrail.co.uk/css/OfficialNationalRailmaplarge. pdf). Zoom in on a local area.
● Display the map from the Keighley and Worth Valley railway (www. kwvr.co.uk/visit/find-us.html). In the film *The Railway Children* (from 1970), Oakworth Station was used as the main set. The children can see the train line on the map.
● For the Keighley and Worth Valley railway, there is only one route out from Keighley to Oxenhope and back again. So, if the lines became blocked at one of the stations, there is no other route around.
● Now, choose another railway map (ideally a local example) and ask the children how they would travel from one station to the next. If one of the stations became blocked, could they find a way around?

Paired work

● Display the rail network that the class has chosen. You could display this on screen, print it out or collect leaflets from the local railway.
● In pairs, the children play the routes game, using Photocopiable page 33 'Train routes'. Can they find the shortest route between two stations? Which lines must they follow?
● One of the pair then says that a particular station is closed, can they find another way around?

Differentiation
● Support: Less confident learners may need support to plan one route between five stations.
● Challenge: More confident learners could plan routes around the rail network between more than ten stations.

Review

● Bring the class together and ask three pairs of children to demonstrate how they travelled from one station to another and then changed their route, when one was blocked.
● Make the analogy that the railway is a network of stations and that the internet is a network of computers.
● The computers on a network are called 'servers', they serve out information.
● Make the analogy that the information in websites is shared by the servers. This information is delivered in a way people can understand (World Wide Web) and the delivery method is the rail network (the internet).

Curriculum objectives
● To understand computer networks including the internet; how they can provide multiple services, such as the World Wide Web; and the opportunities they offer for communication and collaboration.
● To use technology safely, respectfully and responsibly.

Lesson objectives
● To send and receive messages using paper.
● To send and receive messages using online tools.
● To compare sending and receiving messages using physical methods and online tools.
● To use an analogy to describe how data can be broken into packets of data.

Expected outcomes
● Can send and receive messages using different methods.
● Can use the paper chase analogy (for example in *The Railway Children*) to show how web pages can be broken into smaller packets of data.

Resources
Photocopiable page 'Nursery rhyme message' from the CD-ROM; photocopiable page 34 'Secret messages'; *The Railway Children* by Edith Nesbit

Packets of data

Using a 'paper chase' analogy from the story, children think about breaking up the data that makes up a web page into smaller packets. The data is sent and received and reconstructed into the original web page.

Introduction
● Introduce the lesson by displaying a railway network map (for example, the London tube map www.tfl.gov.uk/maps/track/tube).
● Recapping on the previous lesson, invite two children to each choose a station. Ask: *Can you find a route between the stations? If there was a blockage (it could be a broken-down train), how could you navigate from one to the other?*
● Explain that railways and canal networks move people and goods around. Similarly, the internet moves data around.

Whole-class work
● Read in the story (Chapter 11), where the children watch a 'Hare and Hounds' paper chase. Explain that this could be thought of as a trail of data, like a railway network.
● Using photocopiable page 'Nursery rhyme message' from the CD-ROM, the children are given individual words from the rhyme. They stand in a line and pass jumbled-up words from the front to the back. The child at the back reassembles the words.
● Remind the children that they are 'servers, who serve each other with data'.
● Repeat the activity, but this time choose a child in the middle to be a 'blockage' and not take the words. The children should see how the information gets stuck at that point.
● Ask: *How could you improve this system?*
● Next, the children stand in two lines. Choose one child to stand at the end, in between the two lines.
● Pass the words down the two lines, giving each line a piece at random. The child at the end receives the same message, but via two routes.
● Again, choose a child who will be a blocker on one line. This time the child before the blocker can instead pass the paper across to the opposite line. In this way, the data still travels along the opposite line to get to the end.

Paired work
● The children can send online messages to one another using a simple online tool called 'Today's meet' (http://todaysmeet.com/).
● The children need to consider how they can be responsible and respectful online.
● Using photocopiable page 34 'Secret messages', the children post and decipher coded messages.

> **Differentiation**
> ● Challenge: More confident learners will be able to code their own messages.
> ● Support: Less confident learners may need support to set up the online room and to decipher the coded messages.

Review
● Bring the class together and, using photocopiable page 34 'Secret messages', ask the children for their answers to the coded questions.
● How do they think the data in their online messages travelled from one computer to another? Explain that by using the internet (a huge network of computer servers, all joined together), the data could be sent via many different routes, avoiding blockages.
● Elaborate that when the data was sent from one computer, it was broken down into smaller pieces called packets and reassembled at the end, on the other computer. The web page is part of the World Wide Web, which is how we can understand the data. The method to transfer the data is the internet.

Curriculum objectives
● To understand computer networks including the internet; how they can provide multiple services, such as the World Wide Web; and the opportunities they offer for communication and collaboration.
● To use technology safely, respectfully and responsibly.

Lesson objectives
● To describe how packets of data can be transported on the internet.
● To describe how data can be transported using a protocol to organise them.
● To create a simple model to describe how web pages are formed from packets.

Expected outcomes
● Can describe how data are transported on the internet, including packets and the notion of a protocol.
● Can create a simple model to describe how the web pages are formed from packets.

Resources
Photocopiable page 35 'Hare and hounds'; interactive activity 'What's my address?' on the CD-ROM; photocopiable page 'Packets of data (1)' from the CD-ROM; photocopiable page 'Packets of data (2)' from the CD-ROM; *The Railway Children* by Edith Nesbit

Protocols

Following on from learning about packets of data, the children think about the process of breaking up the data for a web page and reconstructing it in another place. For this to work, a 'protocol' must be followed, in order for the sender and receiver to make sense of the data.

Introduction
● Explain that, on the internet, every web page and email is sent and received as 'packets of data'.
● Remind them that the packets are sent by the best route, and if there is a blockage on that route, the packets can go another way.
● To warm up the class, use photocopiable page 35 'Hare and hounds' to act out a paper chase and find the quickest and most efficient route. First, leave one trail of pieces of paper for the children to follow. Then, leave several trails of pieces of paper that follow more than one route to the same destination.

Whole-class work
● Explain that, when an email is sent, the network breaks it into a 'packet'. The packet contains the sender's address, the recipient's address, the total number of packets and the number of that individual packet.
● Ask the children to explain why they think the packets need an address?
● Use the interactive activity 'What's my address?' on the CD-ROM for children to add an address to the front of the parcel.
● Ask the children why it might be useful to add the sender's address.
● Finally, if the person was sending a large item, they might send it in smaller pieces, so the recipient would need to know how many parcels to expect.

Paired work
● In pairs, the children use the interactive activity to add their addresses and the packet information.

Whole-class work
● Explain that in order to make sense of the packets of data, a 'protocol' is used to put the packets into an order.
● Using photocopiable page 'Packets of data (1)' from the CD-ROM, choose a child to number the squares on the picture. Let them decide how to number them. Do not let the class see the picture.
● They cut the picture into 32 pieces and place into four envelopes.
● Send the four envelopes to another child who puts them together on their grid using photocopiable page 'Packets of data (2)' from the CD-ROM. They might be able to figure out how the squares are numbered.
● Now ask the first child to explain how they numbered the squares on the grid. Is it now possible for the recipient to put the picture together?

Paired work
● In pairs, the children use photocopiable pages 'Packets of data (1) and (2)' from the CD-ROM. Ask: *How will you number the squares on the picture? When you know the method, can you put the picture together?*

Review
● Bring the class together, and ask: *Did you find it easy to put the picture together, once you had been told how the squares had been numbered?*
● Explain that the method to put the picture together could be called a 'protocol'.
● Explain that before the idea of all computers using the same protocol, it was not possible for them to communicate with each other.
● Tell the children that when they type an address into the web browser, it begins with 'http://', which stands for 'hypertext transfer protocol'. This means it follows a particular protocol to put the web page together.

■SCHOLASTIC

The binary number system

The data sent between computers is in a binary format of ones and zeros. The children learn about the binary number system. They convert binary numbers into base 10 numbers and vice versa. They try to explain how they are working out their answers.

Introduction
● Introduce the lesson by reminding the children that web pages are broken down into packets of data. This data is sent as binary code, that is, ones and zeros.
● Explain that computers communicate using binary code. In this lesson the children will learn how to count using the binary number system and send messages to each other.

Whole-class work
● Tell the children that computers communicate using ones and zeros. This is because inside they do their calculations using switches that can either be on or off (this is represented by ones for on and zeros for off).
● When computers send their data, the smallest part is a 'binary digit', that is, an on or off, represented by a one or a zero.
● The binary digits or 'bits' can be combined when sharing information. A 'byte' is a binary code containing eight bits, for example 01101111. It is just a way of grouping the information. This is the data that can form a web page or an email, for example.
● Using interactive activity 'Binary quiz' on the CD-ROM, show the children how the columns are organised and the equivalent base 10 numbers, for example 101 in binary (base 2) is equivalent to 5 in decimal (base 10).
● Work through two examples on photocopiable page 36 'Binary numbers' to show how the binary number system works.

Independent work
● In pairs, the children attempt the questions on the photocopiable sheet. Ask: *Can you describe the method you are using?*

Whole-class work
● Bring the class together and review the answers to the photocopiable sheet.
● Use the interactive activity to give further examples, to check for understanding.
● Explain that the eight 'bits' that are combined into a byte have eight columns.
● Using the eight columns means that combinations of numbers up to 11111111 can be stored (this is equivalent to the number 255 in base 10).

> **Differentiation**
> ● Support: Less confident learners may need support to understand how the binary number system works and help to interpret the questions.
> ● Challenge: More confident learners could attempt all the binary number questions and then invent further examples for a partner to try.

Review
● In the story, the family know that the father has been released from prison and is arriving on a particular train. This message could have been sent by the telegraph system, before the news came in the newspaper. Explain how the telegraph system worked using 'on' and 'off' similar to binary '0' and '1'.
● Continue the messaging analogy to explain how Morse code messages can be sent and received. The letters in Morse code are made up of a series of 'dots' and 'dashes' – from simple combinations, much more complex messages can be sent.

Curriculum objectives
• To understand computer networks including the internet; how they can provide multiple services, such as the World Wide Web; and the opportunities they offer for communication and collaboration.
• To use technology safely, respectfully and responsibly.

Lesson objectives
• To know that a byte is a collection of digital information.
• To explain that large volumes of data can be given a prefix, such as, kilobytes, megabytes, gigabytes and larger.
• To recognise examples of kilobytes, megabytes, gigabytes, in everyday life.

Expected outcomes
• Can know that a byte is a unit of digital information.
• Can explain that large volumes of data can be described using terms such as kilobytes, megabytes, gigabytes.
• Can identify examples of digital information in everyday life.

Resources
Photocopiable page 'IP addresses' from the CD-ROM; interactive activity 'Big bytes' on the CD-ROM; *The Railway Children* by Edith Nesbit

What's your address?

The children have learned about sending and receiving data, but how does a computer know where to send it to or from where it has been sent? The children learn that, similar to *The Railway Children*, who live at Three Chimneys, every computer has an address. They learn about IP addresses for computers and look at the addresses where different web pages are held. They also look at the sizes of quantities of data.

Introduction
• Introduce the lesson by reading a section from *The Railway Children* story, which describes the Three Chimneys address where they live.
• Computers also have an address called an IP Address.
• The IP stands for Internet Protocol. The children will recognise protocols from previous lessons.
• Every web page is stored on a computer, which has an IP address. These IP addresses look like a list of numbers, for example, 212.58.244.71. Ask a child to type this into a browser address bar. Which web page appears?

Paired work
• Explain that the children are going to type in different IP addresses into a web browser. Using photocopiable page 'IP Addresses' from the CD-ROM, they find out the IP address of the computer, which holds the web page.

Whole-class work
• Bring the class together and demonstrate how to find out an IP address for a computer. Type into the search box (on the Google search page) the words 'my IP'. It will return a number, which is the address of that computer.
• Explain that every time they search using Google or Bing, the search is 'tagged' with their address. This is similar to the activity the children did using the parcel analogy, writing the sender's address on the outside.
• Explain that this raises questions such as: *Can we search for things anonymously? Does Google know about every search we do?*
• If the search word 'weather' is typed into the search box, the IP address may be used to guess the location, in order to give a localised weather report.
• Remind the children that all of the information on a web page is sent as ones and zeros, the digital bits that combine to form bytes. The larger the web page, the larger the number of bytes.
• Larger numbers of bytes can be called 'megabytes', that is, 1,000,000 bytes or 'gigabytes', that is, 1,000,000,000 bytes.
• Larger numbers of bytes can be represented as terabytes (TB), petabytes (PB), exabytes (EB), zettabytes (ZB) to yottabytes (YB).
• More information can be found at: www.stanford.edu/class/cs101/bits-gigabytes.html

Differentiation
• Support: Less confident learners may need support with making the analogy between the house address and IP address and help entering the numbers correctly.
• Challenge: More confident learners will be able to make the analogy between house addresses and IP addresses. They will be able consider the implications for all of their searches being recorded by a search engine provider.

Review
• Bring the class together and look at the names for large numbers of bytes on interactive activity 'Big bytes' on the CD-ROM.
• Ask the children to describe where they have heard the terms kilobytes (KB), megabytes (MB) and gigabytes (GB) in everyday life. For example, it might be on adverts for computers or USB memory sticks.
• Remind the children that they have been learning about IP addresses being similar to house addresses.

The Railway Children today?

The children look at the changes in technology since the time of the story. They think about how *The Railway Children* story might be different if it was set in modern times.

Curriculum objectives
● To understand computer networks including the internet; how they can provide multiple services, such as the World Wide Web; and the opportunities they offer for communication and collaboration.
● To use technology safely, respectfully and responsibly.

Lesson objectives
● To retell a story and describe how the development of technology has benefitted everyday life (for example, the technological improvements in *The Railway Children* and since that period).
● To discuss how technology in modern life can affect our health in both positive and negative ways.
● To use technology safely and responsibly.

Expected outcomes
● Can discuss the health and safety aspects of using technology.

Resources
Photocopiable page 37 '*The Railway children* storyboard'; interactive activity 'How has it changed?' on the CD-ROM; interactive activity 'New technologies – good or bad?' on the CD-ROM

Introduction
● Introduce the lesson by asking: *How would* The Railway Children *story be different if it was set today? How have the railways changed? Do we still have station masters?*
● Explain that trains can be tracked using global positioning systems (GPS) and that train timetables and live updates are available online. Also, people can be tracked using their mobile phones.
● Using interactive activity 'How has it changed?' on the CD-ROM, gather all the ideas about how technology has changed; for example, if the story was set today the children could have used mobile phones to call the station or police to alert them about a landslip.
● Ask the children to look around the classroom for ideas of how technology has changed, and then ask them to think of changes outside of school and in their homes.

Whole-class work
● Explain that the children are going to make a modern-day version of the story. Can the children use the same themes of justice and kindness in their story plan? Will the children have the same characters? How will they talk?

Independent work
● The children use photocopiable page 37 '*The Railway children* storyboard' to sketch a modern version of the scenes.
● In each scene, they decide whether modern technology would change what happens. They can add speech bubbles to describe what the children might be saying.
● At the end of the storyboard planning, they need to add a short sentence, 'I think new technology is (better/worse) for us because...' Explain that the children need to think about whether technology is having a positive effect on them or actually has some negative implications.

Differentiation
● Support: Less confident learners may need support to rethink the story to include modern technology. They could choose one scene from the story, think how one new technology is now used and decide whether it is helpful or not helpful.
● Challenge: More confident learners will be able to plan their story board, adding speech bubbles to annotate the action in the scenes. They will be able to critically comment on whether modern technology is beneficial or has some detrimental effects on their lives.

Review
● Bring the class together and ask four children to share their stories. Ask: *How have you changed the story to include new technologies?*
● Ask whether they think new technologies are all beneficial. For example, one advantage is that now they can find out about events around the world, via the World Wide Web, but in the story, news was delivered by newspaper.
● Ask them if they think there are any technologies that are not beneficial? For example, sitting in front of screens means people might not be getting enough exercise. Also, disposing of old equipment can increase pollution.
● The children have considered how to use technology responsibly – so does using computers and mobile phones give more opportunity for bullying?
● Allow the children time to consider the questions and give 'for' and 'against' arguments. To structure the discussion, use interactive activity 'New technologies – good or bad?' on the CD-ROM to allow the positive and negative sides of the arguments to be displayed and considered.

Curriculum objectives
● To understand computer networks including the internet; how they can provide multiple services, such as the World Wide Web; and the opportunities they offer for communication and collaboration.
● To use technology safely, respectfully and responsibly.

Lesson objectives
● To describe the internet in terms of a global network.
● To explain the difference between the World Wide Web and the internet.

Expected outcomes
● Can explain what the World Wide Web and the internet are and explain the difference.

Resources
Photocopiable page 33 'Train routes' from previous lessons; photocopiable page 34 'Secret messages' from previous lessons; interactive activity 'Binary quiz' on the CD-ROM; photocopiable page 38 'Binary numbers again'; photocopiable page 39 'Binary codes'

Railway children: Assess and review

The children review their learning. They look at binary numbers again and think about the internet as a global network and how the World Wide Web is the service using that network.

Introduction
● Introduce the lesson by reminding the children that the railway is a network of train lines taking people from one place to another. Display a rail map (for example, www.firstgreatwestern.co.uk/Your-journey/Route-Maps).
● Play the railway routes game again, using photocopiable page 33 'Train routes' using different stations.
● Ask: *Can you plan a route between two stations and then find another route, if one was blocked? Thinking about train routes, can you give a definition of the 'internet' and explain how it works to a partner?*

Individual work
● Use the interactive activity 'Binary quiz' on the CD-ROM to give three examples of binary numbers as base 10 numbers.
● Using photocopiable page 38 'Binary numbers again', the children read binary numbers and convert them into base 10 numbers and vice versa.
● Ask: *Can you convert a binary number into a base 10 number? Can you convert a base 10 number into a binary number?*

Paired work
● Using photocopiable page 39 'Binary codes', the children think of a question which a partner has to answer in binary and base 10.

Whole-class work
● Bring the class together and choose pairs to read out their questions and then give the answers in binary and base 10 numbers.
● Explain that the person credited with inventing the World Wide Web is Sir Tim Berners-Lee. He enabled computers to communicate using the HTTP (hypertext transfer protocol) and using the language HTML (hypertext mark-up language).
● Watch the BBC clip about the development of the World Wide Web: www.bbc.co.uk/education/clips/zr3b4wx
● Ask: *Can you explain the difference between the World Wide Web and the internet?*

Differentiation
● Support: Less confident learners may need support to understand that the internet is the network of computers connected together and the World Wide Web is the system running on the internet to share information.
● Challenge: More confident learners will be able to give a clear definition of the World Wide Web and the internet and describe the difference between them. They will be able to convert binary numbers to base 10 and vice versa.

Review
● Bring the class together and recap learning.
● Discuss how there have been huge technological changes since *The Railway Children* was written.
● Remind children that computers communicate using binary and that all websites have an IP address.
● Discuss how technology can be beneficial but also detrimental.

Train routes

- Write the name of the station you are travelling from and to.
- Describe your route and whether you have to change routes.

1. I am travelling from _____ and going

to _____.

This is my shortest route:

_____

_____

Suddenly, there is a blocked station at _____.

My new route is: _____

_____

2. I am travelling from _____ and going

to _____.

This is my shortest route: _____

_____

Suddenly, there is a blocked station at _____.

My new route is: _____

_____

I can work out the shortest route between two stations and find a way around a blocked station.

How did you do?

Secret messages

A secret message can be sent using a secret code.

This is a substitution code, where one letter is replaced by another.

A	B	C	D	E	F	G	H	I	J	K	L	M
c	g	p	s	h	y	o	r	t	d	u	v	q
N	O	P	Q	R	S	T	U	V	W	X	Y	Z
b	l	f	k	e	a	x	j	n	i	z	m	w

■ Write your message below.

■ Now encrypt it using the code.

■ Give your coded message to someone else to decode.

I can write a secret message and decipher a secret message.

How did you do?

PHOTOCOPIABLE

Name: _____   Date: _____

Hare and hounds

- Play the 'Hare and hounds' game outside or in a large room.

Your teacher will be the hare.

One route:

- Follow a single route of paper, then make a sketch of it below.

More than one route:

- Follow each route of paper. Which was the fastest route? Sketch it below.

I can follow a route and sketch it.
I can follow multiple routes and decide which is the fastest.

How did you do?

Binary numbers

■ Work out which numbers go in the spaces below.

8	4	2	1		
0	1	0	1	=	5
1	0	0	1	=	9
0	1	1	1	=	
0	0	0	1	=	
1	0	0	0	=	8
1	1	1	1	=	

8	4	2	1		
				=	12
				=	3
				=	14
				=	6
				=	2
				=	0

■ Now fill in these spaces.

128	64	32	16	8	4	2	1		
								=	32
0	0	1	0	1	0	0	1	=	
								=	65
0	1	1	0	1	0	1	0	=	
								=	50
1	0	0	0	0	0	0	1	=	
								=	255

I can change binary numbers into base 10 numbers.
I can change base 10 numbers into binary numbers.

How did you do?

The Railway Children storyboard

Scene 1: Arriving at Three Chimneys	Scene 2: Visiting the station	Scene 3: Reading the newspaper with the father's trial information
Scene 4: The paper chase and boy stuck in the tunnel	Scene 5: Stopping the train	Scene 6: The father coming home and information in the newspaper

■ I think modern technology is better/worse for us, because...

_____

_____

I can describe how technology has changed since the Victorian age.

How did you do?

Binary numbers again

■ Fill in the blanks below.

128	64	32	16	8	4	2	1		
								=	11
								=	122
								=	15
								=	160
								=	205
								=	245

128	64	32	16	8	4	2	1		
0	0	0	1	0	0	1	0	=	
1	0	1	1	0	1	0	0	=	
0	1	0	0	1	0	1	0	=	
1	0	0	1	0	0	0	0	=	
0	0	1	0	0	0	1	0	=	
0	1	1	0	0	0	1	1	=	

I can change binary numbers into base 10 numbers.
I can change base 10 numbers into binary numbers.

How did you do?

PHOTOCOPIABLE

Binary codes

- Write five questions below. Each must have a numeric answer.

For example:

How many months are there in a year?

- Swap pages with your partner.
- Ask him or her to work out the answers and write them in binary.
- Swap back and convert the binary number into base 10. Did your partner get the right answer?

	Question	Answer in binary	Answer in base 10	Is it correct?
1				
2				
3				
4				
5				

I can solve problems, then convert binary to base 10 numbers and base 10 to binary numbers.

How did you do?

China and India

In these lessons, the children consider internet filtering, searching online, being discerning in the content they find and its reliability. They see that different countries (for example, China and India) have different Google search home pages and they think about the ranking of the results to a web search. The children look at Wikipedia pages, how they work and consider their reliability. They compare the main site with the Simple English Wikipedia site and see the difference in the pages. They consider bias and also what makes an effective presentation.

Expected prior learning

● The children will have searched online using key search words. They will have used Boolean terms, such as, '+' and '-' to narrow a search and also used the 'advanced search' features.
● When looking at Wikipedia, they will know that many people edit the pages, though they may not have considered the process, nor spent time reviewing the information for bias.
● The children will have presented before, though not in a 'Pecha Kucha' style, using images and with a limited time to speak.

Chapter at a glance

Subject area
• Communication

National Curriculum objective
• To use search technologies effectively and be discerning in evaluating digital content. • To use technology safely, respectfully and responsibly; recognise acceptable/unacceptable behaviour; identify a range of ways to report concerns about content and contact.

Week	Lesson objectives	Summary of activities	Expected outcomes
1	• To explain how to use a computer safely. • To know there are different types of browser. • To know that browsers have safety features included in them. • To describe why browsers have safety features.	• Children establish what facts they already know about China. • They look at the Google homepage for China and discuss whether every country has access to the same information. • They look at the safety features built into browsers. • They research some amazing facts about China.	• Can explain how to use technology safely. • Can describe safety features that are included in internet browsers.
2	• To define internet filtering. • To know that schools may filter the content. • To discuss why filtering has advantages and disadvantages. • To know how to search using specific, appropriate keywords. • To explain how to narrow a search, by changing the search criteria.	• Children are introduced to the term 'internet filtering'. • They discuss the advantages of filtering and whether what they view through the school computers is filtered. • They discuss whether countries/governments should filter information. • They look at why family-friendly and safe-search filters are used.	• Can discuss the advantages and disadvantages of internet filtering. • Can show how to narrow an internet search by selecting different search criteria.
3	• To know how to search using specific, appropriate keywords. • To evaluate the results of a keyword search. • To be discerning in evaluating the content found using a search. • To know that particular words can be found on web pages, using a search tool. • To find particular words on a web page using the search tool.	• Children establish what facts they already know about India. • They look at the Google homepage for India and discuss whether every country has access to the same information. • They search for information about Indian traditions and evaluate the results.	• Can be discerning in evaluating the content found using a search. • Can use the search on a web page to locate particular words.

■SCHOLASTIC

Week	Lesson objectives	Summary of activities	Expected outcomes
4	• To discuss whether the important information is displayed in Simple English Wikipedia compared to Wikipedia. • To explain why there is a need for Simple English Wikipedia. • To know that wiki pages can be edited. • To be able to change the bias of a website by changing the text and images, using software tools.	• Children research the life and death of Gandhi using Wikipedia and Simple English Wikipedia. • They describe the differences between Wikipedia and Simple English Wikipedia. • They consider why there is a need for Simple English Wikipedia. • They find out that Wikipedia can be edited.	• Can compare the detailed and simple versions of Wikipedia to identify if the important information is present. • Can model changing the bias and purpose of a website, using software tools.
5	• To explain the importance of giving concise presentations, while including the important information. • To create criteria for an effective presentation. • To create a presentation based on effective, self-authored criteria. • To evaluate other children's presentations, based on self-authored criteria.	• Children find out more about the death of Gandhi. • They look at the criteria for an effective presentation. • They try a 'Pecha Kucha' style presentation. • They evaluate the presentations using the criteria.	• Can present relevant information, in a concise way. • Can evaluate other children's presentations, using given criteria.
6	• To explain what bias is, through giving relevant examples. • To know that websites may contain bias. • To analyse websites to decide whether they are biased. • To explain how to choose appropriate search keywords and justify their selection.	• Children collect evidence using the 'Book Creator' feature of Simple English Wikipedia. • They discuss the advantages and disadvantages of Book Creator. • They analyse Wikipedia articles to find fact or opinion. • They explain how to choose appropriate keywords.	• Can describe how websites may contain bias. • Can choose and justify appropriate search keywords to locate information.
Assess and review	• Assess and review the half term's work.	• Children search for information on India. • They evaluate the results of their search. • They locate words on a web page using the search tool. • They present using a 'Pecha Kucha' style.	• Assess and review.

Overview of progression
● The children will begin by recording their knowledge of China and India, before researching online to gather facts about the countries and the people.
● They will have searched online before, so will return to earlier learning and progress their evaluation of the content they find.

Creative context
● The lessons link closely to the English curriculum, by explaining and discussing their understanding of what they have read, including through formal presentations and debates. They retrieve, record and present information from non-fiction, making comparisons across different texts.
● They prepare to read aloud and to perform, showing understanding through intonation, tone and volume so that the meaning is clear to an audience. They provide reasoned justifications for their views.
● Linking to the geography curriculum, they learn about China's and India's major cities and climates.
● Linking to the history curriculum, the children learn about famous figures such as Mahatma Gandhi and the British rule of India.

Background knowledge
● The children will have knowledge of China and India through the news and for some through family links.
● Their learning about internet filtering will build on their current knowledge of the school internet filtering compared with their access to the web outside of school.
● The children have presented information and have considered what makes an effective presentation, so they will learn about other presentation styles.

Curriculum objectives
● To use search technologies effectively and be discerning in evaluating digital content.
● To use technology safely, respectfully and responsibly; recognise acceptable/ unacceptable behaviour; identify a range of ways to report concerns about content and contact.

Lesson objectives
● To explain how to use a computer safely.
● To know there are different types of browser.
● To know that browsers have safety features included in them.
● To describe why browsers have safety features.

Expected outcomes
● Can explain how to use technology safely.
● Can describe safety features that are included in internet browsers.

Resources
Photocopiable page 49 'Our Google home page'; photocopiable page 50 'Different web browsers'

China

In this lesson, the children think about what they already know about China and then research online. They look at the different Google search home pages for the UK and for China and compare them. Considering different web browsers, they explore the safety features that are available.

Introduction
● Ask the children what they already know about China.
● Display ideas using an online 'sticky note' wall, for example, Padlet.com.
● Use the sticky note wall as an assessment tool, showing what the children know at the start of the topic and returning at the end to add new knowledge.

Whole-class work
● Display the Google homepage for China (Hong Kong) (www.google.com. hk/). Does it look different to the UK website (www.google.co.uk)?
● Ask: *Do you think that every country accesses the same information?*
● Using photocopiable page 49 'Our Google home page', they draw what a home page for their town or school would look like and invent a web address. They then list examples of other Google search web addresses.
● Display the Google home pages for China and the UK, then search using the word 'censorship'. On the Chinese page, the results will be a mixture of those in Chinese and in English. The children will see that the English Wikipedia page is listed (http://en.wikipedia.org/wiki/Censorship).
● On the English Google results page, they will see a list of articles, including the same Wikipedia link. So, each country will produce different results for a search. However, some websites will rank highly in many countries.

Paired work
● Using two different web browsers, for example Internet Explorer, Google Chrome or Mozilla Firefox, the children list the common features and differences, using photocopiable page 50 'Different web browsers'. Areas to consider include bookmarking, browser settings, how to search and so on.

Whole-class work
● Explain that web browsers have safety features built in to them. For example, Mozilla Firefox (www.mozilla.org/en-US/firefox/security/) has features such as blocking pop-up windows, which are often used for advertising. Google Chrome has advice for safe browsing, by setting the 'Safe Search' as a default (www.google.com/safetycenter/families/start/).

Paired work
● Using the notes you made on their thinking about China, can the children think of three key questions they would like to ask? For example: *What is the population? How big is China? Does everyone have a mobile phone?*
● They then research three amazing facts about China to share with the class.

Review
● Bring the class together and ask ten children to state their research question, the search words they used and then the fact they found.
● Ask ten other children to describe the differences between the two web browsers. Did they find one easier to use than the other?
● Explain that, to stay safe when online, the children should always be careful.
● Explain that when using the World Wide Web, there is, most likely, filtering in school and Google Safe Search, to help protect them from finding inappropriate material, but it is not completely safe and if they access the World Wide Web outside of school or without Safe Search, they need to be even more careful.
● Ask: *Should web browsers should have filtering automatically activated or should it be up to the user to enable the features?*

Curriculum objectives
● To use search technologies effectively and be discerning in evaluating digital content.
● To use technology safely, respectfully and responsibly; recognise acceptable/ unacceptable behaviour; identify a range of ways to report concerns about content and contact.

Lesson objectives
● To discuss whether the important information is displayed in Simple English Wikipedia compared to Wikipedia.
● To explain why there is a need for Simple English Wikipedia.
● To know that wiki pages can be edited.
● To be able to change the bias of a website by changing the text and images, using software tools.

Expected outcomes
● Can compare the detailed and simple versions of Wikipedia to identify if the important information is present.
● Can model changing the bias and purpose of a website, using software tools.

Resources
Photocopiable page 54 'Gandhi facts'; interactive activity 'Gandhi facts' on the CD-ROM

Mahatma Gandhi

The children look at Wikipedia and the information that it holds about Mahatma Gandhi. They discuss how the pages are edited and refined. Looking the Simple English Wikipedia, they compare the text with the main Wikipedia site. They understand that the pages can be edited.

Introduction

● Explain that they will be focusing on a famous Indian person named Mahatma Gandhi.
● Demonstrate an online search to find out about Gandhi. Ask the children which search words you should use?
● On the list of search results, show that the Wikipedia entry is most likely to be very near the top. Why do the children think this is?
● Explain that Google gathers information on all the websites using 'web crawlers', pieces of software that visit the websites and follow the links, gathering information and returning it to Google.
● The information is 'ranked' or ordered depending on complex algorithms.
● Advertisers can also buy space. Demonstrate a search for 'advertising on Google' and the page returned shows space that advertisers can purchase.

Paired work

● Ask the children to research the life and death of Gandhi. They record the information on photocopiable page 54 'Gandhi facts'.
● They record the facts and the websites where they found the information. However, explain that they are not allowed to use Wikipedia this time.
● Once complete, they choose one fact and write it in large text on the sheet.
● Children can use the interactive activity 'Gandhi facts' on the CD-ROM to check if their research has made them experts on Gandhi!

Whole-class work

● Ask the children to share their fact about Gandhi. Display each fact written (on the page in large text) on the wall of the classroom. If the children have chosen the same fact, then it may be more likely that the information is correct.
● Explain that Wikipedia is a huge collection of facts that people have brought together. When another person reads the information, if they think it is incorrect, then they change it.
● Ask: *Do you think the information will become more or less accurate*?
● Reinforce the idea that Wikipedia should be used alongside other pieces of information, to ensure accuracy.
● Ask the children to look at the Wikipedia page for Gandhi. Do the facts they have located support the information on the page?

Whole-class work

● Tell the children that there is a 'Simple English Wikipedia' (http://simple.wikipedia.org).
● Display the home page on the screen and then search for 'Gandhi'. Can they see the difference between the simple page and the full Wikipedia page.
● To help with this comparison, use http://oranchak.com/againbutslower.com which displays the pages side-by-side.
● What do the children think are the main differences between the main Wikipedia and Simple Wikipedia websites?

Review

● Bring the class together and ask the children why they think there is a need for Simple English Wikipedia?
● Explain that wiki pages can be edited by anyone, so the children could make changes to Wikipedia (though some pages on Wikipedia are protected).
● If they felt a page was biased, they could change the bias, by altering the

Curriculum objectives
● To use search technologies effectively and be discerning in evaluating digital content.
● To use technology safely, respectfully and responsibly; recognise acceptable/unacceptable behaviour; identify a range of ways to report concerns about content and contact.

Lesson objectives
● To explain the importance of giving concise presentations, while including the important information.
● To create criteria for an effective presentation.
● To create a presentation based on effective, self-authored criteria.
● To evaluate other children's presentations, based on self-authored criteria.

Expected outcomes
● Can present relevant information, in a concise way.
● Can evaluate other children's presentations, using given criteria.

Resources
Photocopiable page 55 'Our effective presentation criteria'; photocopiable page 'Pecha Kucha planning' from the CD-ROM; stop watches

Effective presentations

Giving presentations is an important skill, so this week the children think about 'What makes an effective presentation?' They produce their own criteria to use within the lesson. Using a style of presentation called 'Pecha Kucha', they research the death of Gandhi and prepare one slide to share. They evaluate their presentations using their criteria.

Introduction
● Introduce the lesson by sharing two videos of Mahatma Gandhi's funeral:
   ● www.history.com/videos/history-rewind-gandhis-funeral-1948#history-rewind-gandhis-funeral-1948
   ● www.britishpathe.com/video/funeral-of-gandhi/
● Ask: *What facts can you remember about Mahatma Gandhi?*

Whole-class work
● Explain to the children that they will be creating a presentation on Gandhi, using a special format called 'Pecha Kucha'. The name comes from the Japanese for 'chit chat' and it consists of 20 slides of pictures, which are displayed for 20 seconds.
● For some children, it may be difficult to talk for over six minutes. Therefore, an alternative method would be for each child to choose an image about Gandhi and talk for 20 seconds about it.
● Ask: *What do you think would make an effective presentation?*
● Collect suggestions, for example, 'the words match the image' or 'they include at least one fact'.
● From the list, compile the five criteria for an effective presentation. The children add these to photocopiable page 55 'Our effective presentation criteria'.

Independent work
● Each child researches an image related to Gandhi online.
● Using photocopiable page 'Pecha Kucha planning' from the CD-ROM, the children compose the words they will say.

Whole-class work
● You will need to bring together the images that the children have chosen into one presentation in a shared network area or a collaborative presentation, for example Google docs.
● Once the children have shared their images, compile the presentation with each image on a separate slide.

Paired work
● In pairs, the children practise reading words for their image. They time each other to make sure that they can speak their words in 20 seconds.
● They need to check their effective presentation criteria to assess whether their partner is following them.

Review
● Bring the class together and organise the children into the order of the presentation slides.
● Each child takes turns to say their words, while their Gandhi image is displayed.
● The children evaluate each presentation, using the presentation criteria that they authored at the beginning of the lesson.
● When everyone has presented, ask the class whether they enjoyed the 'Pecha Kucha' style of presentation.
● Conclude the lesson by highlighting that they self-authored their own criteria and then used them to create and evaluate their presentations.

Curriculum objectives
● To use search technologies effectively and be discerning in evaluating digital content.
● To use technology safely, respectfully and responsibly; recognise acceptable/ unacceptable behaviour; identify a range of ways to report concerns about content and contact.

Lesson objectives
● To explain what bias is, through giving relevant examples.
● To know that websites may contain bias.
● To analyse websites to decide whether they are biased.
● To explain how to choose appropriate search keywords and justify their selection.

Expected outcomes
● Can describe how websites may contain bias.
● Can choose and justify appropriate search keywords to locate information.

Resources
Photocopiable page 'Checking for bias' from the CD-ROM

Is it biased?

The children look at ways to discern whether a site is biased. They use the Simple English Wikipedia to make a book and decide whether this helps them to understand the information.

Introduction
● Introduce the lesson by displaying the Simple English Wikipedia page for Mahatma Gandhi (https://simple.wikipedia.org/wiki/Mahatma_Gandhi).
● In the side bar menu on the left of the page is an option called 'Print/export' then 'Make a book'.
● Select 'Make a book' and you are taken to the page asking 'Start book creator'. Once pressed the Gandhi page is displayed again, but this time, it has a box at the top for the book creator.
● Pages can be added by selecting the 'Add this page to your book' link.
● Choose another link on the page such as 'Gujarati', then select 'Add linked wiki page to your book'.
● Continue to add one more page, then select 'Show book'.
● The book creator tool gathers the information from each page and places into the book. This can be given a name, for example 'The life of Gandhi' and a subtitle, which could be the child's name.
● Select Download and select from the dropdown menu 'e-book pdf'. It will say it is rendering the book, then change page to say 'Rendering finished'. Select 'Download the file' to save the document to the computer.
● The output file is a 'pdf' so, when you view it, you can see that it's a table of contents, then the information from each page. This has collected the evidence together in one place.
● You can now search the document using the 'Find' tool in the menu.

Paired work
● In pairs, the children research the life of Gandhi, using Simple English Wikipedia and gather pages together using the book creator tool.

Whole-class work
● Bring the class together and ask whether they think the book creator helps them to research the topic.
● Explain that they are going to look for bias in the documents, by searching for particular words.
● They will choose part of the document to read aloud to listen for whether it sounds fair. If they would feel uncomfortable saying the words, it may be biased.
● They will search for words like: 'always', 'never', 'obviously', 'certainly', 'definitely', 'undoubtedly', 'activist', 'protest' and so on. Does this make the page look like it favours a particular viewpoint?
● Check the references – where has the information come from? Is it reliable?

Paired work
● In pairs, the children read through their book. They search for keywords and check the links.
● Using photocopiable page 'Checking for bias' from the CD-ROM, they record the tests they have carried out on the text.

Review
● Bring the class together and ask where the children thought they may have discovered bias. Wikipedia is edited by many people, so the intention is that the articles should be impartial and not biased. However, this process may take time and small changes may alter the bias of an article.
● Conclude the lesson by playing the video on reliability from the Childnet resources (www.childnet.com/resources/the-adventures-of-kara-winston-and-the-smart-crew/chapter2).

Curriculum objectives

● To use search technologies effectively and be discerning in evaluating digital content.
● To use technology safely, respectfully and responsibly; recognise acceptable/ unacceptable behaviour; identify a range of ways to report concerns about content and contact.

Lesson objectives

● To know how to search using specific, appropriate keywords.
● To evaluate the results of a keyword search.
● To be discerning in evaluating the content found using a search.
● To find particular words on a web page using the search tool.

Expected outcomes

● Can be discerning in evaluating the content found using a search.
● Can use the search on a web page to locate particular words.

Resources

Photocopiable page 'Searching for information on India' from the CD-ROM; photocopiable page 'Pecha Kucha planning' from the CD-ROM

China and India: Assess and review

The children research facts about India, recording and justifying their search words, before creating a short presentation to share their learning.

Introduction

● Remind the children about the facts they collected about India. They shared their original knowledge about India in the earlier lesson. Return to these notes to add newly acquired knowledge.
● Ask: *What have you learned about India?*
● Collect together the new facts and display them. Can children see how they have learned more about the country and its people?

Whole-class work

● Remind the children of the work they did using a 'Pecha Kucha' presentation about Gandhi. Explain that today they are going to prepare another 'Pecha Kucha' presentation. They will divide the work between the class and each present one slide, containing one large image. They will talk for 20 seconds.
● Ask: *What is important for an effective presentation?*
● The children need to search for facts about India and record them using photocopiable page 'Searching for information on India' from the CD-ROM.
● Divide the class into groups to research broad themes; for example the country, food and drink, famous Indian politicians and sport.
● In each group, the children individually research the topic and choose a slide.
● Ask: *Which search words will you use and how will you decide which links to follow from your page of results?*
● They need to record which key words they used for searching and how they decided upon the links to follow from the results the search page displays.
● On the websites they find, they can then use the 'Find' tool to search within the page.

Independent/paired work

● Allow the children time to research their chosen topic and to select the image for their slide.
● Again, you will need to gather the images together into one presentation.
● They then write the words they are going to say to accompany their picture, using photocopiable page 'Pecha Kucha planning' from the CD-ROM, and practise the timing.
● In pairs, they practise presenting to each other before the class comes together to present the 'Pecha Kucha' style presentation.

Differentiation

● Support: Less confident learners may need support to select the search words to use. They may need help to draft the words they are going to use and check that they clearly share the facts.
● Challenge: More confident learners will be able to research their topic, locate an image and relevant information. They will be able to plan and draft the words they will use and review the content to ensure that it conveys the facts.

Review

● Organise the class in order of the slides in the presentation. You will need to group the topics, for example the sport slides should be together.
● The children should present their slide, keeping in mind the criteria they had drafted for an effective presentation (in week 5).
● Once complete, ask: *How did you find the information? Did you use the 'Find' tool on a page to locate particular words, showing whether the content you found was relevant?*
● Would they approach the task differently if they did it again or had more time?

Our Google home page

■ Design a Google home page for your school or town.

What could the web address be? Add this to your sketch.

[Blank drawing box]

■ List examples of Google search web addresses for France, Germany, Australia, New Zealand and the USA.

_____

_____

_____

_____

_____

I can look at Google home pages for different countries and recognise the format.

How did you do?

Different web browsers

■ Write the names of two web browsers and draw their logos below. Note some features of each browser, for example, how do you search, access settings, or add bookmarks?

Browser 1 name	Browser 2 name
Logo	Logo
Features of browser 1	Features of browser 2

Similarities between the two browsers are:

_____

Differences between the two browsers are:

_____

I can compare the features of two web browsers.

How did you do?

PHOTOCOPIABLE

Name: _____   Date: _____

For and against filtering

■ Write your reasons for and against filtering the content of the World Wide Web.

For filtering	Against filtering

I can think of reasons for and against filtering the content of the World Wide Web.

How did you do?

Seasons of Splendour search

■ Search for information about the book *Seasons of Splendour* by Madhur Jaffrey.
The search words I will use are:

_____

_____

_____

_____

_____

On the results page, the links I will look at are:

_____

_____

_____

The reasons I chose them are:

_____

_____

My *Seasons of Splendour* facts are:

_____

_____

_____

_____

I can research online and carefully consider which results I choose.

How did you do?

Word detective

The website I have chosen is called: _____

The web address is: http:// _____

The ten words to find are:

_____

_____

_____

_____

_____

_____

I can use the 'Find' search tool in a browser to locate particular words.

How did you do?

Name: _____ Date: _____

Gandhi facts

■ Draw a sketch of Mahatma Gandhi below.

From my research online, my Mahatma Gandhi facts are:

1. _____

2. _____

3. _____

4. _____

5. _____

On which websites did you find the facts?

■ Write one of the facts that you have found in large text on the back of this sheet.

I can research about Mahatma Gandhi online and record the facts.

How did you do?

PHOTOCOPIABLE

SCHOLASTIC
www.scholastic.co.uk

Name: _____ Date: _____

Our effective presentation criteria

In an effective presentation, I would:

SEE: 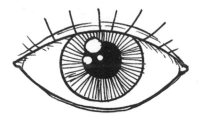   HEAR:

From all our ideas, we think the five most important features of an effective presentation are:

1. _____

2. _____

3. _____

4. _____

5. _____

I can create my own criteria for an effective presentation.

How did you do?

Kensuke's Kingdom

This chapter engages the children in a theme around the author Michael Morpurgo and especially his book *Kensuke's Kingdom*. The children use and combine a wider range of tools and software to collect and present data. They use an online voting tool to gather the answers to a class survey. They filter the data collected using a flat file and refine their questions, based upon feedback. The children consider the importance of the human–computer interface, by reviewing and designing different questionnaire forms. They describe how 'useable' an interface is and how it could be improved.

Expected prior learning

- The children will have collected data using tally charts and created pictograms and bar charts.
- They will have used web browsers to access the World Wide Web, though they may not have considered how these are designed for the user.
- They will have written for different audiences and will apply this learning to creating questionnaires.

Chapter at a glance

Subject area
• Data and information

National Curriculum objective
• To select, use and combine a variety of software (including internet services) on a range of digital devices to design and create a range of programs, systems and content that accomplish given goals, including collecting, evaluating and presenting data and information.

Week	Lesson objectives	Summary of activities	Expected outcomes
1	• To describe the difference between software and hardware. • To know that software is designed for particular users. • To describe how a piece of software is designed for particular users. • To explain how to complete a simple questionnaire. • To discuss what makes a good question. • To create a series of questions related to a particular author's work (for example, Michael Morpurgo).	• Children are introduced to Michael Morpurgo as an author and search for facts about him. • They look at different web browsers and how they are designed for different users. • After reading the opening of *Kensuke's Kingdom* by Michael Morpurgo, children create a comprehension questionnaire. • They discuss what makes a good question and write some related to the story.	• Can describe how a piece of software has been designed for the user. • Can design a simple questionnaire.
2	• To create a simple questionnaire, relating to an author (for example, Michael Morpurgo), using an online tool. • To review a simple questionnaire to decide if the questions can be answered using an online tool. • To describe the features of an online tool to identify the human–computer interface design. • To describe the importance of human–computer interface design.	• Children continue to read *Kensuke's Kingdom* and create a questionnaire. • They decide whether an online tool could be used. • They recognise the importance of human–computer interface design.	• Can use an online tool to create a simple questionnaire. • Can explain the importance of human–computer interface design.
3	• To use an online tool to collect questionnaire data. • To evaluate if the data is collected more efficiently using online tools compared to in person. • To display the data gathered using an online tool, for different audiences.	• Children discuss and the research the plight of orang-utans. • They investigate online to find facts and opinions about orang-utans. • They use an online tool to collect data and evaluate whether data collected online is more efficient than face-to-face.	• Can use an online tool to collect questionnaire data. • Can use an online tool to display questionnaire data.

Week	Lesson objectives	Summary of activities	Expected outcomes
4	• To create a questionnaire, based upon a fictional book (for example, by Michael Morpurgo) using an online tool for two particular audiences. • To explain how a questionnaire can be designed for a particular audience. • To use an online questionnaire to collect data. • To manipulate data collected using an online tool.	• Children create a questionnaire on Japan and the Second World War. • They collect data and analyse it in a flat file. • They apply a filter to the data. • They use an online tool to create a questionnaire for different audiences.	• Can use an online tool to create a questionnaire for two different audiences. • Can collect and manipulate questionnaire data.
5	• To define an infographic. • To review examples of infographics and discuss their effectiveness, using given criteria. • To create a simple, paper-based infographic (themed upon a fictional book, for example, by Michael Morpurgo).	• Children look at how data can be presented, for example, pictograms. • The look at examples of infographics in everyday life. • They create a simple infographic related to the content of *Kensuke's Kingdom*.	• Can examine and evaluate examples of infographics. • Can create a simple infographic.
6	• To create an infographic using online tools or software. • To research information, using a search engine, to locate information. • To present information in different ways as an infographic (themed upon a fictional book, for example, by Michael Morpurgo). • To explain the importance of human–computer interface design.	• Children use an online tool to create an infographic. • They present information as an infographic based on *Kensuke's Kingdom*. • They describe the importance of human–computer interface design.	• Can research a specific topic and present using an infographic. • Can explain the importance of human–computer interface design.
Assess and review	• Assess and review the half term's work.	• Children create a simple questionnaire using an online tool. • They review and improve the questionnaire. • They discuss the features of an online tool to identify how it is designed for the user. • They recognise the importance of human–computer interface design.	• Assess and review.

Overview of progression

● The children progress their knowledge of web browsers, thinking about their design for a user.
● They look at online tools and evaluate the design of the 'human–computer interface'.
● They develop their questioning skills and refine their questions based upon feedback.

Creative context

● The lessons link closely to the English curriculum; the children present to different audiences and evaluate fact verses opinion.
● Linking to maths, the children begin to decide which representations of data are most appropriate and give reasons to justify their answers.
● For geography, the story of *Kensuke's Kingdom* involves sailing around the world, so the children can trace the route and at the same time think about the different climates of the countries passed.
● Linking to history, children learn about the Second World War and the nuclear bomb on Nagasaki.

Background knowledge

● The children will have created bar charts and pictograms. The chapter focuses on how the online tools can be used and about the human–computer interface.
● The children will have considered how software is designed for the user and may have used more than one browser to access the World Wide Web.
● They will have experienced comprehension questions, though they may not have written their own nor used an online tool to gather the feedback.

Web browser design

The children are introduced to the author, Michael Morpurgo, and in particular one of his stories *Kensuke's Kingdom*. The children look at websites using different web browsers and think about how they are designed for the user. Based on the opening to the story, they create questions to ask each other about what is happening. They then think about what makes a 'good' question?

Introduction
● Introduce the lesson by asking the children if they have heard of the author Michael Morpurgo. They may have heard about *War Horse*, a book that has been successfully adapted into a play and a film.
● Display Michael Morpurgo's website http://michaelmorpurgo.com/about-michael-morpurgo. What job did he have before becoming a writer?
● Read the opening of *Kensuke's Kingdom* by Michael Morpurgo.

Whole-class work
● Explain that web browsers display web pages. However, different web browsers can have different designs and features intended for different users.
● Show the Michael Morpurgo website on two different browsers.

Paired work
● Using two different web browsers, allow the children to investigate facts about Michael Morpurgo. They record their findings using photocopiable page 65 'About Michael Morpurgo'.
● They write a short evaluation of the two browsers, which helps them think about the design.

Whole-class work
● Bring the class together and ask their opinions of the different browsers. Were they intuitive to use? Did the children find features that they had not used before?
● Explain that they are going to create a simple comprehension questionnaire about the start of the book.
● Read the opening passage again and ask three children to think of a question.
● Record the questions and display them for the class. Can the children infer the characters' thoughts and motivations by asking questions?
● Ask what makes a 'good' question? The children may reply with criteria such as using simple words or asking about something interesting.

Paired work
● In pairs, the children create a series of questions related to the story, using photocopiable page 66 'Kensuke's Kingdom questions' (the children can read the first pages of the text of the book online at http://clubs-kids.scholastic.co.uk/products/31 Click 'Look inside').
● They ask their partner the questions to see whether they can answer them.
● Finally, they order the questions from most easy to most difficult.

Review
● Bring the class together and collect ten different questions. Could they rank them from easy questions to more difficult questions?
● Ask the class to answer the questions. You can differentiate this by giving the more confident children the challenging questions.

Curriculum objectives
● To select, use and combine a variety of software (including internet services) on a range of digital devices to design and create a range of programs, systems and content that accomplish given goals, including collecting, evaluating and presenting data and information.

Lesson objectives
● To create a simple questionnaire, relating to an author (for example, Michael Morpurgo), using an online tool.
● To review a simple questionnaire to decide if the questions can be answered using an online tool.
● To describe the features of an online tool to identify the human–computer interface design.
● To describe the importance of human–computer interface design.

Expected outcomes
● Can use an online tool to create a simple questionnaire.
● Can explain the importance of human–computer interface design.

Resources
Photocopiable page 67 'Kensuke's Kingdom more questions'; Kensuke's Kingdom by Michael Morpurgo

Creating questionnaires

The children continue with the *Kensuke's Kingdom* theme. They use an online tool to answer verbal questions before creating their own quiz. They begin to discuss the 'human–computer interface' design.

Introduction
● Introduce the lesson by continuing to read *Kensuke's Kingdom* and discuss how Kensuke helps Michael.
● Following on from the previous lesson, the children create a simple true or false questionnaire relating to the text.
● Collect the children's questions together and display them. Select a question and children vote true or false, by raising their hands.

Whole-class work
● Using the online questioning tool, Socrative, log in as a teacher (http://socrative.com/). This will give you a 'room number'.
● The children log in at Socrative as students (http://socrative.com/). They then enter your room number.
● Once logged in, select the 'Single question activities' and then 'True/false'.
● Start the activity of asking questions and ask the children to vote 'true' or 'false' for their answers.
● Ask the children to evaluate how they found the activity, how was it different using the online tool?
● Another method of asking questions is multiple choice. In the 'Single question activities' section of Socrative, there is an option to ask multiple choice questions. By default, it offers responses of 'A, B, C, D or E'.
● Ask a multiple-choice question to gauge opinion; for example, *How friendly was Kensuke when Michael first arrived on the island? Was he A: very friendly B: friendly C: neither friendly nor unfriendly D: unfriendly or E: very unfriendly?*

Paired work
● In pairs, the children write ten questions on *Kensuke's Kingdom*. They could be true or false or multiple-choice questions. They record the questions using photocopiable page 67 '*Kensuke's Kingdom:* More questions'.

Whole-class work
● Children can vote on their favourite class question. Using Socrative, select 'Short answer' then 'Single student response' and 'Anonymous students'.
● Pairs choose a question from their ten and type it into their computers. The question will appear on the teacher screen.
● Once every pair has added a question, review the questions with the class before selecting to vote on which one they liked best.
● Ask one of the children who voted for the most popular question to explain why they chose it.

Review
● Ask children about using the online tool to collect answers: *Do you think it helps the process or could there be disadvantages?* For example, Socrative requires internet access.
● Ask the children to look at the design of the Socrative page: *How is it designed for the user? For example, has it got clear text? Are the instructions easy to understand? Is the language appropriate for children or adults?*
● Explain that the 'human–computer interface' is very important to enable a person to be able to use the online tool.

Curriculum objectives
● To select, use and combine a variety of software (including internet services) on a range of digital devices to design and create a range of programs, systems and content that accomplish given goals, including collecting, evaluating and presenting data and information.

Lesson objectives
● To use an online tool to collect questionnaire data.
● To evaluate if the data is collected more efficiently using online tools compared to in person.
● To display the data gathered using an online tool, for different audiences.

Expected outcomes
● Can use an online tool to collect questionnaire data.
● Can use an online tool to display questionnaire data.

Resources
Photocopiable page 68 'Orang-utan facts'; *Kensuke's Kingdom* by Michael Morpurgo

Orang-utans

In the *Kensuke's Kingdom* story, there are orang-utans. The children research orang-utans using online searches. They gather the information to create an online quiz. The class then completes the quiz to gather the data. They consider the differences between collecting the data face-to-face and online.

Introduction
● In the story *Kensuke's Kingdom*, it describes the orang-utans in the forest. What do the children know about orang-utans?
● Ask them which words they would use to locate information about orang-utans. Display www.orangutans-sos.org/kids/orangutan_facts.
● Ask: *Does orang-utan mean 'person of the forest'? Are orang-utans an endangered species?*

Paired work
● In pairs, the children investigate online to find facts and opinions about orang-utans.
● Using photocopiable page 68 'Orang-utan facts' they construct a short questionnaire using true or false or multiple choice questions.

Whole-class work
● Bring the class together and ask for an example of each style of question.
● Using Socrative (http://socrative.com/), login as a teacher and demonstrate how to create a new quiz. Select 'Manage quizzes' then 'Create a quiz'.
● Give the quiz a name and ensure that the 'Enable sharing' box is ticked.
● Select the style of question – multiple choice or short answer.
● When all the questions have been added, select 'Save'.
● Write down the 'SOC' number (this means the quiz can be shared).

Paired work
● In pairs, the children use the questions from the photocopiable sheet to create an online quiz using Socrative.
● Once the children have finished creating their quiz, they should write down their 'SOC' number.

Whole-class work
● Bring the class together and import one of the children's quizzes. This is carried out by selecting 'Manage quizzes' then 'Import quiz', which then prompts for the 'SOC' number. Type in the number and then save.
● Allow the children to log in on http://socrative.com/ as a 'Student' and enter the room number.
● On the teacher's computer, on the main page, select 'Start quiz' and use the drop-down menu to choose the quiz.
● Start the quiz and allow the children to complete the questions.

Differentiation
● Support: Less confident learners may need support to manipulate the online tools and to locate appropriate information.
● Challenge: More confident learners will be able to use online tools to create their own quizzes and then answer other children's quizzes. They will research appropriate information about orang-utans and convert it into questions.

Review
● Once the quiz is complete, bring the class together and select 'End activity'.
● Select 'Download' and an .xls spreadsheet file can be kept as a record.
● Ask the children about the human–computer interface – is it easy to use Socrative online to create a quiz?
● Ask them whether they think the data can be collected more efficiently using online tools than face to face. What might be a disadvantage?

Writing for different audiences

The children consider writing for different audiences. They create a quiz to ask the class about their knowledge of the Second World War and Japan. The data is then displayed as a flat file, using an online spreadsheet tool, which can be manipulated using a filter to analyse the responses.

Introduction

● Introduce the lesson by asking the children about the characters in the story. They are Kensuke, a 75-year-old Japanese man, and Michael, a 12-year-old English boy. In the story, they have different approaches to living on the island.
● Explain that creating resources for children and adults can be very different.
● Can they imagine what style of resource an older person would prefer? How about a younger person?

Whole-class work

● Ask the children what they know about Japan and in particular what they know about Japan during the Second World War.

Paired work

● In pairs, the children research Japan in the Second World War using photocopiable page 69 'The Second World War and Japan facts', to record facts and then write five questions for a quiz.
● Once complete, they log into Socrative (http://socrative.com/) as a teacher and add their questions to a new quiz. (They record the 'SOC' number, so the quiz can be shared).

Whole-class work

● Bring the class together and select one quiz from one pair of children for the whole class to complete.
● Download the report as a spreadsheet and then display as a flat file database.
● Try different filtering questions and options to filter answers.

Paired work

● Ask the children to look at the type of questions they asked. They may have used mostly knowledge-style questions, such as: *What happened after...? How many...?* and so on.
● Using photocopiable page 70 'Evaluation questions' children rewrite three questions in their questionnaire. They use more evaluation-style questions, such as: *Which is more important...? What is more moral...? What is better...?*

Differentiation

● Support: Less confident learners could adjust their questionnaire for younger learners, for example, for Year 4 children.
● Challenge: More confident learners will be able to adapt their questionnaire to be more challenging for themselves and others. They can ask more 'evaluation' style questions, rather than 'knowledge' recall questions. You could adjust the main questions by asking them to focus on the use of the nuclear bomb on Japan.

Review

● Bring the class together and ask children to share their new questions.
● Ask the class to comment on the success of their new questions as more or less challenging.
● Can the children give feedback on how to improve the questions?

Curriculum objectives

● To select, use and combine a variety of software (including internet services) on a range of digital devices to design and create a range of programs, systems and content that accomplish given goals, including collecting, evaluating and presenting data and information.

Lesson objectives

● To create a questionnaire, based upon a fictional book (for example, by Michael Morpurgo) using an online tool for two particular audiences.
● To explain how a questionnaire can be designed for a particular audience.
● To use an online questionnaire to collect data.
● To manipulate data collected using an online tool.

Expected outcomes

● Can use an online tool to create a questionnaire for two different audiences.
● Can collect and manipulate questionnaire data.

Resources

Photocopiable page 69 'The Second World War and Japan facts'; photocopiable page 70 'Evaluation questions'

Curriculum objectives
● To select, use and combine a variety of software (including internet services) on a range of digital devices to design and create a range of programs, systems and content that accomplish given goals, including collecting, evaluating and presenting data and information.

Objectives
● To define an infographic.
● To review examples of infographics and discuss their effectiveness, using given criteria.
● To create a simple, paper-based infographic (themed on a fictional book).

Expected outcomes
● Can examine and evaluate examples of infographics.
● Can create a simple infographic.

Resources
Interactive activity 'Bar graph' on the CD-ROM; interactive activity 'Word clouds' on the CD-ROM; photocopiable page 'My chocolate pictogram' from the CD-ROM

Infographics

Infographics are a way of representing data visually. The children look at examples of infographics, such as pictograms and word clouds. They create pictograms based on a class survey.

Introduction
● Introduce the lesson by asking: *What is a pictogram?* Explain that pictograms are one way of representing data.

Whole-class work
● Carry out a survey of favourite chocolate bars. Ask for the names of five bars and then ask the children to vote for their favourite.
● Collect the results and then display the numbers on the screen, using the interactive activity 'Bar graph' on the CD-ROM.
● Using photocopiable page 'My chocolate pictogram', the children complete a table and a pictogram of the chocolate bar survey.
● Ask children to compare their pictogram to the electronic bar graph. Which one is most suited to the audience of their class? Which one do they think would suit an adult audience?

Paired work
● In pairs, the children look online using the safe search (http://primaryschoolict.com/) to search for examples of 'infographics'.
● One website that posts an infographic every week is: http://edutech4teachers.edublogs.org/category/infographic-of-the-week/.

Whole-class work
● Select three children to define an infographic (a way of representing data visually). Infographics are often used in the news and in newspapers and magazines, to share the data in an attractive, interesting and accessible way.
● Display a word cloud example from the interactive activity 'Word clouds' on the CD-ROM.
● Word clouds are simple infographics that display the words from a text. The more often a word appears, the larger it is represented.
● Two word cloud generators are: Wordle (http://www.wordle.net/ – requires Java) and Tagxedo (www.tagxedo.com/ – requires Microsoft Silverlight).
● On the Tagxedo website, select 'Create' and on the new page, select 'Load'. Now paste text from your document into the box. Text can be cut and pasted from another source. Alternatively, a website address can be added to the search box. For example, text from *Kensuke's Kingdom* could be cut and pasted from the electronic sample book (http://clubs-kids.scholastic.co.uk/products/31 – select 'Look inside').
● Using the 'Shape' button, the outline shape of the cloud can be changed, for example, into a speech bubble or the shape of a country.

Paired work
● The children locate their favourite website or a page from Wikipedia on their favourite topic, then they cut and paste the text into the 'Load' box.
● Which shape do they think is appropriate for their word cloud?

Differentiation
● Support: Less confident learners may need support to locate the text to create a word cloud. They may need help to identify an appropriate shape to use.
● Challenge: More confident learners will be able to find and select text to add to the word cloud. They should be able to decide upon an appropriate outline shape.

Review
● Bring the class together and share four different word clouds that the children have created.

Curriculum objectives
● To select, use and combine a variety of software (including internet services) on a range of digital devices to design and create a range of programs, systems and content that accomplish given goals, including collecting, evaluating and presenting data and information.

Lesson objectives
● To create an infographic using online tools or software.
● To research information, using a search engine, to locate information.
● To present information in different ways as an infographic (themed on a fictional book).
● To explain the importance of human–computer interface design.

Expected outcomes
● Can research a specific topic and present using an infographic.
● Can explain the importance of human–computer interface design.

Resources
Paper plates and newspapers; photocopiable page 71 'Infographic research'

Digital infographics

The children engage in infographics by tearing plates and newspapers to represent the data. They move on to thinking about digital infographics. Using an online tool, they create infographics based on their research. They evaluate the human–computer interface and describe why it is important.

Introduction
● Introduce the lesson by asking the children how many had breakfast that morning? Do they think it was a healthy breakfast? In the story of *Kensuke's Kingdom*, Michael woke and found the food and drink he needed.
● Give each child a paper plate and ask them to tear the plate to show the proportion of children they think had a healthy breakfast. Once torn, they write on the plate a list of criteria for a healthy meal. Then, on the other piece of plate, ask them to write a list of criteria for an unhealthy meal.
● Select three children to explain why the have torn their plate in that proportion and what their criteria are for a healthy meal.

Independent work
● Give each of the children a page from a newspaper. Ask: *What proportion of the page do you think is fact and what is opinion?*
● Allow them time to tear, cut or colour the page, so that they can display an answer to the question.

Whole-class work
● Ask three children to hold up their newspaper and explain how they have organised the data.
● Tell them that they have created an infographic – a way of representing data visually. They have collected the data in an approximate way, but they can show others how much of the page they think is factual.
● Explain that the children can also use digital tools to represent data.
● Go to the Piktochart website (http://piktochart.com/), this is an online tool to help create infographics. Allow the children time to look at examples in the galley showcase http://piktochart.com/gallery/showcase/.

Paired work
● In pairs, the children decide on a topic to research. For example, they could choose a topic from *Kensuke's Kingdom*.
● They research the information using a search engine and record what they find on photocopiable page 71 'Infographic research'.
● Using Piktochart, they experiment with creating an infographic.

Differentiation
● Support: Less confident learners may need support to research their topic and then translate the data into an infographic.
● Challenge: More confident learners will be able to research a topic, using appropriate keywords, then create an infographic using an online tool. Ask them to justify why they have represented the data in that format.

Review
● Bring the class together and share five of the children's infographics.
● Ask the children to explain how they created the infographic and why they chose that format. Can they comment on the success of their solution?
● Ask them about their experiences of using the online software. Did you find the tool intuitive to use? Were the controls clear?
● Remind them of the importance of the 'human–computer interface'. The company who designed the tool needed to think carefully about who would be using it. Explain that the company would have spent a long time listening to feedback and improving the design.

Curriculum objectives
● To select, use and combine a variety of software (including internet services) on a range of digital devices to design and create a range of programs, systems and content that accomplish given goals, including collecting, evaluating and presenting data and information.

Lesson objectives
● To create a simple questionnaire.
● To display the data.
● To describe the features of an online tool to identify the human–computer interface design.
● To describe the importance of human–computer interface design.

Expected outcomes
● Can use an online tool to create a simple questionnaire.
● Can explain the importance of human–computer interface design.

Resources
Photocopiable page 'My book blurb' from the CD-ROM

Kensuke's Kingdom: Assess and review

Children use the online questionnaire tool to ask questions about the story *Kensuke's Kingdom*.

Introduction
● Introduce the lesson by asking the children to describe the 'blurb' of a book.
● Read the blurb for *Kensuke's Kingdom* (http://clubs-kids.scholastic.co.uk/products/31). Ask: *Does it make the story sound interesting?*

Group work
● In small groups of four, the children write their own blurbs for the story. Can they make it sound exciting and keep it to less than 100 words? They write their blurb using photocopiable page 'My book blurb' from the CD-ROM.
● They then create an online questionnaire to ask three questions about the blurb. For example, 'Does the opening sentence grab the reader's attention?' They add their questions to the photocopiable sheet.
● Using Socrative (http://socrative.com) the group can then log in as a teacher and create a new quiz (recording the 'SOC' number).
● They add each question as a multiple-choice question, using the responses 'A = Strongly agree' to 'E = Strongly disagree'.
● The group try out their questions and review them.

Whole-class work
● The class completes the surveys of each group. In order to do this, import the quiz from the first group (using their 'SOC' number). The first group read out their blurb and then the children complete the questionnaire.
● While the class is completing the questions, if you select 'Live results', the children will be able to see the responses appearing online.
● Ask: *Were the questions clear and easy to understand? How could you improve your questions? How is the online quiz tool designed to help the user? Why is it important that the human–computer interface design is suited to the needs of user?*

Group work
● Children take time to review their questionnaire to improve the questions.

Whole-class work
● The groups share their revised questionnaire with the class and explain how they have modified it, based on the feedback they received.

> ### Differentiation
> ● Support: Less confident learners may need support to create the questionnaire for the blurb. They will need support to write their book reviews and to add the simple questionnaire to evaluate it.
> ● Challenge: More confident learners should be able to create a book review and associated questionnaire to evaluate the review. They should take critical feedback and, based upon this, improve their work.

Review
● Bring the class together and ask two children to share their book reviews, their questionnaires and explain how they acted on the feedback.
● Ask the children to explain what the 'human–computer interface' is.
● Ask them to explain why 'human–computer interface' design is important.

About Michael Morpurgo

Ten facts about Michael Morpurgo:

1. _____

_____

2. _____

_____

3. _____

4. _____

5. _____

6. _____

7. _____

8. _____

9. _____

10. _____

I used two web browsers called:

_____ and _____

I liked the _____ feature of the _____ web browser,

because _____

I liked the _____ feature of the _____ web browser,

because _____

I liked the _____ feature of the _____ web browser,

because _____

I can use more than one web browser to access online information.

How did you do?

Kensuke's Kingdom questions

Eight questions about the opening of the *Kensuke's Kingdom* story.

1. _____

_____

2. _____

_____

3. _____

_____

4. _____

_____

5. _____

_____

6. _____

_____

7. _____

_____

_____

8. _____

_____

_____

■ Write the questions numbers below, in order of most difficult to easiest questions.

_____, _____, _____, _____, _____, _____, _____, _____

I can create questions based on a story.

How did you do?

Name: _____ Date: _____

Kensuke's Kingdom: More questions

■ Write your questions for your online quiz below.

1. _____

_____

2. _____

_____

3. _____

_____

4. _____

_____

5. _____

_____

6. _____

_____

7. _____

_____

8. _____

_____

9. _____

_____

10. _____

_____

I can write true/false and multiple-choice questions.

How did you do?

Orang-utan facts

■ Write five orang-utan facts.

1. _____

2. _____

3. _____

4. _____

5. _____

■ Now write five questions to raise awareness about the orang-utan situation in the world. You can use true or false or multiple-choice questions.

_____

_____

_____

_____

_____

■ Add your questions to the Socrative quiz.

My 'SOC' number for the quiz is: _____

I can research online and create quiz questions based on my results.

How did you do?

PHOTOCOPIABLE

SCHOLASTIC
www.scholastic.co.uk

The Second World War and Japan facts

- Write ten facts that you have found about Japan in the Second World War:

1. _____

2. _____

3. _____

4. _____

5. _____

6. _____

7. _____

8. _____

9. _____

10. _____

- Write five quiz questions on the back of the sheet.

My 'SOC' number is: _____

I can research online and create a series of questions.

How did you do?

Evaluation questions

■ Use the prompts below to write three 'evaluation'-style questions.

Which is more important...?

What is more moral...?

What is better...?

Is there a better solution to...?

What do you think about...?

Can you defend your position about...?

Do you think...is a good or bad thing?

What changes to...would you recommend?

Do you believe...?

How would you feel if...?

What are the consequences of...?

■ Write your questions here.

1. _____

_____

2. _____

_____

3. _____

_____

I can revise my questions to ask more evaluation-style questions.

How did you do?

Infographic research

My topic for research is: _____

The facts I have found are: _____

_____

_____

_____

_____

■ A sketch of my infographic would look like:

I can research online and represent the findings in an infographic.

How did you do?

Greek mythology

In this chapter children create a Greek mythology–themed maze game using Scratch. Using the plan-create-evaluate format, the children consolidate and extend their skills and understanding, working with multiple variables, repeat until loops and two-way selection when designing, writing and debugging their game.

Expected prior learning

● The children are familiar with Scratch from previous chapters and have been building their skills, knowledge and understanding of the Scratch language and many of the programming concepts. These skills will be developed further in this chapter. The children will need to know some of the more popular Greek myths, such as Theseus and the Minotaur as the sample game for this chapter is based on this story.

Chapter at a glance

Subject area
• Algorithms and programming

National Curriculum objective
• To design, write and debug programs that accomplish specific goals, including controlling or simulating physical systems; solve problems by decomposing them into smaller parts. To use sequence and repetition in programs; work with variables and various forms of input and output. To use logical reasoning to explain how some simple algorithms work and to detect and correct errors in algorithms and programs.

Week	Lesson objectives	Summary of activities	Expected outcomes
1	• To identify what makes an effective maze game and write criteria. • To brainstorm ideas for their own maze game based on a Greek myth. • To identify an audience. • To plan their maze game using a paper template. • To explain what elements they have included to ensure their maze game will be effective for the player.	• Children understand what makes an effective maze game. • They plan their own maze game based on a Greek myth.	• Can understand what makes an effective maze game. • Can plan a simple maze game using a given paper template.
2	• To identify the assets they need to create for their game. • To understand the importance of creating appealing assets within a game. • To create sprites, backgrounds and sounds for their animation. • To carefully name their assets and understand why that is important.	• Children discuss what makes an effective game. • They plan, create and collate the assets for their own game.	• Can plan and create the assets needed for their maze game. • Can use multimedia tools to create appealing assets for their game.
3	• To decompose their game into smaller programmable parts. • To plan the code for each part of their maze game. • To test and debug their code.	• Children match Scratch scripts to desired actions. • They plan code for their game. • They debug their code with a partner.	• Can use logical thinking to decompose their maze game into smaller parts. • Can design and write programs to create a maze game.
4	• To plan the use of sequences of two-way selection and repeat until loops to create efficient programs. • To implement sequences of two-way selection and repeat until loops to create efficient programs. • To work collaboratively to debug their code.	• Children understand how two-way selection and loops are used within the Scratch example game and then apply them to their own game. • Program their game and debug their code.	• Can use simple repeat until loops and two-way selection where appropriate. • Can work collaboratively to test and debug their programs.

■SCHOLASTIC

Week	Lesson objectives	Summary of activities	Expected outcomes
5	• To understand how multiple variables can be used to make their game more interesting for the player. • To use multiple variables to add scores, timers and lives as appropriate. • To test and debug their code as they write it. • To work collaboratively to debug their code.	• Children understand how variables can be created and added to their game to create lives, scores and timers. • They apply their knowledge to create their own variables. • They finish programming their game and debugging their code.	• Can use multiple variables where appropriate to create an effective game. • Can work collaboratively to test and debug their programs.
6	• To give and receive constructive feedback. • To evaluate their own game and others' games using their own criteria, as determined in Lesson I. • To discuss how they would change their approach if undertaking a similar task in the future.	• Children play each other's games and give and receive feedback. • They improve their work after feedback. • They evaluate their work and their approach to the task.	• Can evaluate their own and others' work. • Can evaluate their own approach to the task.
Assess and review	• Assess and review the half term's work.	• Create a tutorial for others on how to design and create a maze game using Scratch.	• Assess and review.

Overview of progression

• Throughout the lessons the children build upon their knowledge and understanding of programming using Scratch and of the creative process. They begin by considering what makes an effective maze game before planning and designing their own Greek mythology–based game. They then create and collect the assets they need for their game and plan their code. They are introduced to repeat until loops, multiple variables and two-way selection and evaluate both their completed game and their own approach to the task.

• Throughout the chapter, the children apply and develop their knowledge and understanding of programming by using their decomposition and problem-solving skills to achieve their planned outcomes and actions, working collaboratively to debug their work as needed.

Creative context

• The lessons have links to the mathematics curriculum as the children use logical thinking, problem solving and decomposition to write and debug their code. Programming movement of the sprites within the game in particular links to maths as the children apply angles, numbers and x and y coordinates. The computing lessons also draw on the children's learning in English through their written work in planning, creating and evaluating their game. The lessons also develop the children's spoken language as they are encouraged to share and explain their work verbally, including creating a tutorial for others to follow in the assess and review task.

• The lessons have links to the art curriculum as the children use the inbuilt paint tools to draw their own sprites and backgrounds.

Background knowledge

• From the work they have already completed in earlier years, the children will be confident designing and creating programs in Scratch. They have used single variables, broadcast blocks, If statements and repetition previously and this chapter extends their skills in Scratch and develops their understanding of programming.

• Having assessed the children's understanding in previous units, in this chapter assess the children's ability to create a maze game. Adjust the task as necessary, creating a simplified version for some children if needed.

• It is important to be a relatively able user of Scratch for this chapter and be familiar with how to create a maze game and use the example game used throughout the chapter.

• The lessons in this chapter assume the use of Scratch 1.4, although other versions, including the online version, could be used.

Curriculum objectives

● To design, write and debug programs that accomplish specific goals, including controlling or simulating physical systems. To solve problems by decomposing them into smaller parts; use sequence and repetition in programs; work with variables and various forms of input and output. To use logical reasoning to explain how some simple algorithms work and to detect and correct errors in algorithms and programs.

Lesson objectives

● To identify what makes an effective maze game and write criteria.
● To brainstorm ideas for their own maze game based on a Greek myth.
● To identify an audience.
● To plan their maze game using a paper template.
● To explain what elements they have included to ensure their maze game will be effective for the player.

Expected outcomes

● Can understand what makes an effective maze game.
● Can plan a simple maze game using a given paper template.

Resources

Photocopiable page 81 'Maze game ideas'; media resource 'Example maze game plan' on the CD-ROM; photocopiable page 82 'Maze game plan'; Scratch sample file 'Theseus and the Minotaur' (opened from the Quick links section of the CD-ROM)

Planning a maze game

The children establish criteria for an effective maze game and then decide upon a Greek myth on which to base their own game. They then plan their game, identifying the audience.

Introduction

● Remind the children of previous animation and quiz work they have completed in Scratch and explain that over the next few lessons they will be creating a maze game based on Greek mythology.
● Display and play the Scratch file 'Theseus and the Minotaur', opened from the Quick links section on the CD-ROM, on the whiteboard.
● Highlight and discuss features such as losing lives (variables), moving Theseus (with arrow keys), If statements (if reach minotaur, win message broadcast/if hit edge lose a life), and so on.

Whole-class work

● Invite the children to share what they know about maze games and what makes an effective maze game. You can use the Scratch example file to help.

Group/paired work

● Ask the children to come up with the top three elements that an effective maze game contains.
● You could use a think-pair-share activity if you wish (the children think for themselves, discuss with partner, share back to class).

Whole-class work

● Ask volunteers to share their ideas and as a class come up with around five key elements for an effective maze game should have. Write these on the whiteboard and save them for use in Week 6.
● Ask them to share what they know about Greek myths.

Independent/paired work

● Give each child or pair photocopiable page 81 'Maze game ideas' and ask them to brainstorm ideas for their maze game. Then they share ideas with a partner who helps them to choose one idea for their game.

Whole-class work

● Encourage children to consider who will be the audience for their game, that is, who will be most likely to play it.
● Give out photocopiable page 82 'Maze game plan' and ask the children to write a summary of their idea and their audience in the space provided.
● Display media resource 'Example maze game plan' on the CD-ROM, and discuss the plan for the 'Theseus and the Minotaur' game.

Independent/paired work

● Ask the children to complete their maze game plan. Continue to display the example plan on the whiteboard to help them.

Differentiation

● Support: Less confident learners may benefit from adult support to develop their ideas and could use the 'Theseus and the Minotaur' example, focusing on planning a simple game with one background only and one variable.
● Challenge: Encourage more confident learners to include more complex elements such as multiple variables, for example lives and a score.

Review

● Pair up the children and ask them to talk through their plan.
● Assess the children's progress by reviewing the maze game plans and children's explanations.

Curriculum objectives

● To design, write and debug programs that accomplish specific goals, including controlling or simulating physical systems. To solve problems by decomposing them into smaller parts; use sequence and repetition in programs; work with variables and various forms of input and output. To use logical reasoning to explain how some simple algorithms work and to detect and correct errors in algorithms and programs.

Lesson objectives

● To identify the assets they need to create for their game.
● To understand the importance of creating appealing assets within a game.
● To create sprites, backgrounds and sounds for their animation.
● To carefully name their assets and understand why that is important.

Expected outcomes

● Can plan and create the assets needed for their maze game.
● Can use multimedia tools to create appealing assets for their game.

Resources

Photocopiable page 83 'My game assets'; completed photocopiable page 82 'Maze game plans' from last lesson; Scratch sample file 'Theseus and the Minotaur'; microphones to record sounds if wished

Collecting and creating assets

This week, the children will plan, create and collect the assets they need for their maze game, giving consideration to how their sprites, sounds and backgrounds will appeal to their audience. They will also be reminded of the need to name their assets carefully.

Introduction

● Recap last week's work with the children and give out their completed photocopiable page 82 'Maze game plan'.
● Show the 'Theseus and the Minotaur' game on the whiteboard.

Whole-class work

● Explain that they will be planning, collecting and creating the assets needed for their games. Check the children's understanding of the word 'assets' (they are the game components, for example sprites, backgrounds, sounds).
● Ask the children to identify and share the assets in the 'Theseus and the Minotaur' game. Write these on the whiteboard.
● Ask the children what they think the most important assets are. Encourage them to realise that the characters are the most important.
● Look at characters from commercial games and ask what these characters have in common (bold colours, simple shapes).
● Discuss how designing assets that are simple and appealing to the audience is important. Also discuss simple but effective sound, background and button creation.

Independent/paired work

● Give out photocopiable page 83 'My game assets'.
● The children complete the assets sheet for their game.
● Once the children have finished, ask them to talk through their assets with a partner, give each other feedback and make any adjustments necessary.

Whole-class work

● Using the 'Theseus and the Minotaur' game as an example, discuss why it is important to name and keep track of the assets as they create them.

Independent/paired work

● Ask the children to create or collect their assets.
● Encourage them to save their work regularly.

Differentiation

● Support: Less confident learners may benefit from working in pairs, or with an adult to plan, create and collect their assets. They should create simple assets and use those within the Scratch program as necessary.
● Challenge: More confident learners will be able to plan and create their assets with ease. They should be encouraged to take time to create assets that are as appealing to their audience as possible. They can also help others.

Review

● Ask the children to show some of the assets they are pleased with.
● Review the key learning points from today's work, asking: *Why is it important that we keep assets simple? Why should assets be named?*

Curriculum objectives

● To design, write and debug programs that accomplish specific goals, including controlling or simulating physical systems. To solve problems by decomposing them into smaller parts; use sequence and repetition in programs; work with variables and various forms of input and output. To use logical reasoning to explain how some simple algorithms work and to detect and correct errors in algorithms and programs.

Lesson objectives

● To decompose their game into smaller programmable parts.
● To plan the code for each part of their maze game.
● To test and debug.

Expected outcomes

● Can use logical thinking to decompose their maze game into smaller parts.
● Can design and write programs to create a maze game.

Resources

Scratch sample file 'Theseus and the Minotaur'; photocopiable page 'What do the scripts do?' from the CD-ROM; photocopiable page 84 'Code matching'; photocopiable page 85 'My game code'

Writing game code

This lesson sees the children planning the code for their game. First, they are asked to match up Scratch blocks to the correct action and then break down the writing of their game code into smaller parts (decomposition). They work through their code, matching desired actions to Scratch scripts, which will help them to program their game systematically and with fewer errors.

Introduction

● Give out photocopiable page 'What does the script do?' from the CD-ROM and photocopiable page 84 'Code matching', which show scripts and actions from the 'Theseus and the Minotaur' game. On the first page they say what script does and on the second they match scripts to the code.
● Ask the children to work in pairs to complete the two tasks.
● You may wish to give them access to the game file to help them with this and future tasks.

Whole-class work

● Use the 'Theseus and the Minotaur' Scratch file game (opened from the Quick links section of the CD-ROM) to point out the correctly matched actions and scripts, talking through what each one is showing.
● Take extra time to go through any common misunderstandings, as most of the children will use these scripts in their own games.
● Give out the photocopiable page 85 'My game code' and explain, using the example, how the children should complete the worksheet.
● Explain to them that they should focus on the main game and that, for now, not to worry about writing scripts for any timers, scores, lives and so on (unless they wish to try), as these variables will be covered in the next lesson.

Independent/paired work

● The children work through the worksheet independently, working collaboratively if needed.
● Encourage them to imagine that they are playing the game and to follow it through step-by-step, thinking 'what needs to happen next'.
● Once they have finished, ask them to swap with a partner and check each other's code to help with the debugging process.

Whole-class work

● If there are any common issues that arise from the task above, spend time as a class going over some of the key maze game concepts.
● This is a good time to point out any issues. For example, they will need to make their character move back (move −10 steps) before changing the lives by −1, or the lives will go down by more than one. You can demonstrate these issues by changing the scripts around to show the children what happens.

Differentiation

● Support: Encourage less confident learners to focus on the more simple game instructions, using one screen only rather than multiple screens and play buttons. Depending on their level, they could create a simple version of the game for them to use as reference, removing potentially difficult elements.
● Challenge: More confident learners should be able to plan more complex code with confidence and independence. Encourage them to logically work out code and look at two-way selection and variables (covered in later lessons).

Review

● If you have noticed children writing interesting code, ask them to share it with their peers.
● As a class, come up with top tips for writing maze game code.
● Review the children's progress through the work they complete and their confidence in the class discussion.

Curriculum objectives

● To design, write and debug programs that accomplish specific goals, including controlling or simulating physical systems. To solve problems by decomposing them into smaller parts; use sequence and repetition in programs; work with variables and various forms of input and output. To use logical reasoning to explain how some simple algorithms work and to detect and correct errors in algorithms and programs.

Lesson objectives

● To plan the use of sequences of two-way selection and repeat until loops to create efficient programs.
● To implement sequences of two-way selection and repeat until loops to create efficient programs.
● To work collaboratively to debug.

Expected outcomes

● Can use simple repeat until loops and two-way selection where appropriate.
● Can work collaboratively to test and debug their programs.

Resources

Completed photocopiable page 85 'My game code' from Week 3; Scratch sample file 'Theseus and the Minotaur'

Writing and debugging more complex code

This week, the children program their maze game in Scratch using the coding plans they created last lesson. They are also taught how to use two-way selection and repeat until loops if they are using these in their planned game. They plan and program these into their game and debug the code as they go.

Introduction

● Recap last week's work with the children and give out completed photocopiable page 84 'My game code'.
● Explain that they will be starting to program their game in Scratch and that you are going to discuss a few sections of code they may need to know.

Whole-class work

● Display the Scratch resource "Theseus and the Minotaur' and highlight the 'if/else' section of code on the 'Theseus' sprite.
● Explain that this means, 'if this happens, then do this, otherwise, do this'.
● Show the comments and explain this is known as two-way selection. Write this term on the board.
● Discuss why this is efficient use of code (no need to create multiple If statements).

Independent/paired work

● In pairs, ask the children to come up with their own examples of where they might use this block in a different way in their own games.
● Ask a few volunteers to share their ideas with the class.

Whole-class work

● Highlight where the 'repeat until' section of script is on the stage
● Explain that it means, 'repeat untpostil this happens'.
● Show the comments and explain that this is known as a repeat until loop. Explain that this means that it is repeating the action until the condition (timer=0) is met.
● Discuss why this is efficient use of code (no need for multiple repetitions, it just keeps going *until* the condition is met).

Independent/paired work

● In pairs, ask the children to come up with their own examples of where they might use this block in a different way in their own games.
● Ask a few volunteers to share their ideas with the class.
● The children can add the instances they would use these two blocks to photocopiable page 85 'My game code'.
● For the remainder of the lesson, the children program their planned scripts into Scratch, working collaboratively to debug.
● Point out the use of the 'forever' block and 'nested if statements' .

> ### Differentiation
> ● Support: Less confident learners may need adult or peer support when programming their game.
> ● Challenge: Encourage more confident learners to help others to debug their work and improve their own work by considering how they can make their games more effective and their code more efficient, using multiple selection and nested If statements.

Review

● Ask for a few volunteers to share their work and, as a class, give feedback.
● Review with the children their progress during the lesson and, if unfinished, ensure that they know what they need to do at the start of the next lesson.

Curriculum objectives

● To design, write and debug programs that accomplish specific goals, including controlling or simulating physical systems. To solve problems by decomposing them into smaller parts; use sequence and repetition in programs; work with variables and various forms of input and output. To use logical reasoning to explain how some simple algorithms work and to detect and correct errors in algorithms and programs.

Lesson objectives

● To understand how multiple variables can be used to make their game more interesting for the player.
● To use multiple variables to add scores, timers and lives as appropriate.
● To test and debug their code as they write it.
● To work collaboratively to debug their code.

Expected outcomes

● Can use multiple variables where appropriate to create an effective game.
● Can work collaboratively to test and debug their programs.

Resources

Scratch sample file 'Theseus and the Minotaur'; photocopiable page 86 'My variables'

Adding scoring, timers and lives

This week, the children are introduced formally to using multiple variables, such as scores, lives and timers in their Scratch game. They define and assign their planned variables and continue to work collaboratively to write and debug their code.

Introduction

● Remind the children that last week they started programming their game and looked at multiple selection and loops.
● Explain that in this lesson they will be using variables – understanding what they are and how they can use them in their game. Write the word 'variables' on the board for emphasis.

Whole-class work

● Recap that a variable is something in the game that is a changeable value and can be anything that the computer needs to remember and change. They will have come across this term if they have studied earlier units.
● Display the Scratch sample file 'Theseus and the Minotaur' on the whiteboard and ask the children to identify what they think might be the variables in the game (timer, lives). They will probably have come across these in their exploratory work of the game.
● As a class, talk through the code and how it is working, that is, when the timer and lives are set, when they decrease and how the program makes them do this, what happens when they reach 0, how they are shown/hidden.
● Ask the children to come up with other variables that could be used in this game, or that they wish to use in their own game (score and health are popular).
● Demonstrate, or ask a confident learner to demonstrate, how to make a variable and show/hide it.
● Give out photocopiable page 86 'My variables' and go through the example with the children.

Independent/paired work

● Ask the children to plan their own variables on the photocopiable sheet.
● When they think they have finished, they should explain to their partner what variables they are using and how these will work.
● Ask one or two volunteers to share their ideas with the class.
● For the remainder of the lesson, the children program their variables into their game, as usual, working collaboratively to debug any errors that arise after testing.

Differentiation

● Support: Less confident learners may need additional adult or peer support in understanding how variables work and planning and programming their own variables. They could be encouraged to stick to one variable if necessary.
● Challenge: More confident learners will be able to plan and use multiple variables with confidence and can share their understanding with others.

Review

● Use a think-pair-share activity to assess understanding of working with multiple variables and how variables work in a game, asking questions such as: *What is a variable? Explain how you can create multiple variables in Scratch? Why are variables important in a game?*

Curriculum objectives

● To design, write and debug programs that accomplish specific goals, including controlling or simulating physical systems. To solve problems by decomposing them into smaller parts; use sequence and repetition in programs; work with variables and various forms of input and output. To use logical reasoning to explain how some simple algorithms work and to detect and correct errors in algorithms and programs.

Lesson objectives

● To give and receive constructive feedback.
● To evaluate their own game and others' games using their own criteria, as determined in Lesson 1.
● To discuss how they would change their approach if undertaking a similar task in the future.

Expected outcomes

● Can evaluate their own and others' work.
● Can evaluate their own approach to the task

Resources

Photocopiable page 87 'Game feedback'; criteria for an effective maze game as established by the class in lesson 1; photocopiable page 'Game evaluation' from the CD-ROM

Sharing and evaluating games

This week, the children will review each other's work, playing each other's games and giving and receiving constructive feedback. They improve their work after feedback and reflect on what they have achieved and learned during this chapter, including evaluating their approach to the task and how they might adjust this in the future.

Introduction

● Display a volunteer's maze game, or a maze game of your choice, on the whiteboard.
● Remind the children of the criteria they established in Lesson 1 for what makes an effective maze game.
● Invite a child to come up and play the game.
● Using 'what went well' and 'even better if', discuss as a class how this game meets the criteria for effective maze games and how it could be improved.

Whole-class work

● Explain that they will be giving and receiving constructive feedback for each other's games.
● Give out the photocopiable page 87 'Game feedback' and pair up the children whose work is of a similar standard.

Independent/paired work

● Ask the children to play their partner's game and complete photocopiable page 87 'Game feedback' for their partner's game.
● Once they have both finished, they swap sheets and discuss the feedback they have given each other, making it clear how they have suggested they could improve their game in some small way.
● They then improve their game in the way discussed.

Whole-class work

● Give out photocopiable page 'Game evaluation' from the CD-ROM.
● You may wish to go through the questions as a class and discuss how they can be answered. The last two questions, which deal with the children's approach to the task, are purposefully challenging.

Independent work

● The children should answer the questions in as much detail as possible.
● They can use the photocopiable sheet to help them, although encourage them to write their own ideas too.

Differentiation
● Support: Encourage less confident learners to give simple, clear and helpful feedback. They may need support in making the changes suggested. They may also need additional adult help in completing the evaluation sheet.
● Challenge: Challenge more confident learners to give highly detailed, specific feedback to improve the quality of the game and increase the efficiency of the code. Encourage them to write high-quality, thoughtful evaluations of their work and their own approach.

Review

● Bring the children together and select some of the games to show and play. Ask the children to talk through their games as they are played, discussing how feedback helped them to improve their game further.
● Hopefully, you will have time to show all the games. Try to at least discuss each game with each child, which will help you with assessment of the chapter's work.
● Assess the children's understanding by reviewing the maze games, the evaluations and the review discussion with you.

Curriculum objectives
● To design, write and debug programs that accomplish specific goals, including controlling or simulating physical systems. To solve problems by decomposing them into smaller parts; use sequence and repetition in programs; work with variables and various forms of input and output. To use logical reasoning to explain how some simple algorithms work and to detect and correct errors in algorithms and programs.

Lesson objectives
● To understand what is required in a tutorial.
● To share ideas about what makes an effective maze game.
● To explain why planning is an important part of game design.
● To demonstrate their knowledge and understanding of creating a maze game in Scratch.
● To explain why feedback is an important part of the process.

Expected outcomes
● Can explain to others the process of designing, creating and reviewing a maze game using Scratch.
● Can demonstrate their understanding of developing a maze game using Scratch to others.

Resources
Photocopiable page 'Maze game tutorial planning' from the CD-ROM; screen recording software (such as Jing), or video recording equipment

Greek mythology: Assess and review

This week, the children apply the knowledge, skills and understanding they have developed using Scratch to a different programming tool. This will help to consolidate their learning and provide an opportunity for them to demonstrate their understanding of programming and of implementing algorithms with different programs. Assessment and observation of the children's work will allow you to make adjustments to future learning of this topic, as you deem appropriate.

Introduction
● Discuss with the children what they have learned about creating a maze game using Scratch during this chapter. You could do this as a think-pair-share activity.
● Explain that for this assessment task they will be creating a video tutorial for other children to follow to demonstrate to them how to design, create and review a maze game using Scratch.

Whole-class work
● Show the children one or two video tutorials you have found that are effective. You could use the tutorials on http://info.scratch.mit.edu/Video_Tutorials, although these are short.
● Discuss with the children why these tutorials are effective and how they can use these elements in their own tutorials. (They are clear, to the point and so on.)
● Give out photocopiable page 'Maze game tutorial planning' from the CD-ROM and explain to the children how they should prepare their plan. They can work in pairs or small groups for this activity.
● You may also need to explain to the children how to use the equipment you have chosen for them to record their tutorials.

Independent work
● Ask the children to complete the photocopiable sheet.
● Once they have finished, they should complete their tutorial and save it in a folder/area you can access as directed.

Differentiation
● Support: Less confident learners may benefit from working in small groups or with additional adult support.
● Challenge: Encourage more confident learners to create a more in-depth, easy-to-follow tutorial and include explanations of two-way selection, loops and variables.

Review
● The video tutorials are an ideal opportunity for you to assess the children's understanding of the process of designing and creating a maze game using Scratch.

Maze game ideas

■ Use the space below to brainstorm possible ideas for your maze game.

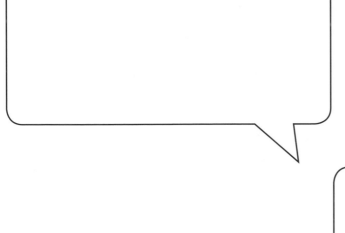

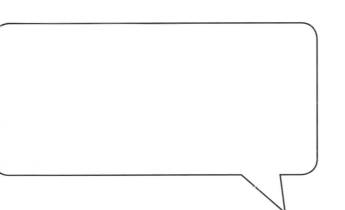

I can brainstorm ideas for a maze game.

How did you do?

Maze game plan

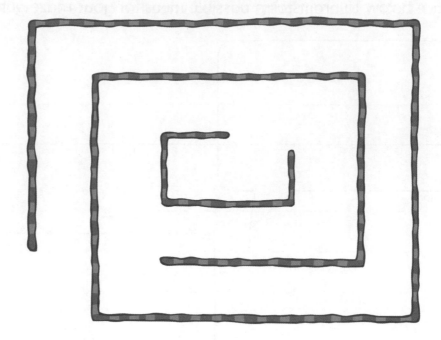

■ The plans for my maze game.

Game title: _____

Target audience: _____

Characters: _____

_____

Aim of the game: _____

_____

How does the player win/lose? _____

_____

Controls: _____

_____

_____

I can plan a maze game.

How did you do?

PHOTOCOPIABLE

My game assets

■ Write down ALL the different parts that you need to create and collect for your game below.

Characters: _____

_____

Game objects: _____

_____

_____

Sounds: _____

_____

Buttons: _____

_____

_____

Backgrounds: _____

_____

Text: _____

_____

_____

I can plan the assets needed for my maze game.

How did you do?

Code matching

■ Match the Scratch script to the correct action by writing the action number in the correct box.

Action

1. Control/move sprite with arrow keys.

2. If touching minotaur, then say 'You have defeated the minotaur!'

3. If touching maze, then lose a life.

4. Put the pen down on the screen (so it will draw).

5. Set the starting position of a sprite.

6. When the play button is clicked, broadcast a message to start the game.

7. When the message to start the game is received, change to the Labyrinth background.

Script

I can understand which Scratch scripts perform which actions.

How did you do?

My game code

■ Use the table below to plan the code for your game. The first box shows an example.

Action	Scratch script	Where the code goes
When the game starts, instructions show	When green flag clicked, show 'instructions' background	Stage

I can plan the actions and scripts needed for my Scratch maze game.

How did you do?

My variables

■ Use the table below to plan the variables you will use in your game. The first box shows an example.

Variable	What needs to happen
Lives	Set 3 lives at start of game. When touch maze, lose life. When 0 lives left, display 'game over' and stop game.

I can plan the variables needed for my Scratch maze game

How did you do?

PHOTOCOPIABLE

Name: _____ Date: _____

Game feedback

Your name: _____

Name of your partner:

_____

■ Play your partner's game. Give them feedback on their game using the questions below.

What went well?

_____

_____

_____

_____

What did you like about the game? (Be specific)

_____

_____

_____

_____

What would make it even better?

_____

_____

_____

_____

I can evaluate a maze game.
I can give constructive feedback to a partner.

How did you do?

The Arctic and the Antarctic

The children find out about the North Pole, before learning about Shackleton and his expeditions to the South Pole. They plan itineraries for journeying from place to place and evaluate their partner's plans. Finally, they link their studies to e-safety, to remind them that if they encounter a website that upsets them, they should tell someone they trust.

Expected prior learning

● The children will have searched online for information, using specific keywords. They transfer that knowledge to searching maps. They will have seen many search results pages, though they may not have thought about how they choose which links to follow.

● Using presentation tools, the children share their learning by using screen captures and note-taking skills.

Chapter at a glance

Subject area
• E-safety

National Curriculum objective
• To use search technologies effectively and be discerning in evaluating digital content. • To use technology safely, respectfully and responsibly; recognise acceptable/unacceptable behaviour; identify a range of ways to report concerns about content and contact.

Week	Lesson objectives	Summary of activities	Expected outcomes
1	• To know that search engines can be used to locate information. • To discuss the need for carefully choosing search keywords. • To share the results of a search and be discerning in the information that is located.	• Children find out about animals that live in the Arctic using their search skills. • They find out about global warming from three different websites. • They discuss whether web filtering is beneficial or could lead to reduced safety online.	• Can search effectively to locate information. • Can evaluate digital content located via web searches.
2	• To search for particular given information, using an online mapping tool or software. • To use online mapping tool or software to locate places visited.	• Children locate places using Google maps. • They measure distances between places. • They customise a map of their route to school.	• Can search for information using online maps.
3	• To know that online mapping tools can create a tour on a map. • To create a personalised map for a specific purpose. • To evaluate the information shown on a personalised map. • To create a tour, using an online mapping tool.	• Children find out about Shackleton and his Antarctic journey. • They study a customised map of the journey. • They create a customised map of significant places of their lives.	• Can create personalised maps for a specific purpose. • Can create a tour for a specific audience, using an online map.
4	• To retell a story using an online map. • To manipulate images captured from an online mapping tool, to annotate important features.	• Children explore further Shackleton's journey. • They annotate a map of his journey. • They discuss what they would take to the Antarctic and compare their list with the contents of Scott's hut.	• Can retell a story using online maps. • Can manipulate images of maps.

Week	Lesson objectives	Summary of activities	Expected outcomes
5	• To plan an itinerary for a journey using an online mapping tool and websites. • To plan an itinerary for a journey using relevant websites. • To evaluate an itinerary for an expedition, using given criteria. • To create a presentation to describe an expedition, using online mapping tools and related websites. • To evaluate digital content located via web searches.	• Children plan an itinerary for a school visit. • They use websites to find information. • They use online tools to prepare a presentation of their itinerary.	• Can plan an itinerary for a journey using online maps and related websites. • Can evaluate digital content located via web searches.
6	• To describe acceptable behaviour online. • To know whom to contact, if someone behaves in an unacceptable manner online. • To know how to report concerns about content or contact online.	• Children plan a tour of their school using images. • Using an online map of the school the children create a custom tour. • They discuss unacceptable behaviour online and what they would do if they experienced this.	• Can recognise acceptable behaviour online. • Can identify ways to report concerns about content or contact.
Assess and review	• Assess and review the half term's work.	• Planning an itinerary for a journey. • Using websites to find information for the journey and developing note-taking skills. • Evaluating the content located via the web searches.	• Assess and review

Overview of progression

● The children progress their knowledge of searching the web and using maps. To add to their skills, they create custom maps, which are another way of presenting information.
● They begin to think more about the search rankings of the results returned by search engines.
● They continue to develop their learning about staying safe online, by reminding themselves that if they encounter upsetting material, they should tell someone.

Creative context

● The lessons link closely to the English curriculum, through identifying new vocabulary related to the Arctic and Antarctic and the animals living there. The children follow a chronological account of Shackleton and his expedition. They learn about how a story can be told using maps and how the route can relay the events.
● Linking to maths, the children learn about time through looking at the number of days needed to travel to a destination. The mapping tools allow distances to be measured and the travel between them compared.
● There are links to geography through studying maps.

Background knowledge

● The children will have previously learned about searching online and using appropriate keywords. They will have learned about narrowing searches, using Boolean operators ('+' and '−').
● They may have used maps before or seen maps used on a SatNav. However, they may not have searched using keywords or thought about planning an itinerary. Their note-taking skills from their English lessons will help them gather information.
● The children will know that they receive a list of web links when searching online and have thought about which ones to follow. Ask them to think about whether they ever go on to the second page of results?

Curriculum objectives
● To use search technologies effectively and be discerning in evaluating digital content.
● To use technology safely, respectfully and responsibly; recognise acceptable/ unacceptable behaviour; identify a range of ways to report concerns about content and contact.

Lesson objectives
● To know that search engines can be used to locate information.
● To discuss the need for carefully choosing search keywords.
● To share the results of a search and be discerning in the information that is located.

Expected outcomes
● Can search effectively to locate information.
● Can evaluate digital content located via web searches.

Resources
Photocopiable page 97 'Arctic websites'; photocopiable page 98 'Global warming websites'

The Arctic

The children look at websites about the Arctic and research information about it. They find out about search engines and how information is collected.

Introduction
● Show a short video of BBC's programme *Frozen Planet* or a similar example. Ask: *What do you think life would be like there? How are animals adapted to the cold temperatures?*

Whole-class work
● Ask: *If you wanted to find out more about the animals at the North Pole, which keywords would you use to search the web?*
● Demonstrate searching the web, using the suggested keywords. The websites will be ranked according to how the search engine uses the web crawler information.
● Select one of the websites found and model asking questions about the page. For example: *Is the writing easy to understand? Does it relate to the purpose of the search? Can you tell whether it is a reliable website?*
● Remind the children about looking at website addresses to see whether they are familiar, for example, the BBC or an ending like 'ac.uk' or '.edu'.

Paired work
● Using photocopiable page 97 'Arctic websites', the children research animals that live in the Arctic.
● They record the web address and information about the animals. They also make a note of the keywords they used and why they chose the websites. Was it the top website? Did it look most interesting? Did the description seem to match?

Whole-class work
● Bring the class together and let the children share information Which animal did they study? Which websites did the information come from? Why did they choose those websites?
● Using photocopiable page 98 'Global warming websites', ask children to find and record three pieces of information about global warming. Allow the children time to work together in pairs to discuss the information they find.
● Report back using three points as before but this time, ask them to explain whether they thought the websites agreed with each other.
● The websites containing information about Arctic animals are probably factual, with little bias. However, for global warming, different people or organisations may use different facts to support their point of view.
● The children need to check the sources of the websites, by looking at the web address and the links. Also, they should check whether the sites have an 'About' section, which might explain further about the organisation.

Differentiation
● Support: Less confident learners may need support to select the keywords to use to search for animals at the North Pole and for global warming. Once the websites have been located, they may need help to decipher the information into notes.
● Challenge: More confident learners will be able to visit websites and record the main reasons why they would trust the website. They should also be able to explain why they should refine a search to make it more accurate.

Review
● Ask one pair of children to present a website that supports global warming and another pair to present a site against it.
● How did the children decide which websites to choose from the list given by the search engine?
● How did they decide whether they trusted the website?

Using online maps

Curriculum objectives
● To use search technologies effectively and be discerning in evaluating digital content
● To use technology safely, respectfully and responsibly; recognise acceptable/ unacceptable behaviour; identify a range of ways to report concerns about content and contact.

Lesson objectives
● To search for particular given information, using an online mapping tool or software.
● To use online mapping tool or software to locate places visited.

Expected outcomes
● Can search for information using online maps.

Resources
Photocopiable page 99 'Planning routes'

Children use online maps to view places and take screenshots to collect information. They are introduced to the explorer Shackleton and his expeditions to the South Pole.

Introduction
● Introduce the lesson by displaying a map of London using an online map. Can the children recognise any famous landmarks?
● Then display a map of the local town. Can they see places they recognise?

Whole-class work
● Tell the children that they will be using mapping tools.
● Display on the computer a web browser and type in 'maps.google.co.uk'.
● Type the school postcode into the search box on the map.
● In the browser window, you can select the 'Satellite' image of the map.
● A first-person view of the area can be seen using 'Street view'.

Paired work
● Working in pairs, let the children search for their home addresses and places they visit on their way to and from school.
● When the children find a place of interest, they take a screenshot.

Whole-class work
● Display the map of the school and explain that the maps tool can give us directions or a route from one place to another.
● Select 'Directions', type the name of a local road and see the route that the map suggests.
● By default, the map will have selected a route for driving, change this to walking (by selecting the icon of the person walking).
● The map will suggest a route and give an approximate time for completion.

Paired work
● Using photocopiable page 99 'Planning routes', the children record the distance between places and how long it would take.

Whole-class work
● If the school has 'Google apps for education', then the children can have their own accounts to make a customisable map.
● If not, demonstrate how to create a map.
● From the settings cog select 'My places' then select 'Create map'.

Paired work
● If the children have a Google account, let them create a custom map of their journey to school, using the Google marker and line tools.

Differentiation
● Support: Less confident learners may need support locating their home and to chose when and where to collect screenshots.
● Challenge: More confident learners will be able to follow their route from home to school, collecting screenshots. They decide the size of the intervals and explain why they chose these.

Review
● Bring the class together and display the map of Shackleton's journey (http:// bit.ly/shackletonmap). Explain that Ernest Shackleton was a famous explorer who travelled to the Antarctic (South Pole).
● Can the children see how the Google map has been customised?
● Ask the children why customising maps might be useful to them and to other people who are learning about the world.

Curriculum objectives
● To use search technologies effectively and be discerning in evaluating digital content
● To use technology safely, respectfully and responsibly; recognise acceptable/unacceptable behaviour; identify a range of ways to report concerns about content and contact.

Lesson objectives
● To know that online mapping tools can create a tour on a map.
● To create a personalised map for a specific purpose.
● To evaluate the information shown on a personalised map.
● To create a tour using an online mapping tool.

Expected outcomes
● Can create personalised maps for a specific purpose.
● Can create a tour for a specific audience, using an online map.

Resources
Photocopiable page 100 'Shackleton facts'; photocopiable page 101 'My life journey'; interactive activity 'My life journey' on the CD-ROM

Recording significant events

Looking again at customised maps, the children find out more about Shackleton and his travels identifying the significant places in his journeys. They record the significant events in their lives and try to link them with locations, using maps.

Introduction
● Introduce the lesson by displaying the map of Shackleton's journey (http://bit.ly/shackletonmap). What do the children know about Ernest Shackleton?
● Explain that they have ten minutes to search online to find three facts about Shackleton. Which keywords will they use to search?

Paired work
● In pairs, the children search for the information about Shackleton. They record their notes using photocopiable page 100 'Shackleton facts'.
● Once they have three facts, they explain why they chose those websites.

Whole-class work
● Bring the class together and share the information that they have found. Do the facts cover a wide range of information about Shackleton's life?
● Could the research have been divided into different areas, so that a bigger picture of his life could have been constructed?
● Returning to the map of Shackleton's journey, explain that it covers the significant events and places that he visited.
● From the icons menu, below the search bar, select 'Add marker' and then select the significant place. You can give the marker a name and add a short description.
● Ask the children to think about their own lives, what have been the significant events?

Paired work
● In pairs, the children use photocopiable page 101 'My life journey', and record ten events that were significant, for example, birth place, first birthday, first visit to the seaside or cinema.
● The children create their own custom maps, charting their life and adding markers and descriptions.
● Alternatively, they can capture screenshots of maps or use interactive activity 'My life map' on the CD-ROM.

Whole-class work
● Bring the class together and share their life stories.
● How did they search for the locations? Did they know the place name or postcode? Did they need to refine their searches to find the correct place.

Differentiation
● Support: Less confident learners may need support to identify the significant events. They should create three points for each event – 'Name of event', 'Where?' and 'When?'
● Challenge: More confident learners should be able to identify ten events in their lives and justify why they have chosen them. They can then search the maps to locate the places relevant to the events and take screenshots or add markers to a custom map.

Review
● Display Shackleton's map (http://bit.ly/shackletonmap).
● Ask them to use the map as a prompt to describe the significant events of Shackleton's journey to a Year 4 child.
● The map can help to structure planning, writing and editing a tour for a specific audience. Tell the children that, in the following lessons, they will be creating tours for others to follow.

Curriculum objectives
● To use search technologies effectively and be discerning in evaluating digital content.
● To use technology safely, respectfully and responsibly; recognise acceptable/ unacceptable behaviour; identify a range of ways to report concerns about content and contact.

Lesson objectives
● To retell a story using an online map.
● To manipulate images captured from an online mapping tool, to annotate important features.

Expected outcomes
● Can retell a story using online maps.
● Can manipulate images of maps.

Resources
Photocopiable page 102 'Shackleton's journey'; photocopiable page 103 'What would I take to the Antarctic?'

What would you take to the Antarctic?

The children use maps to tell a story. They plot Shackleton's journey on a map and, using the Google World Wonders website, look inside the explorer Scott's hut and see the supplies and items he had. They make a comparison to today, thinking about which supplies they would take to the Antarctic.

Introduction
● Display the map of the Antarctic and see how there are other countries nearby such as Chile. Which is the nearest town to the South Pole?

Whole-class work
● Explain that Shackleton travelled to Antarctica and had many difficult times. From his diary, we know that he became trapped in the ice, had to drag his ships, had to wait on Elephant Island and walk across the glacier until finally reaching the whaling station.
● Tell the children that a map can be used to tell the story.

Paired work
● The children capture a screenshot of the Antarctic map or save an image.
● Using a tool such as Evernote Skitch or the Paint program, they can add arrows and labels to show the progress of Shackleton's journey in 1909.
● Using photocopiable page 102 'Shackleton's journey', the children record five facts about the expedition. Once found, they can add the information to their map (using the Paint program or another annotation program).

Whole-class work
● Choose two pairs of children to share their maps. Do they contain the same information? How did they decide upon the websites to visit?
● Explain that, even though Google have not completed their photographic coverage of the whole world, they do have interesting examples for Antarctica.
● On the Google World Wonders website, they have three images of the outside of Shackleton's hut (www.google.com/culturalinstitute/entity/%2Fm% 2F09txk5?projectId=world-wonders).
● On the same web page, there is a link to Captain Scott's hut (another famous Antarctic explorer from the same time period). Click on 'Street view Show all 4' to see Scott's hut. Click on the interior view.

Paired work
● Using photocopiable page 103 'What would I take to the Antarctic?' the children list the items they would take on an expedition to the Antarctic.
● Now let the children explore the hut and take screenshots of images that interest them.
● They can manipulate the images by using the Paint program.
● Are the items they would take in the hut?

Differentiation
● Support: Less confident learners may need support to identify the essential items they would need in the Antarctic and how to spell the words. They may also need help using the software to manipulate the images.
● Challenge: More confident learners will be able identify the items they would take to the Antarctic and compare them with Scott's hut. They will be able to describe how the technology has changed since the early 20th century.

Review
● Bring the class together and ask three pairs of children to list the items they would take to the Antarctic. Can they show or describe what they saw in the hut and how it is different?
● Explain that technology has changed greatly since Shackleton's time, but the essentials of food and warmth still remain.

Curriculum objectives
● To use search technologies effectively and be discerning in evaluating digital content.
● To use technology safely, respectfully and responsibly; recognise acceptable/unacceptable behaviour; identify a range of ways to report concerns about content and contact.

Lesson objectives
● To plan an itinerary for a journey using an online mapping tool and websites.
● To plan an itinerary for a journey using relevant websites.
● To evaluate an itinerary for an expedition, using given criteria.
● To create a presentation to describe an expedition, using online mapping tools and related websites.
● To evaluate digital content located via web searches.

Expected outcomes
● Can plan a itinerary for a journey using online maps and related websites.
● Can evaluate digital content located via web searches.

Resources
Photocopiable page 'Planning our travel' from the CD-ROM; interactive activity 'Our school visit'; photocopiable page 'Itinerary evaluation' from the CD-ROM

Planning a journey

The children continue their learning about maps and plan a journey for an educational visit. They present their itinerary and help to evaluate their own and others' itineraries.

Introduction
● Tell the children they are going to plan an itinerary for a journey, which could be a school visit to a local place or a place abroad.
● Explain that they will use websites to find information for the journey and develop their note-taking skills.
● As a class, use interactive activity 'Our school visit' on the CD-ROM to demonstrate how to plan three journeys. They identify a local place, a place in Europe and a place in the world. They then suggest when and how they will travel. They also need to explain why they think it would be a good place to go.

Whole-class work
● Search online for examples of package holidays or cruises, especially where the itinerary for the places visited is listed.

Paired work
● In pairs, the children plan their school visit. It could be to one destination, where they must then describe the mode they will travel. Using photocopiable page 'Planning our travel' from the CD-ROM, they make notes of the information they gather.
● They take screenshots of the maps to show the locations and use Google 'Street view' to show places of interest.
● Once they have gathered the information, children can pair up to talk through their itinerary to see if it makes sense and give feedback.

Whole-class work
● The tool 'Thinglink' allows the user to add an image, then annotate it with pop-up labels and links to other websites. Demonstrate how to use Thinglink, by inserting a screenshot of a map, and then add links to show places of interest.
● Ask the children to carefully consider how they will search for information to add to their Thinglink presentation. Which keywords will they use?

Paired work
● In pairs, the children use Thinglink to add an image for their visit and add links to relevant websites.
● Pairs join together and evaluate their Thinglink presentations, using photocopiable page 'Itinerary evaluation' from the CD-ROM.

Differentiation
● Support: Less confident learners may need support to use the Thinglink interface and to locate suitable website, using appropriate keywords.
● Challenge: More confident learners will be able to research the travel times and costs of the journeys, using public transport and travel agent websites.

Review
● Bring the class together and ask two pairs (who have worked together) to share their Thinglink presentations and explain why they choose the places of interest and the corresponding websites or images.
● Ask them how they will refine their plans, based on the feedback.
● Explain that the feedback is very important to people putting an itinerary together. It helps them to consider whether they need to change their plans based on the comments.

Curriculum objectives
● To use search technologies effectively and be discerning in evaluating digital content.
● To use technology safely, respectfully and responsibly; recognise acceptable/ unacceptable behaviour; identify a range of ways to report concerns about content and contact.

Lesson objectives
● To describe acceptable behaviour online.
● To know whom to contact, if someone behaves in an unacceptable manner online.
● To know how to report concerns about content or contact online.

Expected outcomes
● Can recognise acceptable behaviour online.
● Can identify ways to report concerns about content or contact.

Resources
Photocopiable page 'My gallery' from the CD-ROM

World wonders

The lesson consolidates the learning about maps and gathering information. The children look at the Google World Wonders website, which has many interesting images and tours. They plan and collect images for their own tour of the school. They present and justify their decisions for including and not including images.

Introduction
● Introduce the lesson by showing the 'Google World Wonders' website.
● The children have visited Scott's hut on this site. Explain that it is a useful resource for seeing images of places that they cannot visit.
● However, the World Wonders website also lets people add their own images. What would happen if an inappropriate picture was added?

Whole-class work
● Give the children time to explore the World Wonders website.
● Explain that they can create a gallery, if they have a Google account. Where would they go and what would they show?

Paired work
● Thinking about the school location and using photocopiable page 'My gallery' from the CD-ROM, the children plan their customised gallery to share. They need to think about the places and what in particular might be interesting to a viewer.
● They can collect images of themselves in different locations around the school, to give examples of interesting places and justify why they think it is appropriate and interesting to share these images.
● What would be an inappropriate image to share? They write their ideas on the photocopiable sheet.

Whole-class work
● Bringing the class together, choose three pairs to describe their collection of images (if possible, display the images). Can they explain why they thought these images would be interesting and why?
● Can they describe what an inappropriate image would be?

Paired work
● Using an online map of the school, the children create a custom tour, using a website such as Thinglink. There are other websites such as Padlet.com that allow a custom background to be added with sticky notes showing places to visit

---

Differentiation
● Support: Less confident learners may need support to identify which images to gather and also how to display them, using a web tool. They may also need help to explain why an image may be inappropriate.
● Challenge: More confident learners will be able to gather the information and images and describe a route to take to view them in a particular order. They can justify why the images are relevant and also why other images may be inappropriate.

Review
● Bring the class together and display examples from at least four pairs of children. Is their tour interesting? Are the images appropriate?
● Can the children remember that when commenting they need to be kind?
● What would they do if someone wrote an upsetting comment? (They should tell someone they trust.)
● Do they know who to tell when at school and when at home?

Lesson objectives
● To plan an itinerary for a journey using an online mapping tool.
● To create a presentation to describe an expedition, using online mapping tools and related websites.
● To evaluate digital content located via web searches.

Expected outcomes
● Can plan an itinerary for a journey using online maps and related websites.
● Can evaluate digital content located via web searches.

Resources
Photocopiable page 'Around the world' from the CD-ROM; *Around the World in Eighty Days* by Jules Verne

The Arctic and the Antarctic: Assess and review

To review the learning, the children use the theme of 'Around the World in Eighty Days' to plan the places they would visit in that time. They collect information to add to their presentation. The children review their learning about what to do if they find upsetting information.

Introduction
● Introduce the lesson by displaying a world map. Tell the children that they are going to plan an 'Around the world in eighty days' itinerary.
● Show an image of the book *Around the World in Eighty Days* by Jules Verne. Explain that the main character, Fogg, is challenged to travel around the world in eighty days. On the Wikipedia page, a simple map shows his route (http://en.wikipedia.org/wiki/Around_the_World_in_Eighty_Days).

Whole-class work
● Ask the class which way around the world they would go. They may suggest going east or west, some might say north or south. When they have planned their routes, they need to be able to justify their choice.
● Share photocopiable page 'Around the world' from the CD-ROM so the children can see the planning table.

Independent work
● The children look at the map and choose their ten places and give approximate dates for their visits. Can they identify a route between the places, for example, an airport or road? Could they travel by sea or river?
● They record the ten places and then begin to collect images for them. They can use screenshots or save images from websites.

Paired work
● In pairs, the children talk through their itineraries and see whether they make sense. Their partner can give advice, by asking how they are going to travel between the places and is it a reasonable route.
● They then begin to organise their images and links using a website such as Thinglink, or by using a presentation tool.

Differentiation
● Support: Less confident learners may need support to navigate the map to find suitable locations to visit. They may need help to read and interpret websites.
● Challenge: More confident learners should be able to plan their journeys and give approximate travel times, based on flight or other transport information websites. They should explain why they have chosen to travel the direction of route around the world.

Review
● Bring the class together and ask three pairs to present their routes.
● Can they get around the world in 80 days? Can they identify how they can travel between places?
● Ask the children to think about whether it would be an enjoyable journey?
● Can they identify which were useful websites to gather information from and were some difficult to use?
● Ask: *What would you do if you were planning a journey and you found a website that upset you?*
● Remind them, if they find something that upsets them, they should tell someone they trust.

Name: _____   Date: _____

Arctic websites

- Search websites to find information about animals in the Arctic.
- Write notes on what you find in the table below.

	Name of animal	Web address	Information about the animal
1			
2			
3			
4			
5			
6			
7			

- What keywords did you use?

_____

_____

_____

I can find information on a subject using the web and evaluate the websites I find.

How did you do?

Global warming websites

- Search websites to find information on global warming.
- Use the table to make notes on what you find.

	Name of website	Web address	Information about global warming
1			
2			
3			

1. Why did you choose these websites?

_____

_____

2. Do the three websites agree with each other?

_____

_____

3. What do they agree about?

_____

_____

4. What do they disagree about?

_____

_____

I can use websites to find information about a subject and evaluate the websites I find.

How did you do?

Name: _____   Date: _____

Planning routes

■ Fill in the table with information about your routes.

	Start place	Finish place	How far is it between the places?	How long would it take to get there?
1				
2				
3				
4				
5				
6				
7				
8				
9				
10				

I can plan a route using an online maps tool.

How did you do?

Name: _____ Date: _____

Shackleton facts

- In 10 minutes, can you find three important facts about Shackleton?

	Fact	Why is it important?	Web address
I			
2			
3			

I can find information quickly using a search engine.

How did you do?

PHOTOCOPIABLE

SCHOLASTIC
www.scholastic.co.uk

Name: _____   Date: _____

My life journey

	Place name	**When?**	**Why was it significant?**
1			
2			
3			
4			
5			
6			
7			
8			
9			
10			

I can list locations of significant events from my own life.

How did you do?

Name: _____ Date: _____

Shackleton's journey

■ Capture an image of the Antarctic map.

Find five facts about Shackleton's journey.

1. _____

_____

_____

2. _____

_____

_____

3. _____

_____

_____

4. _____

_____

_____

5. _____

_____

_____

■ Add your facts to your map to retell the story of Shackleton's journey.

I can retell the story of one of Shackleton's expeditions.

How did you do?

PHOTOCOPIABLE

■SCHOLASTIC
www.scholastic.co.uk

What would I take to the Antarctic?

What I would take to the Antarctic	Why I would take it

I can list the items I would need for a particular destination.

How did you do?

Great journeys

This chapter engages the children in the story *Journey to the River Sea* by Eva Ibbotson with a focus on computer networks, software and services. The children will look at topics within 'How computers work' and 'Communication' such as networks, searching, Web 2.0 tools for collaboration, wikis and blogs. They will consider the term 'multitasking' and think about the 'fetch execute cycle' as a precursor for their future learning in computing.

Expected prior learning

● The children will understand the difference between the internet and the World Wide Web. They will know about video and audio communication (VoIP voice over IP).
● They will recognise what is acceptable and unacceptable behaviour when using online services.
● They will understand the main functions of the operating system.
● They will be able to make judgments about digital content when evaluating it for a given audience.
● The children should understand the potential of collaboration when computers are networked.

Chapter at a glance

Subject area
• How computers work

National Curriculum objective
• To understand computer networks including the internet; how they can provide multiple services, such as the World Wide Web; and the opportunities they offer for communication and collaboration. • To use technology safely, respectfully and responsibly.

Week	Lesson objectives	Summary of activities	Expected outcomes
1	• To describe the World Wide Web and how users connect. • To explain the difference between the World Wide Web and the internet. • To explain how to navigate web pages using a browser. • To explain a hyperlink and how it behaves. • To guide a peer through using a web page.	• Children are introduced to the book *Journey to the River Sea* by Eva Ibbotson. • They make the link with searching on the internet and going on a journey. • They look at how users search using web browsers and hyperlinks and making bookmarks. • They compile a glossary of terms. • They annotate a web page.	• Can outline the key features of the World Wide Web. • Can explain how to use a browser, including navigation via hyperlinks.
2	• To describe different navigational methods. • To explain the relationship between different navigational methods. • To describe the features of a large wiki. • To explain how an entry on a large wiki is created and edited.	• Children research information about Brazil. • They look at the features of web browsers. • They record facts about Brazil from a Wikipedia page. • They present this information in a Wikipedia style format.	• Can explain the relationship between different navigational methods. • Can describe the features of large wikis, such as Wikipedia, and how they are created and edited.
3	• To identify the features of collaborating in person. • To identify the features of collaborating online. • To compare collaborating online and in person and give advantages and disadvantages. • To describe the workflow of using Web 2.0 tools for collaboration.	• Children research a 'great' journey. • They enter information using an 'etherpad'. • They put together for and against arguments for a journey. • They carry out a debate using the etherpad. • They discuss face-to-face and online ways of working collaboratively.	• Can compare collaborating online and in person. • Can give examples of collaboration online using Web 2.0 tools.

Week	Lesson objectives	Summary of activities	Expected outcomes
4	• To identify the features of a physical diary. • To identify the features of a blog. • To know that a blog is a web log. • To be able to contribute a blog post. • To be able to evaluate a blog post contribution.	• Children write diary entries for Maia's journey down the Amazon. • They write blog entries and comment on each others.	• Can explain how a blog works. • Can add a blog post and a comment.
5	• To identify online surveying tools. • To use an online survey tool to collect information. • To create a new survey to collect information. • To describe the advantages and disadvantages of online survey tools.	• Children look at online travel sites and identify places of interest in Brazil. • They write questions to ask prospective travellers to make up a survey.	• Can use an online surveying tool and describe the advantages and disadvantages of using online tools.
6	• To know that computers can multitask. • To describe why multitasking is important. • To predict the future of computing, referring to Moore's law. • To use technology safely and responsibly.	• Children compare how they multitask with how computers multitask. • They look at how technologies have changed over time and Moore's law.	• Can describe how computers can multitask. • Can simply explain Moore's law.
Assess and review	• Assess and review the half term's work.	• Children review their understanding of the World Wide Web. • They explain how to use a browser and navigating between and within web pages.	• Assess and review.

Overview of progression

● The children will know the difference between computer hardware and software and that a web browser is a software tool for accessing the World Wide Web.

● They will have used online collaborative tools, such as wikis, blogs and survey tools before, so they progress in their knowledge of the advantages and disadvantages of using the technology.

● They will know that computers have IP addresses and that the data is sent via the internet. They will now think about how computers enable data to be navigated using hyperlinks.

Creative context

● The lessons link closely to the English curriculum, through studying travel fiction. The children look at diary writing and write a blog. They consider how authors use figurative language to create impact and compare this with the writing style in Wikipedia. The children will retrieve, record and present information from non-fiction.

● Linking to science, the children learn about the nature of the Amazon river and the variety of animals and plants, adapted to their environment.

● Linking to geography, they learn about South America, Brazil and the Amazon river and its environment. They learn about the climate and how the river changes through the year.

Background knowledge

● The children have been learning about computer networks, the internet and the World Wide Web. They need to be able to describe the key features of these components and the relationships between them, for example browsers, URLs and hyperlinks. They should experience different web browsers and identify the similarities and differences between them.

● The children learn about what happens when a user requests a web page in a browser.

● They should be able to describe the opportunities that the World Wide Web offers for communication and collaboration.

Curriculum objectives
● To understand computer networks including the internet; how they can provide multiple services, such as the World Wide Web; and the opportunities they offer for communication and collaboration.
● To use technology safely, respectfully and responsibly.

Lesson objectives
● To describe the World Wide Web and how users connect.
● To explain the difference between the World Wide Web and the internet.
● To explain how to navigate web pages using a browser.
● To explain a hyperlink and how it behaves.
● To guide a peer through using a web page.

Expected outcomes
● Can outline the key features of the World Wide Web.
● Can explain how to use a browser, including navigation via hyperlinks.

Resources
Photocopiable page 113 'Navigating the Amazon'; photocopiable page 114 'Computing glossary'; photocopiable 115 'Navigating a web page'; interactive 'Navigating the web' on the CD-ROM; *Journey to the River Sea* by Eva Ibotson

Journey to the River Sea

The children are introduced to the story *Journey to the River Sea* by Eva Ibbotson with focus on computer networks, software and services.

Introduction
● Show the children the book cover (http://shop.scholastic.co.uk/products/94730). Ask: *What do you think will happen in the story? Where do you think the story is set?*
● Explain that this is a genre of story called 'journey fiction', where the character travels from somewhere safe, has a series of adventures and returns home emotionally richer.
● Read the opening chapter. Make the link with data travelling on the internet, which is also like going on a journey.

Whole-class work
● Ask the children to name some web browsers. Ask: *Why do you think there is more than one?*
● Ask them how they move around from web page to web page. They may suggest typing different search words into a search box, by selecting a hyperlink, bookmarks or the history.
● Demonstrate opening a search page, for example, www.google.co.uk and searching for information about the book *Journey to the River Sea*. How do the children know which text is a hyperlink?
● Can the children define a 'hyperlink'? (a piece of text or an image that links to another part of the web page or to another web page.)
● Demonstrate to the children how to add a bookmark for a page and putting it into a folder of similar bookmarks.

Paired work
● Using photocopiable page 113 'Navigating the Amazon', the children search for information about the Amazon river.

Whole-class work
● Ask five children to share information they have found about the Amazon. Are there words they have found that need defining?
● Explain that they are going to create a glossary and continue to add to it as the lessons progress.

Paired work
● Give out photocopiable page 114 'Computing glossary'. The children define the words and think of least two more words they can add.
● Using photocopiable page 115 'Navigating a web page', the children create a guide to navigate someone through a web page.

Differentiation
● Support: Less confident learners may need support from adults to define the words in the glossary or to find information to help them explain the words with examples.
● Challenge: More confident learners will be able to create a glossary for the suggested words and then add at least five more words, with clear definitions.

Review
● Bring the class together and use interactive activity 'Navigating the web' on the CD-ROM to show the main features of a web page. Can they explain the difference between the internet and the World Wide Web?
● Ask what happens when they want to view a web page? They type a web address (a URL – unique resource locator) into the address bar. In simple terms, the computer sends that address off to a large database (like a phone book), which finds the IP address for the website. Once the computer knows the IP address, it sends a request to that computer for the web page.

Curriculum objectives
● To understand computer networks including the internet; how they can provide multiple services, such as the World Wide Web; and the opportunities they offer for communication and collaboration.
● To use technology safely, respectfully and responsibly.

Lesson objectives
● To describe different navigational methods.
● To explain the relationship between different navigational methods.
● To name and describe the features of a large wiki.
● To explain how an entry on a large wiki is created and edited.

Expected outcomes
● Can explain the relationship between different navigational methods.
● Can describe the features of large wikis, such as Wikipedia, and how they are created and edited.

Resources
Media resource 'The Amazon' on the CD-ROM; photocopiable page 114 'Computing glossary'; photocopiable page 116 'Brazil'; photocopiable page 117 'Wikipedia page layout'; Journey to the River Sea by Eva Ibotson

Wikis

The children continue to find out about the story Journey to the River Sea and think about navigating the web. They look at Wikipedia pages and consider how people collaborate to share information.

Introduction
● Read the next part of Journey to the River Sea, focusing on Brazil.
● What do the children know about Brazil? Show the media resource 'The Amazon' on the CD-ROM. Can they remember any of the facts?
● Remind children about navigation of web pages, using hyperlinks and bookmarks. Ask: How could you use the menu or toolbar to navigate?
● Demonstrate the top menus by opening each one in turn.
● Demonstrate the toolbar icons, by hovering over each button for a description.

Paired work
● Ask the children to locate the Wikipedia page for The Journey to the River Sea and read the overview.

Whole-class work
● Remind the children that Wikipedia is a large wiki. Ask: Can you define a wiki? When you have agreed a definition, ask them to add it to photocopiable page 114 'Computing glossary' from the previous lesson.
● Ask: What are the common features of Wikipedia pages? A heading, subheadings, references, hyperlinks, text, images and a Wikipedia logo.

Paired work
● Using Wikipedia, children research facts about Brazil. Using photocopiable page 116 'Brazil', they record their findings.
● They then present the information to look like a Wikipedia page. They do this on photocopiable page 117 'Wikipedia page layout' or digitally.

Whole-class work
● Ask three children to share the information they have discovered about Brazil. How have they laid out the information to make it look like a Wikipedia page.

Differentiation
● Support: Less confident learners could use the Simple English Wikipedia pages to gather information and then use the template on photocopiable page 117 'Wikipedia page layout' to structure their page.
● Challenge: More confident learners will be able to research the pages of Wikipedia for information about Brazil. They could sketch or design, in word processing software, a 'mock' Wikipedia page.

Review
● Bring the class together and display pages from the story. Ask: How is the information presented differently in Journey to the River Sea?
● Explain that the Wikipedia pages are very factual.
● In the book more emotional and persuasive words are used.
● Show the children how, in Wikipedia, there is a 'sandbox' area (http://en.wikipedia.org/wiki/Wikipedia:Sandbox) to enable people to try out the tools to create a page.
● Select 'Edit' at the top-right of the page, then demonstrate on the screen how to type text, make it bold or italics.

Curriculum objectives
● To understand computer networks including the internet; how they can provide multiple services, such as the World Wide Web; and the opportunities they offer for communication and collaboration.
● To use technology safely, respectfully and responsibly.

Lesson objectives
● To identify the features of collaborating in person.
● To identify the features of collaborating online.
● To compare collaborating online and in person and give advantages and disadvantages.
● To describe the workflow of using Web 2.0 tools for collaboration.

Expected outcomes
● Can compare collaborating online and in person.
● Can give examples of collaboration online using Web 2.0 tools.

Resources
Photocopiable page 118 'Great journeys'; photocopiable page 114 'Computing glossary'; photocopiable page 119 'Debating'

Web 2.0 tools

This week, the children revise their knowledge and experience of Web 2.0 tools. They collaborate online and face-to-face and compare methods.

Introduction

● Introduce the lesson by focusing on a great journey, for example, Apollo 13, or the journeys of Charles Darwin, Christopher Columbus or Shackleton.
● In groups of four, give children ten minutes to research journeys online and record their findings on photocopiable page 118 'Great journeys'.
● Bring the class together and ask for journeys facts and the explanation of why they are 'great'.
● Explain that they are now going to collaborate online to gather the information about one of the journeys and then vote to choose one journey.

Group work

● Set up an 'etherpad' – a collaborative word processing document, to be used by the whole class (http://etherpad.wikimedia.org/).
● Still in groups, children enter their group name at the top right-hand side of the web page.
● On the page, write the heading 'Group 1', then leave a space of five lines, then 'Group 2', then five lines and so on for each group.
● Each group adds their facts.

Whole-class work

● Bring the class together and display the etherpad on the screen.
● Children read the information about the journeys and then vote for the one they find most interesting.

Paired work

● In pairs and using Google or Bing maps, they plot the route of the chosen journey. They add arrows and labels to identify the place names and details.
● They also try and find out the cost and the purpose of the journey.

Group work

● Explain that the children are going to hold a debate. The debate could focus on, for example 'It was a waste of money to put a man on the moon' or 'It would have been better if Columbus had never travelled to America'.
● Organise the class by combining each small group with another, one group 'for' and the other 'against'. They can begin by arguing face-to-face, putting their ideas down on photocopiable page 119 'Debating'. After ten minutes, switch to using the etherpad to debate. Do they find it easier or more difficult?

Differentiation
● Support: Less confident learners may need support to research the facts and see how they can have advantages and disadvantages.
● Challenge: More confident learners should be able to research facts about a journey and organise them into counter arguments of 'for' and 'against'. They will be able to use the online tools to collaborate and organise their thoughts.

Review

● Bring the class together and select one child from each group. Ask them to summarise the debate.
● Ask them to describe the differences between working face-to-face and online.
● What could be the advantages of being online? (People could be located in different places or even working at different times.)
● Remind the children about using video communication tools (voice over the internet services, VoIP). In this way it is possible to talk with someone remotely and try to identify their body language using the video connection.

Curriculum objectives
● To understand computer networks including the internet; how they can provide multiple services, such as the World Wide Web; and the opportunities they offer for communication and collaboration.
● To use technology safely, respectfully and responsibly.

Lesson objectives
● To identify the features of a physical diary.
● To identify the features of a blog.
● To know that a blog is a web log.
● To be able to contribute a blog post.
● To be able to evaluate a blog post contribution.

Expected outcomes
● Can explain how a blog works.
● Can add a blog post and a comment.

Resources
Photocopiable page 'Maia's diary' from the CD-ROM; interactive activity 'Amazon journey' on the CD-ROM; *Journey to the River Sea* by Eva Ibbotson

Blogs

In *Journey to the River Sea*, Maia and Finn travel up the Amazon river. The children imagine what it would be like to be them and write diary entries and create a blog post.

Introduction
● Discuss the ending of the story, where Maia is described as being back 'safe' but not 'home'.
● Encourage children to imagine Maia's physical and emotional journey. Would there have been times when she would have been frightened?

Whole-class work
● Use interactive activity 'Amazon journey' on the CD-ROM or display a map of the Amazon river.
● Add labels to parts of the route and suggest a date that Maia reached that point (they can invent the locations and the dates).

Paired work
● In pairs, using photocopiable page 'Maia's diary' from the CD-ROM, the children write short diary entries for the locations on the map.

Whole-class work
● Ask three children to read out a diary entry. Ask another child to give feedback on each one.
● Remind the children that feedback must be kind, specific and helpful.
● The children have been introduced to blogs in previous lessons. Can they identify the features of a blog?
● Prior to the lesson, set up a blog for the class to use. Edublogs (https://edublogs.org/) enables the children to have a try.
● Demonstrate how to create a new blog entry and use one of the children's examples of a diary entry for the text.
● Ask: *Would you use a public blog to record all of the same information as a diary?* It might be that the diary has their intimate thoughts.

Paired work
● In pairs, the children contribute to the blog, by writing a blog post linked to the story. How have they repurposed the information for a wider audience? Who do they think might read the blog?
● Once the blog entry has been posted, they should select another pair's entry and read it carefully.
● They now add a comment for their peers, making sure that it is 'kind, specific and helpful'.

Differentiation
● Support: Less confident learners may need support to imagine a scene from the story and put it into words. They may need help to rewrite the information for a new purpose.
● Challenge: More confident learners will be able to improvise their diary entries, based upon the story. They should think how the main character might write in their diary, before repurposing the information for a public blog post.

Review
● Bring the class together and select five children to read their blog posts and the associated comment. Is the comment kind, specific and helpful?
● Can the children explain the advantages and disadvantages of using a blog instead of a diary.

Curriculum objectives
● To understand computer networks including the internet; how they can provide multiple services, such as the World Wide Web; and the opportunities they offer for communication and collaboration.
● To use technology safely, respectfully and responsibly.

Lesson objectives
● To identify online surveying tools.
● To use an online survey tool to collect information.
● To create a new survey to collect information.
● To describe the advantages and disadvantages of online survey tools.

Expected outcomes
● Can use an online surveying tool and describe the advantages and disadvantages of using online tools.

Resources
Photocopiable page 'Amazon adventure planning' from the CD-ROM; photocopiable page 'Tourist survey' from the CD-ROM

Planning an expedition

Many travel companies offer experiences of travelling along the Amazon and visiting Brazil. The children look at example expeditions and then plan an expedition themselves. They use an online surveying tool to gather information and to help the tourist to plan their journey.

Introduction
● Explain that the children will be researching websites of travel companies and then surveying the class to find out which destinations along the journey they would like to visit.

Whole-class work
● Demonstrate an online search using search words, such as, 'Amazon', 'expedition' and 'Brazil'.
● Show the results page and ask the children to identify which sites they think belong to travel companies. Why do they think that?

Group work
● The children research travel company websites and plan for six places they would like to visit, using photocopiable page 'Amazon adventure planning' from the CD-ROM.
● They capture screenshots of the destinations, map locations, price information or testimonials of people who have stayed there, for example.

Whole-class work
● Using photocopiable page 'Tourist survey' from the CD-ROM, the groups plan questions to ask travellers interested in their tour.
● Set up a 'Socrative' account (http://www.socrative.com/). Demonstrate on the screen how to login and create a new quiz.

Group work
● In groups, children add their questions to the survey (each group can use one account).
● Once complete, they can test out their survey by one child logging in as a student (http://m.socrative.com/) and entering the Socrative room number.
● Editing the survey, they add their chosen destinations from their list. They add a description and an image.
● Once complete, they evaluate their survey and check for accuracy.
● Groups swap and compare each other's surveys.
● A results summary is emailed to the group who constructed it.

> ### Differentiation
> ● Support: Less confident learners may need support to structure their survey and help to create the text descriptions of the places to visit.
> ● Challenge: More confident learners will be able to research the destinations, take notes and gather images. They should construct a user survey to gather information. Once complete, they can create an itinerary for the user.

Review
● Bring the class together and ask one group to show their online survey.
● From the results, they could plan an itinerary for that group, once they know how many in the group, the month they wish to travel, which destinations they wish to visit and so on.
● Ask the children about the process of negotiating which places to choose when face-to-face and then describing them in the survey, imagining their end user and their needs.

Curriculum objectives
● To understand computer networks including the internet; how they can provide multiple services, such as the World Wide Web; and the opportunities they offer for communication and collaboration.
● To use technology safely, respectfully and responsibly.

Lesson objectives
● To know that computers can multitask.
● To describe why multitasking is important.
● To predict the future of computing, referring to Moore's law.
● To use technology safely and responsibly.

Expected outcomes
● Can describe how computers can multitask.
● Can simply explain Moore's law.

Resources
Photocopiable page 'Multitasking cards' from the CD-ROM; photocopiable page 'SCARF' from the CD-ROM

Changes in technology

The children are encouraged to think about the changes in technology. They think about how computer processors can multitask and why that is important. They are introduced to 'Moore's law' and the 'fetch execute cycle'.

Introduction
● Introduce the lesson by asking: *Can you do more than one thing at one time?*
● In pairs, ask the children to think of where they can do more than one thing at a time and to demonstrate it to their partner.

Whole-class work
● Display the poem 'The Road Not Taken' by Robert Frost as an example of a poem with a journey theme.
● Choose one child to read the poem aloud. Can they read the poem aloud and sort cards into an order? Using photocopiable page 'Multitasking cards' from the CD-ROM, the child orders the card set 1, while glancing up at the display to read the poem. They repeat with sets 2 and 3.
● Explain that the children are multitasking in the same way that a CPU may be processing the instructions for one application, then switching to processing the instructions for another application. Operating systems, such as, Windows or OSX, appear to 'multitask' different applications, because they appear to be running more than one at once. The CPU is actually switching between each application very quickly, which gives the impression that they are running at the same time.

Paired work
● In pairs, research online to find other poems about journeys and try switching between reading the poems and sorting cards.

Whole-class work
● Bring the class together and explain that modern CPUs, memory and components are becoming faster so the operating system can multitask more applications and switch between them more quickly. Therefore, the user can do more work, more quickly.
● Explain that a simple prediction of how the technology is changing is called 'Moore's law'. Gordon Moore (co-founder of the processor manufacturer, Intel) looked at how computer processing power had increased and predicted that processor speeds would continue to double every two years.
● Moving into Key Stage 3, the children will learn further about the CPU and how it follows a 'fetch execute cycle'. This is where the processor 'fetches' an instruction, 'decodes' the instruction and then 'executes' the instruction. The instructions can be thought of as the lines in the program.

Paired work
● Using the acronym SCARF, the children consider how technology has become: Smaller, Cheaper, more Accurate, more Reliable and Faster. Using photocopiable page 'SCARF' from the CD-ROM, they think about the technology around them and how it has changed.

Differentiation
● Support: Less confident learners may need support to think of five examples of technology and use the SCARF criteria to recognise changes.
● Challenge: More confident learners will be able to consider how technology has changed and think of, at least, ten examples.

Review
● Share examples of how technology has changed.
● Summarise the learning about multitasking and computer CPUs, memory and components becoming faster and more efficient.

Curriculum objectives
● To understand computer networks including the internet; how they can provide multiple services, such as the World Wide Web; and the opportunities they offer for communication and collaboration.
● To use technology safely, respectfully and responsibly.

Lesson objectives
● To explain the difference between the World Wide Web and the internet.
● To explain how to navigate web pages using a browser.
● To explain a hyperlink and how it behaves.
● To guide a peer through using a web page.

Expected outcomes
● Can outline the key features of the World Wide Web.
● Can explain how to use a browser, including navigation via hyperlinks.

Resources
Photocopiable page 'Tour of Brazil' from the CD-ROM; photocopiable page 'Web tour guide' from the CD-ROM

Great journeys: Assess and review

The children return to thinking about accessing the World Wide Web and navigating the web pages. They create a guide for a younger child, on how to navigate a web page.

Introduction
● Introduce the lesson by telling the children that they are 'tour guides' for Year 4 children. They are going to describe a tour of Brazil and explain how to navigate a web page.
● In pairs, ask the children to explain how they access the World Wide Web, for example, using a web browser.
● Ask: *How do you access the World Wide Web?*

Independent work
● Using photocopiable page 'Tour of Brazil' from the CD-ROM, the children use an outline map of Brazil and label the places that they will show the Year 4 children. They research the places using the web and ensure that the language and vocabulary they use is appropriate for younger children.

Whole-class work
● Bring the class together and ask five children to describe the places they have chosen and the reasons why.
● To travel between the places, they will need to use a network of travel routes, for example, air, rail, road or river. Can they identify how they would travel between the places?
● The internet is a global network of computers, analogous to the travel networks. The data travels from one place to another. Can the children define the internet and the World Wide Web?
● Ask: *What is the difference between the World Wide Web and the internet?*

Paired work
● Explain to the children that they will be tour guides for the web browser and web pages. Using photocopiable page 'Web tour guide' from the CD-ROM, the children sketch a browser and web page and label it. They include a glossary for the labelled parts. Alternatively, they could use software to capture screenshots and add labels (for example, using the software 'Skitch').
● They need to explain how the user can travel from one page to another (hyperlinks, bookmarks, history, menu commands, keyboard shortcuts, tool bar buttons).

Differentiation
● Support: Less confident learners may need support to define the difference between the World Wide Web and the internet and to understand that there are several ways to navigate from web page to web page.
● Challenge: More confident learners will be able to describe the key features of the World Wide Web and the methods used to navigate from one web page to another.

Review
● To conclude the chapter, ask the children to imagine the future of technology and how they can access the World Wide Web. One example is Google Glass (http://www.google.co.uk/glass/start/), where the user wears special glasses to view the web controlled by voice commands and the blinking of eyes. How do the children think we will access information in 5, 10 or 20 years' time?

Name: _____ Date: _____

Navigating the Amazon

■ Search for information about the Amazon river.

Find as many interesting facts as you can.

_____

_____

_____

_____

_____

_____

_____

_____

I can research online to find out about the Amazon river.

How did you do?

Computing glossary

- Define the words listed.
- Add your own words and define those too.

Web browser: _____

Web page: _____

Hyperlink: _____

Bookmark: _____

Menu: _____

Image: _____

Text: _____

Keyboard shortcut: _____

- What is the difference between the internet and the World Wide Web?

_____

_____

_____

I can define computing words.

How did you do?

PHOTOCOPIABLE

Name: _____   Date: _____

Navigating a web page

- Sketch your web page below.
- Add labels to describe each part.

I can sketch a web page and explain the function of each part.

How did you do?

Name: _____ Date: _____

Brazil

■ Using Wikipedia, research facts about Brazil.

■ Which topics would be interesting for your class?

_____

_____

My facts about Brazil are:

_____

_____

_____

_____

■ What are the common features of the Wikipedia pages?

_____

_____

I can research facts about Brazil and recognise the common features of the Wikipedia pages.

How did you do?

PHOTOCOPIABLE

Wikipedia page layout

Wikipedia logo		Search box
	Heading	Image
Navigation menu	Text	
	Subheading	
	Text	
	Subheading	
	Text	
	References	
	External links	

I can create a web page in the style of a Wikipedia page.

How did you do?

Name: _____   Date: _____

Great journeys

Which great journey have you chosen? _____

Facts about the journey

1. _____

_____

_____

2. _____

_____

_____

3. _____

_____

_____

4. _____

_____

_____

5. _____

_____

_____

This journey is a great journey because:

_____

_____

I can research information about a journey of my choice.

How did you do?

PHOTOCOPIABLE

SCHOLASTIC
www.scholastic.co.uk

Debating

The great journey we have chosen is:

_____

_____

The issue we are debating is:

_____

_____

For	Against

I can research about a great journey and debate an issue relating to it.

How did you do?

Fantasy worlds

In this chapter, the children create their own fantasy animation using the Alice programming language. They transfer the skills they have learned from creating programs in Scratch to a new programming environment and, in doing so, develop their computational thinking, problem-solving and coding skills. They are encouraged to make use of repetition and selection as appropriate and are introduced to procedures.

Expected prior learning

● The children have been working in Scratch in previous chapters. These lessons build on the existing knowledge, skills and understanding they have already developed by challenging them to transfer their learning to another programming language.

Chapter at a glance

Subject area
• Algorithms and programming

National Curriculum objective
• To design, write and debug programs that accomplish specific goals, including controlling or simulating physical systems; solve problems by decomposing them into smaller parts. To use sequence and repetition in programs; work with variables and various forms of input and output. To use logical reasoning to explain how some simple algorithms work and to detect and correct errors in algorithms and programs.

Week	Lesson objectives	Summary of activities	Expected outcomes
1	• To solve problems using different methods. • To understand that there are many different programs that can be used to accomplish a task. • To use logical reasoning to determine how algorithms could be implemented with a different program and predict the outcome.	• Children revisit their previous work using Scratch. • They investigate Logo and other programming languages. • They report back to class their findings.	• Can understand that problems can be solved in different ways. • Can transfer knowledge and understanding about algorithms and programming to a second programming language.
2	• To understand the basic Alice 2.4 interface. • To plan, create and test programs to solve a number of different challenges. • To know how to use templates to select a scene. • To know and understand how to add, orient and move objects in simple ways in Alice 2.4. • To explain to a beginner the Alice 2.4 interface and how it can solve problems in different ways to Scratch.	• Children look at the Alice programming language. • They select backgrounds, objects and methods to create a new 'world'. • They share their findings with each other.	• Can create algorithms to plan a number of different outcomes. • Can execute algorithms using a second programming language.
3	• To design and plan a short animation using Alice 2.4. • To give and receive constructive feedback. • To list the assets needed for their animation. • To use Alice 2.4 to set the scene for their animation, selecting appropriate scenes and adding objects.	• Children consider what a fantasy world means. • They brainstorm ideas. • They write a textual storyboard for one of their ideas. • They make changes based on feedback.	• Can plan a short story animation using a given template. • Can add suitable assets to a program for their planned story animation.

Week	Lesson objectives	Summary of activities	Expected outcomes
4	• To plan the instructions needed by Alice 2.4 to implement their short story plan. • To use Alice 2.4 to create their planned program. • To test and debug their program as necessary. • To use loops and selection. • To explain how Alice 2.4 differs from and is similar to Scratch.	• Children begin to program their fantasy world, including objects, backgrounds and methods. • They explore adding two methods together, If Else, Loop and While commands. • They work collaboratively to solve problems. • They compare Alice with Scratch.	• Can design and write a program to implement their short story plan. • Can use loops (repetition) and selection to make their program more efficient.
5	• To work collaboratively to test and debug their program. • To add suitable comments to their program. • To know and understand the term 'procedure'. • To explain how procedures are used in Alice 2.4.	• Children use procedures in their programs. • They add comments. • They complete their animation and work collaboratively to debug errors.	• Can add useful comments to their program. • Can understand and explain that procedures can be used to make a program more efficient.
6	• To know how to save and export their animation and code so it can be viewed by anyone. • To present their animation to the class. • To give and receive constructive feedback. • To discuss the differences between Scratch and Alice 2.4. • To evaluate the use of both programs for different purposes.	• Children export their animation and print their code. • They evaluate a partner's animation and evaluate their own. • They compare Alice with Scratch.	• Can present their work to their classmates. • Can explain the importance of selecting the right program for a given purpose.
Assess and review	• Assess and review the half term's work.	• Children choose an element of Alice to explain in a one-page guide.	• Assess and review.

Overview of progression
• Throughout this chapter, the children build upon their knowledge and understanding of designing and developing programs. They begin by considering and evaluating different programming languages before being introduced to the Alice 2.4 interface and planning their own fantasy-world-based animation. They then create and debug their program, using selection, repetition and procedures as appropriate. Finally, they share their work with the class before comparing and evaluating the use of both Alice and Scratch.
• The children apply and develop their knowledge and understanding of programming by using decomposition, logical thinking and problem solving to plan, create, debug and evaluate their animation.

Creative context
• The lessons have links to the mathematics curriculum as the children use logical thinking, problem solving and decomposition to write and debug their code. Programming movement of the objects within Alice 2.4 also requires the children to use direction and distance measurements.
• The computing lessons should also draw upon the children's learning in English through their written work in planning, creating and evaluating their game and also to develop their spoken language as they are encouraged to share and explain their work verbally.

Background knowledge
• From work in earlier years, the children will be confident in using Scratch as a programming language and will be familiar with implementing algorithms, coding and using selection and repetition.
• From assessing the children's understanding in previous units, you will need to assess the children's capability in creating the animation in Alice. You can then adjust the task as necessary, creating a simplified version for some children if needed.
• It is important that you are familiar with Alice 2.4 and are familiar with creating a basic animation.
• Screencasts are available showing you how to use Alice (https://www.youtube.com/watch?v=zq4Xpv4gDIk) and further tutorials are available from http://www.cs.duke.edu/csed/alice09/tutorials.php

Curriculum objectives

● To design, write and debug programs that accomplish specific goals, including controlling or simulating physical systems; solve problems by decomposing them into smaller parts. To use sequence and repetition in programs; work with variables and various forms of input and output. To use logical reasoning to explain how some simple algorithms work and to detect and correct errors in algorithms and programs.

Lesson objectives

● To solve problems using different methods.
● To understand that there are many different programs that can be used to accomplish a task.
● To use logical reasoning to determine how algorithms could be implemented with a different program and predict the outcome.

Expected outcomes

● Can understand that problems can be solved in different ways.
● Can transfer knowledge and understanding about algorithms and programming to a second programming language.

Resources

Photocopiable page 129 'Program discovery'; three to five different programming languages and short activities such as those available at the time of writing at http://www.tynker.com/hour-of-code/, http://learn.code.org/hoc/1, http://www.transum.org/software/logo/, https://code.google.com/p/blockly/, https://www.touchdevelop.com/, http://www.crunchzilla.com/code-monster, http://www.transum.org/software/logo/

Testing programs

In this first lesson, the children will be introduced to the fact that different programs can be used to write code and achieve similar outcomes in different ways. Having used Scratch to program previous animations, quizzes and games, they are challenged with working out how to use other programming software to perform a variety of tasks, problem solving, predicting outcomes and debugging. They then make and share simple evaluations of programs.

Introduction

● Remind the children that in previous lessons they have been using Scratch to create programs, such as quizzes, animations and games.
● Explain that there are many other programs they can use to write code.
● Invite the children to share their knowledge of other programming software and explain that they will be investigating others today.

Whole-class work

● Ask a volunteer to be a human robot and ask the rest of the class to come up with an algorithm to make the robot move backwards and forwards.
● Discuss as a class that an algorithm is intended to be executed by a human and a program is intended to be executed by a computer. We can use programming to implement the algorithm, in this case making an object on a computer move backwards and forwards.
● Ask another volunteer to quickly demonstrate how to do make the cat move backwards and forwards in Scratch by clicking the green flag.
● As they do so, discuss that they are moving blocks of code to create code (the script) that can be executed by clicking the green flag.
● Show the children Logo, and ask them to work out how to move the turtle backwards and forwards.
● Explain that the algorithm of moving backwards and forwards is implemented in different ways by the two programs – there is a different interface and the user has to input the instructions in different ways.

Group/paired work

● Allocate different programs to different groups. Give out photocopiable page 129 'Program discovery' and ask the children to work through the tasks, taking their time to work out how each task might be implemented with the program you have asked that group to investigate.
● Emphasise that this is their opportunity to discover how things work – you are not going to show them. They are going to explore the programs themselves.
● Stress that they need to use their problem-solving, logical thinking and debugging skills, and need to listen to ideas and be persistent.

Differentiation

● Support: Less confident learners should be given one of the more straightforward programs and may benefit from mixed-ability groupings or adult support when working through the task sheet.
● Challenge: More confident learners can be given one of the more complex programs. Encourage them to move beyond the task sheet quickly and be creative in discovering what they can do with the program.

Review

● Ask each group to share what they have learned with the rest of the class.
● As a class, discuss which programs were most effective for what purposes and why having different programming software is useful (gives choice, achieve different outcomes, aimed at different audiences, can be used on different devices and so on).
● Assess the children's progress by their work during the small group activity, their showcase to their peers and class discussion.

Curriculum objectives
● To design, write and debug programs that accomplish specific goals, including controlling or simulating physical systems; solve problems by decomposing them into smaller parts. To use sequence and repetition in programs; work with variables and various forms of input and output. To use logical reasoning to explain how some simple algorithms work and to detect and correct errors in algorithms and programs.

Lesson objectives
● To understand the basic Alice 2.4 interface.
● To plan, create and test programs to solve a number of different challenges.
● To know how to use templates to select a scene.
● To know and understand how to add, orient and move objects in simple ways in Alice 2.4.
● To explain to a beginner the Alice 2.4 interface and how it can solve problems in different ways to Scratch.

Expected outcomes
● Can create algorithms to plan a number of different outcomes.
● Can execute algorithms using a second programming language.

Resources
Photocopiable page 130 'Exploring the Alice program'; Alice 2.4 installed on the computers – available from http://www.alice.org/index.php

Adventures in Alice

This week, the children are introduced to the Alice interface. They spend some time undertaking an independent guided exploration of the program in pairs before sharing what they have discovered with their peers.

Introduction
● Recap last week's lesson with the children and show them the Alice interface.
● Ask them to share what they can see/are interested in knowing more about.
● Use this discussion as an opportunity to show the children how to create a new world, choosing a background template, add and choose objects, click on an object to bring up the object tree, add a couple of methods to the 'my first method' area and play their animation.

Whole-class work
● Explain that in this lesson they will be exploring how to use Alice and experimenting with what they can do with the software.
● Emphasise that, similar to last week, they will need to find things out for themselves and should use their problem-solving, logical thinking and debugging skills.

Paired work
● Give out photocopiable page 130 'Exploring the Alice program' and explain that they will be using this to guide them through the program.
● Go through the first task as an example and highlight how to click 'done' once an object has been added and how to put an unwanted method in the 'bin'.
● Encourage the children to work collaboratively to complete the tasks, helping each other as they go. It would be helpful to watch for any children who find interesting and useful aspects of the program, and then share these with the group later.

Group work
● Match up pairs of children and ask them to share what they have learned with each other. They should work collaboratively to debug any errors in each other's work.

Whole-class work
● Depending on progress, go through the task sheet, or ask pairs to share what they have discovered.
● If you wish, you could create a collaborative, class animation using the collective learning of the class.

Differentiation
● Support: Less confident learners may benefit from working in mixed-ability pairs or from adult support to help them to work through the task sheet, perhaps providing further scaffolding to their exploration of Alice.
● Challenge: More confident learners will be able to work independently and with confidence to explore Alice. They should be encouraged to be creative in finding out what the program can do, creating more complex methods, perhaps using the 'do together' command and adding more objects. Encourage them to share their learning with the group.

Review
● Ask the children to come up with a 'quick fire' quiz for each other. One child comes up with a 'how do you?' question and another answers it. For example, 'How do I move only part of an object?' and the second child shows them. You can do this as a whole class or in pairs/small groups.

Curriculum objectives
● To design, write and debug programs that accomplish specific goals, including controlling or simulating physical systems; solve problems by decomposing them into smaller parts. To use sequence and repetition in programs; work with variables and various forms of input and output. To use logical reasoning to explain how some simple algorithms work and to detect and correct errors in algorithms and programs.

Lesson objectives
● To design and plan a short animation using Alice 2.4.
● To give and receive constructive feedback.
● To list the assets needed for their animation.
● To use Alice 2.4 to set the scene for their animation, selecting appropriate scenes and adding objects.

Expected outcomes
● Can plan a short story animation using a given template.
● Can add suitable assets to a program for their planned story animation.

Resources
Photocopiable page 131 'Fantasy world ideas'; photocopiable page 132 'Textual storyboard'

Planning a fantasy world animation

This week, the children design and plan a short animation based on a fantasy world of their own choosing. They will brainstorm and choose their idea before creating a simple textual storyboard, receiving feedback from their peers and adjusting their ideas as appropriate. The children will then begin their animation in Alice, selecting their scene and adding their chosen objects.

Introduction
● Display Alice on the board and remind the children that last week they were exploring how to use Alice to create programs.
● Ask the children to share their learning from last lesson, recapping how to add objects, add a few methods and play their animation as a minimum.

Whole-class work
● Explain that in the next few lessons they will be creating an animation and that this week they will be brainstorming and choosing their idea, creating a textual rather than a visual storyboard, and perhaps even beginning their animation.
● Ask the children to consider what a 'fantasy world' means. Encourage them to make reference to books they may have read.

Independent/paired work
● Give out photocopiable page 131 'Fantasy world ideas' and ask the children to brainstorm different fantasy worlds they could use in their animation.
● Pair up the children and ask them to share their ideas with their partner, helping each other to narrow down their ideas to one final idea.

Whole-class work
● Ask a few children to share their ideas with the class to check understanding and ask them to consider what they need to do next before getting started on their animation (work out what objects they will use/plan what will happen).
● Give out photocopiable page 132 'Textual storyboard' and go through the example with the children.

Independent/paired work
● Ask the children to complete their textual storyboard, including listing the assets, and then explain it to a partner who can consider questions such as: *Does the animation make sense? What else could/should be included?*
● The children can then make adjustments based on their partner's feedback.
● Some children may finish this quickly and can proceed to beginning their animation, adding objects and methods as appropriate.

Differentiation
● Support: Encourage less confident learners to create a simple yet effective animation. They may benefit from mixed-ability pairings or further adult support when creating their textual storyboard.
● Challenge: More confident learners should be able to plan a more complex animation, including more objects, greater interactions and perhaps adding sounds and effects.

Review
● Ask the children to consider how the textual storyboard they completed is different to the visual storyboards they have completed in the past. The textual storyboard is simply a different way of creating a storyboard and it is useful for them to explore different methods. Ask: *Which do you prefer?* You could create a poll if you wish.
● Invite willing children to share their ideas with the rest of the class for further feedback.
● Measure the children's progress through the textual storyboard activity, which outlines the children's plans for their animation.

Programming in Alice

This week, the children program their animation in Alice. They are shown how to use different buttons to enable the use of different programming elements, including repetition (loops) and selection. Finally, they compare Alice to Scratch and evaluate both programs and their potential use.

Curriculum objectives
● To design, write and debug programs that accomplish specific goals, including controlling or simulating physical systems; solve problems by decomposing them into smaller parts. To use sequence and repetition in programs; work with variables and various forms of input and output. To use logical reasoning to explain how some simple algorithms work and to detect and correct errors in algorithms and programs.

Lesson objectives
● To plan the instructions needed by Alice 2.4 to implement their short story plan.
● To use Alice 2.4 to create their planned program.
● To test and debug their program as necessary.
● To use loops and selection.
● To explain how Alice 2.4 differs from and is similar to Scratch.

Expected outcomes
● Can design and write a program to implement their short story plan.
● Can use loops (repetition) and selection to make their program more efficient.

Resources
Completed photocopiable resource 132 'Textual storyboard' from last lesson; Alice 2.4

Introduction
● Recap last week's work with the children and give out the completed photocopiable page 132 'Textual storyboard'.
● Explain that in this lesson, if they did not do so last lesson, they will be starting to program their animation in Alice and that you are first going to discuss a few elements they may need to know.

Whole-class work
● Display Alice on the whiteboard and add any object. Explain that you wish to make things happen at the same time. Does anyone know how to do this?
● Show them how to add two methods and then use the 'Do together' button to make them happen at the same time, by dragging the 'Do together' button on to the methods area and then dragging in the two methods.

Whole-class work
● Depending on your class's confidence, you can repeat the above with the If/Else, Loop and While commands. Note that you need to go into the 'functions' tab to action the proximity methods used below. Functions are simply methods (or procedures – see Week 5), that can perform calculations.
● If/Else – using selection, this shows that if the bunny is within 1 metre of the robot, then the robot should say 'hello', otherwise, do nothing.

● Loop – showing the use of repetition, this loop makes the bunny move up, move down and think five times.

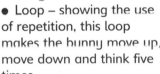

● While – showing another way of using repetition, this while loop makes the bunny move up, move down and think five times *while* it is within 1 metre of the robot.

● Discuss why using these commands is helpful (helps to make code more efficient, avoids unnecessary code that can slow down the computer).

Independent/paired work
● For the remainder of the lesson, the children program their Alice animation, working both independently and collaboratively to solve problems.

Differentiation
● Support: Less confident learners may need additional adult or peer support when programming their animation and can focus on creating a simple animation well.
● Challenge: Encourage more confident learners to make use of the additional commands discussed above.

Review
● Discuss with the children the progress they have made on their animation.
● Discuss how Alice is comparable to and differs from Scratch in terms of how the program implements their desired outcome (or algorithm). Ask: *Which is easier to code and why? Which has the better result and why?*

Curriculum objectives
● To design, write and debug programs that accomplish specific goals, including controlling or simulating physical systems; solve problems by decomposing them into smaller parts. To use sequence and repetition in programs; work with variables and various forms of input and output. To use logical reasoning to explain how some simple algorithms work and to detect and correct errors in algorithms and programs.

Lesson objectives
● To work collaboratively to test and debug their program.
● To add suitable comments to their program.
● To know and understand the term 'procedure'.
● To explain how procedures are used in Alice 2.4.

Expected outcomes
● Can add useful comments to their program.
● Can understand and explain that procedures can be used to make a program more efficient.

Resources
Alice 2.4

Using comments and procedures

In this lesson, the children continue to program their animation and learn how to add comments to their work in Alice. They are also introduced to the term 'procedure'.

Introduction
● Remind children that in the last lesson they started programming their animation.
● Explain that in this lesson they will be learning about using procedures and how they can use them in their Alice animation.

Whole-class work
● Explain that a procedure is a set of commands that can be executed in order to perform a particular task.
● Ask the children to identify the procedure(s) in their animation, which will be any block of code.
● Explain that in Alice we can create our own procedures to save ourselves time and make the code organised and clear. We can do this by creating our own method.
● Show the children how to create their own method, by clicking on the 'create new method' button, naming their method and then adding in the commands needed to achieve the outcome (in this case a bunny hop).
● Show the children how to add an additional event to execute the new method. The example below shows that by pressing the enter key the bunny hop procedure will run.

Independent/paired work
● Ask the children to experiment with creating their own methods (procedures) in Alice and adding additional events to execute them.
● When they think they have finished, they should explain to a partner what procedures are and how they have created and used a new procedure in their work. Their partner can help them to debug their procedure if necessary.

Whole-class work
● Ask the children to recall and share why comments are useful in a program. (They help anyone who is viewing or editing the code to see what each part of code is doing and why.)
● Show the children how to add comments to their work in Alice.
● Firstly drag a comment tile (//) from the far right-hand side of the commands at the bottom of the screen.
● Add the comment to the relevant point and type in a meaningful comment.

Independent/paired work
● For the remainder of the lesson, the children should work on finishing their animation, adding comments and procedures as appropriate and working collaboratively to debug any errors that arise.

> **Differentiation**
> ● Support: Less confident learners may need additional adult or peer support in understanding and creating procedures.
> ● Challenge: More confident learners can be stretched to create multiple procedures with confidence and complete their animation to a high standard.

Review
● Ask the children quick-fire questions to demonstrate their understanding. For example: *What is a procedure? How is a procedure known in Alice? How can a procedure be created/executed in Alice. Why are comments important? How could this (example) comment be improved?* Assess children's progress through their use of procedures and comments and contribution to the class discussions.

Curriculum objectives

● To design, write and debug programs that accomplish specific goals, including controlling or simulating physical systems; solve problems by decomposing them into smaller parts. To use sequence and repetition in programs; work with variables and various forms of input and output. To use logical reasoning to explain how some simple algorithms work and to detect and correct errors in algorithms and programs.

Lesson objectives

● To know how to save and export their animation and code so it can be viewed by anyone.
● To present their animation to the class.
● To give and receive constructive feedback.
● To discuss the differences between Scratch and Alice 2.4.
● To evaluate the use of both programs for different purposes.

Expected outcomes

● Can present their work to their classmates.
● Can explain the importance of selecting the right program for a given purpose.

Resources

Photocopiable resource 133 'Evaluation of your partner's animation'; photocopiable page 134 'Evaluation of your own animation'; it would be helpful if prior to the lesson you were able to collect the children's finished work into a single area to enable viewing as a class

Showcasing animations

This week, the children export their animation and code before presenting it to the class. They will give and receive constructive feedback and evaluate their own animation and also the two programming languages of Alice and Scratch.

Introduction

● Remind the children that last week they were learning about adding comments and procedures to their animation and that they completed their animation.
● Explain that in this lesson they are going to be exporting their animation so it can be viewed on any computer and printing their code so it can be assessed.
● Show the children how to export their completed animation, recording a video of their animation using the File>Export Video command.
● Show them also how to export the code for printing using File>Export Code for Printing.

Independent/paired work

● Ask the children to export their animation and print off their code.

Whole-class work

● Explain that their next task is to review a partner's work and give them feedback on their animation. They can then use this in their own evaluation, which they will complete later in the lesson.
● Remind the children how to use 'what went well' and 'even better if', or a similar way to review work.

Independent/paired work

● In pairs children watch their partner's animation and give each other verbal feedback and record the main points their partner makes using photocopiable page 133 'Evaluation of your partner's animation' sheet.
● Once they have finished, they should complete photocopiable page 134 'Evaluation of your own animation', incorporating their partner's comments as appropriate into the first two questions.

Whole-class work

● Ask for volunteers to present their animations to the class, encouraging as many children as possible to share their work.
● This can be used as an opportunity to assess the children's understanding and progress and encouraging them to explain their code can help with this further.

Differentiation
● Support: Less confident learners may need adult assistance when completing their feedback sheet and benefit from mixed-ability pairings.
● Challenge: Encourage more confident learners to write high-quality, thoughtful evaluations of their work and to give detailed consideration to the differences between Scratch and Alice and evaluating both programs.

Review

● Discuss with the children what they have learned from completing their animation in Alice.
● Invite them to share their opinions of both Scratch and Alice. Which do you like better and why? What are the pros and cons of each? What projects might you use Alice for instead of Scratch and vice versa?
● Assess the children's progress through their animation, their explanation of their code and their evaluation.

Curriculum objectives

● To design, write and debug programs that accomplish specific goals, including controlling or simulating physical systems; solve problems by decomposing them into smaller parts. To use sequence and repetition in programs; work with variables and various forms of input and output. To use logical reasoning to explain how some simple algorithms work and to detect and correct errors in algorithms and programs.

Lesson objectives

● To plan and create a one page tutorial focused on one aspect of Alice.
● To demonstrate their knowledge and understanding of a chosen aspect of Alice.
● To explain how to use a particular aspect of Alice in an easy to understand way using images and text.
● To contribute to a class 'Guide to Alice'.

Expected outcomes

● Can explain to others how to use one aspect of Alice.
● Can demonstrate their understanding of Alice to others in easy to follow instructions.

Resources

Photocopiable page 135 'Alice tutorial'; an example of an effective and/or non-effective how to guide; suitable word processing software for creating a tutorial

Fantasy worlds: Assess and review

In this lesson, the children will create a one-page tutorial on an aspect of Alice for use by others who are using Alice for the first time. They will build on the understanding and skills they built up in Year 5 Summer 1 when creating a Scratch tutorial, this time creating a paper- or screen-based tutorial rather than a screencast. Creating a tutorial allows the children to demonstrate their knowledge and understanding of Alice, and, as a class, you can create a full 'Guide to Alice'.

Introduction

● Discuss with the children what they have learned about Alice during these lessons. You could make a list of these on the board.
● Explain that they will be creating a class guide to using Alice and that each person, or pair if you prefer, will contribute one page to the guide.

Whole-class work

● Ask the children what they think a one-page guide should include.
● Discuss how the use of images and easy-to-follow text are helpful. Show them examples you have found of effective and/or non-effective how-to guides to illustrate that keeping it simple and clear is important.
● Ask the children to choose which element of Alice they will explain from the list they created earlier (assign these or create your own list prior to the lesson if you prefer).
● Ask the children to access photocopiable page 135 'Alice tutorial'. They use this page to plan the tutorial, making a quick list of instructions they will need to provide and screenshots they will use.

Independent/paired work

● The children should complete the tutorial for their allocated aspect of Alice.
● Once they have finished, they should save it in a folder/area you can access.

Differentiation

● Support: Less confident learners may benefit from working in mixed-ability pairings or with additional adult support. They can be assigned one of the more straightforward aspects of Alice on which to create their tutorial.
● Challenge: Encourage more confident learners to create a tutorial on one of the more complex aspects of Alice, explaining for example how to use selection or repetition.

Review

● You could ask volunteers to compile the guide, or you could do it for them.
● The tutorials are an ideal opportunity to assess the children's understanding of Alice.
● Keep the final guide in a shared area so anyone using Alice can access it. If you wish, you could print it out along with some images of the animations for a display.

Program discovery

Group name _____   Allocated program _____

- What audience do you think your program is aimed at and why?

_____

_____

- What can users create with your program?

_____

_____

- What is good about the program?

_____

_____

- What could be improved?

_____

_____

How do you think the program compares to Scratch for teaching young people how to program?

_____

_____

_____

_____

I can work out how to use a new program.
I can evaluate a program.

How did you do?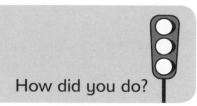

Exploring the Alice program

■ Use the tasks below to help you to understand how to use Alice to write programs.

I. Can you create a new program?

> Hint: If the world is already open, try looking in 'File'. If not, you should see some world templates.

2. Can you choose a template?

Name it: _____

3. Can you add an object?

> Hint: Look for a small green box.

Object added: _____

4. Can you click on the name of the object to bring up the objects methods?

Can you make your object do the following:
Move up I metre. Turn right half a revolution.
Say hello.
Say something else that you decide.

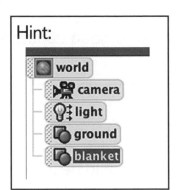

Hint:

5. Add another object. Can you make the new object move towards your first object?

■ What else can you discover that you can do with Alice? Explore the software so you can share your findings with your classmates.

I can explore Alice independently.
I can program Alice to implement algorithms.

How did you do?

PHOTOCOPIABLE   ■SCHOLASTIC
www.scholastic.co.uk

Fantasy world ideas

■ Brainstorm ideas for your fantasy world below.

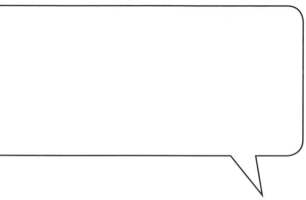

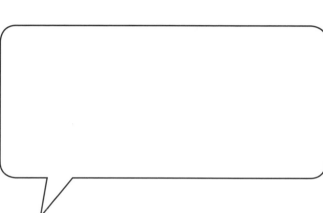

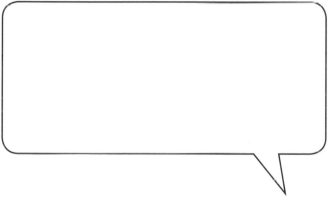

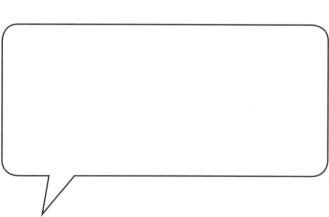

I can brainstorm ideas for a fantasy world.

How did you do?

Textual storyboard

■ Create your own textual storyboard and list the assets you need for your animation. Use the start of the example below to help you.

EXAMPLE

Title: Rabbit and the Astronaut
Textual storyboard:
Rabbit peaks out from behind a rock.
Rabbit says 'boo!' Alien turns.
Alien says 'Who was that?'
Assets needed:
Rabbit
Alien

YOUR ANIMATION

Title:

Textual storyboard:

Assets needed:

I can explore Alice independently.
I can program Alice to implement algorithms.

How did you do?

PHOTOCOPIABLE   ■SCHOLASTIC
www.scholastic.co.uk

Name: _____ Date: _____

Evaluation of your partner's animation

Name of the person whose game you're playing _____

- Look at your partner's animation.
- Give them feedback using the questions below.

1. What went well? (What did you like about the animation? Be specific.)

2. Even better if? (How could the animation be improved? Be specific and remember your partner only has a short time to implement your suggestion.)

I can evaluate an animation.
I can give constructive feedback to a partner.

How did you do?

Name: _____ Date: _____

Evaluation of your own animation

■ Use the questions below to help you to evaluate your animation and the Alice programming language.

1. What are you most pleased with in your animation and why?

_____

_____

_____

2. What would you like to improve about your animation and why?

_____

_____

_____

3. What do you like about using Alice?

_____

_____

_____

4. What do you dislike about Alice?

_____

_____

_____

5. Do you prefer Alice or Scratch for programming? Explain your answer.

_____

_____

_____

I can evaluate my animation.
I can evaluate programming software.

How did you do?

PHOTOCOPIABLE

SCHOLASTIC
www.scholastic.co.uk

Name: _____   Date: _____

Alice tutorial

■ Create a tutorial to explain how to use one aspect of Alice. Use this page to plan your tutorial then create the tutorial on a word processing file.

Aspect of Alice I am creating a tutorial for: _____

Instructions I will need to include in my tutorial	Screenshots I will need to include in my tutorial

I can create a tutorial using images and text.
I can give instructions to others so they can use Alice.

How did you do?

SCHOLASTIC

Africa

In this chapter children look at apps and identify their features. They create paper prototypes and use wireframes to design an app, before using app creation tools to make an app. They consider children in Africa and ask whether they have a different user experience to children in the UK. The children also consider how personal data is shared and the Data Protection Act, copyright and Creative Commons. They then re-evaluate their apps to ensure that they have considered how they are using data and images.

Expected prior learning

● The children will know the difference between hardware and software and their roles within a computer system. They will know that mobile devices use software called 'apps'.
● They will demonstrate responsible use of technologies and online services and know a range of ways to report concerns, if they find material that upsets them.

Chapter at a glance

Subject area
• Data and information

National Curriculum objective
• To select, use and combine a variety of software (including internet services) on a range of digital devices to design and create a range of programs, systems and content that accomplish given goals, including collecting, analysing, evaluating and presenting data and information.

Week	Lesson objectives	Summary of activities	Expected outcomes
1	• To access apps and identify their purposes and common features. • To test apps and describe if the interface is easy to use for a Year 6 child. • To think about user experience. • To discuss to needs of mobile phone users in Africa compared with the UK.	• Children learn that a mobile phone has an operating system and that apps are additional pieces of software. • They discuss their favourite apps and identify the common features of apps. • They start to think about a new app for a Year 6 child and the user experience. • They think about the needs of children in Africa and what kind of app would be useful to them.	• Can compare mobile phone apps and recognise common features. • Can explain what the term 'user experience' means. • Can decompose a larger problem into smaller parts.
2	• To use the 'design thinking process' to plan and design a new app.	• Children name countries in Africa on a map. • They plan an app to inform people about Africa. • They research information about Africa online. • Children use the 'design think' process (empathise, define, ideate, prototype and test) to plan and design their new app.	• Can combine tools using app creation software to create a simple app. • Can explain why user testing and feedback is important.
3	• To use app creation tools to design a home screen for an app. • To feed back on each other's apps. • To think about the user experience.	• Children continue to work on their new app. • They break larger problems into smaller parts. • They use headings, bullets and hyperlinks. • They consider the user experience and test out their apps. • They consider whether children in Africa would need a different design of app.	• Can improve an app design by responding to user feedback. • Can annotate the app to explain the navigation and actions of the buttons.

■SCHOLASTIC

Week	Lesson objectives	Summary of activities	Expected outcomes
4	• To know there are accessible features within apps and why they are important • To identify users who may need accessibility features. • To explain how the accessibility features enable the person to use the app. • Discuss how the accessibility features could be similar or different for users in the UK and Africa.	• Children think about people's different tastes in clothes, music and games. • They discuss how some people might have particular needs, for example, be visually impaired. • They look at accessibility features. • They consider the user experience of children in Africa and whether they would need different accessibility features.	• Can explain why accessibility is important for an app. • Can identify users who may need accessibility features.
5	• To know that apps can collect data. • To identify how apps can collect data.	• Children describe how apps can collect data. • They learn that apps can collect data in less obvious ways, for example, internet searches and location data. • They consider the advantages and disadvantages of collecting data from a mobile device.	• Can identify how data may be collected within an app.
6	• To be able to give a simple definition of copyright. • To know that image, text, video, games can be copyrighted. • To be able to give a simple definition of Creative Commons. • To be able to search for and locate appropriate Creative Commons images, for a specific purpose.	• Children explore how apps can be similar in function. • They are given a simple explanation of copyright. • They learn that images, text, video and games can be copyrighted. • They discuss 'Creative Commons'. • They use Creative Commons to insert images into their apps. • They test and evaluate their apps.	• Can give a simple definition of copyright. • Can explain that there are different Creative Commons classifications. • Can search for Creative Commons images.
Assess and review	• Assess and review the half term's work.	• Children invent a new app for a Year 4 child. • They sketch the app interface and describe the user experience for a Year 4 child. • They consider the needs of a Year 4 child in Africa.	• Assess and review.

Overview of progression

• Children progress their understanding and skills of creating digital content to achieve a specific purpose. They combine software packages and internet services to communicate with a wider audience.
• They make appropriate improvements to their apps, based on feedback.
• They make judgements about the digital content when repurposing it.
• They will develop their understanding of real-world uses of data and information, including copyright and the Data Protection Act and how these things can affect them.

Creative context

• The lessons link closely to the English curriculum, through retrieving, recording and presenting information from non-fiction, through the app information.
• There are also links to the English curriculum through identifying the audience and purpose of their writing.
• The lessons link to geography through learning about Africa, its landscape, people and problems.
• There are links to science when the children learn about the animals and plants of the African countries and how these are adapted to their environment.

Background knowledge

• The children will have used apps on mobile devices and will be aware of common features. They may not have noticed their own 'user experience' as they navigated an app or played a game.
• They will have used digital software tools before, but may not have encountered app creation tools.
• The children will be aware of online surveys and protecting personal information.

Curriculum objectives
● To select, use and combine a variety of software (including internet services) on a range of digital devices to design and create a range of programs, systems and content that accomplish given goals, including collecting, analysing, evaluating and presenting data and information.

Lesson objectives
● To access apps and identify their purposes and common features.
● To test apps and describe if the interface is easy to use for a Year 6 child.
● To think about user experience.
● To discuss to needs of mobile phone users in Africa compared with the UK.

Expected outcomes
● Can compare mobile phone apps and recognise common features.
● Can explain what the term 'user experience' means.
● Can decompose a larger problem into smaller parts.

Resources
Photocopiable page 145 'Common features of apps'; photocopiable page 146 'App interface'; photocopiable page 147 'My new app'

Mobile phone and tablet apps

The children to think about the design and purpose of mobile phone and tablet apps. They think of a design for a new app and consider whether it would need to be changed for a child in Africa.

Introduction
● Ask: *How many of you have a mobile phone? Can you access the World Wide Web on your phone? Do you have a tablet computer? What do you do on your phone or tablet?*

Whole-class work
● Remind the children about operating systems they have seen. Can you name an operating system? (For example, Windows, OSX, Linux)
● Explain that mobile phones have an operating system and that apps are additional pieces of software.
● Ask the children what their favourite apps are? Using sticky notes, write each app name on each note. Display the list of apps on the wall.

Paired work
● In pairs, the children think of a list of five apps they have seen or used. Using photocopiable page 145 'Common features of apps', the children identify the similarities between the apps. They also think about the purposes of the apps.

Whole-class work
● Ask three pairs to share their discussions about the apps. Which apps did they choose and what are the common features?
● The children have previously learned about computers sending and receiving data in binary. The app decodes the binary data to recreate the image, sound or video file.
● Ask the children to choose one of the apps they have looked at and think about what data it would need to send and receive. For example, if it was a football news app, it may send a request for the data of the results. It would then receive the data, which could be text, images and video.

Paired work
● Using photocopiable page 146 'App interface', the children sketch app scenes and label them, for example the home screen, the news screen, the introductory video screen.

Whole-class work
● Ask three pairs of children to feed back with a 'walkthrough' of the app and how the user would experience the different parts (the user experience).
● Now ask them to think about designing a new app for Year 6 children. What would it be and what would it do?
● Using photocopiable page 147 'My new app', the children sketch the home screen and give a basic description of their app idea.

> ### Differentiation
> ● Support: Less confident learners may need support to think of their app from another user's point of view and to design their new app.
> ● Challenge: More confident learners should be able to plan and design a new app, thinking about the user experience.

Review
● Ask children to share their app and briefly describe its purpose.
● Introducing the link to Africa, ask: *If you were designing your app for 11-year-old children in Africa, would it be different? Do the users in Africa have different needs to children in the UK? Would the design need to change and why?*
● The aim is for the children to think about the end-user and their needs.

Curriculum objectives
● To select, use and combine a variety of software (including internet services) on a range of digital devices to design and create a range of programs, systems and content that accomplish given goals, including collecting, analysing, evaluating and presenting data and information.

Lesson objectives
● To use the 'design thinking process' to plan and design a new app.

Expected outcomes
● Can combine tools using app creation software to create a simple app.
● Can explain why user testing and feedback is important.

Resources
Media resource 'Africa' on the CD-ROM; photocopiable page 148 'Empathise – the interview'; photocopiable page 149 'Define – what is the aim?'; photocopiable page 150 'Ideate – my app sketches'; photocopiable page 151 'New app design'

An app for charity

Children create a 'wireframe' sketch for a new app for a charity and research the background information for the screens. They consider the user experience for the people who will be using the app.

Introduction
● Display a large map of Africa and ask the children: *How many countries in Africa can you name?*
● The media resource 'Africa' on the CD-ROM shows some images of Africa to discuss with the children.

Whole-class work
● Explain to the children that they are learning about Africa and about making apps. Could they combine the two areas? Could they create an app to educate Year 6 children about Africa? What would be the purpose of the app? Would it be purely to learn facts about the countries or could it aim to educate people about Africa for a charity?
● Give the children time to think about the problem.

Paired work
● In pairs, the children follow a 'design thinking' process, taken from the Stanford school model (https://dschool.stanford.edu/dgift/). They will 'empathise, define, ideate, prototype and test' their app designs.
● To empathise, they will role play the parts of 'app designer' and 'customer'. The customer could be a person from a charity, a teacher, who would like to teach their children about Africa or a travel agent, who wants to entice people to visit the attractions in various parts of Africa.
● Using photocopiable page 148 'Empathise – the interview', the app designer interviews the customer to get the initial ideas.
● Then they swap roles and ask more questions.
● To define, they use photocopiable page 149 'Define – what is the aim?' Children will summarise what they think their partner is aiming to do.
● To ideate (to think of ideas), they will quickly sketch five ways the app could look, using a simple 'wireframe' template, using photocopiable 150 'Ideate – my app sketches'.
● They then show their sketches to their partner to check whether their ideas matched their partner's thoughts.
● To develop the prototypes, the children research online to gather information about Africa, for example countries, cultural stories, famines, wars, sport, tourism. They should break the research tasks into smaller parts.
● To begin the prototyping process, the children can iterate their designs, to generate a new app design using photocopiable page 151 'New app design'.

Differentiation
● Support: Less confident learners may need support to play the roles of app designer and customers, so they could choose one role to play. They may need help to break the larger problems into smaller parts and to create sketches for the initial designs.
● Challenge: More confident learners will be able to follow the design thinking process, placing themselves in the roles of the app designer and the customer. They should be able to create effective questions to ask and summarise the responses. Expect them to create at least five sketched wireframes to solve the problem.

Review
● Bring the class together and choose three pairs to summarise their ideas and the process they have followed. Do they feel that following the structured 'design thinking' approach helped to clarify the problem and to create more solutions?
● Explain that the children will be developing their prototypes and testing their apps, using software, in the following weeks.

Curriculum objectives
● To select, use and combine a variety of software (including internet services) on a range of digital devices to design and create a range of programs, systems and content that accomplish given goals, including collecting, analysing, evaluating and presenting data and information.

Lesson objectives
● To use app creation tools to design a home screen for an app.
● To feed back on each other's apps.
● To think about the user experience.

Expected outcomes
● Can improve an app design by responding to user feedback.
● Can annotate the app to explain the navigation and actions of the buttons.

Resources
Photocopiable page 'App feedback' from the CD-ROM; example app creation tools: Google app inventor (http://beta.appinventor.mit.edu/), App furnace (http://appfurnace.com/), Blippit (https://www.blippit.co.uk/), Appshed (http://appshed.com/) and Mozilla App maker (https://apps.webmaker.org/)

Prototypes

The children begin to prototype their apps using app creation tools. They gain experience with the tools by making a simple app, based on their own hobbies and interests. They then continue with their African app, finding information and creating the first few screens.

Introduction
● Begin by asking three children to recap their app ideas.
● Explain that they are going to continue developing their app. They can use paper prototypes or begin to use the software.
● This lesson will introduce them to potential app creation software.

Whole-class work
● Explain to the class that they can create their own apps by learning programming languages and using specific software (see resources).
● Before the lesson, register with the tool's website.
● Open the app creation tool and demonstrate how to edit the home screen. Change the title of the home screen, give a description and add navigation such as a button to the next page.

Independent work
● The children create their own app home page. To gain practice, they pick a topic of their hobby or favourite sport, for the app's focus.
● Allow time for them to create three pages (a home screen, page two and page three).
● They preview the apps online, through their web browsers.

Whole-class work
● Bring the class together and ask five children to demonstrate their apps. Can they describe the purpose of their app, the items they have added (buttons, text, images) and who they think the audience for their app might be.
● Once the children have demonstrated their apps, ask them to find a partner and ask for feedback. Remind them to be 'kind, specific and helpful'. They then modify their app, responding to the feedback using photocopiable page 'App feedback' from the CD-ROM.

Paired work
● Returning to the work in the previous lesson on Africa, ask the children to design their home screen for their app.
● Using the information they have gathered, they add further pages to the app.
● As they plan the navigation, they need to break the larger problems into smaller parts. They will need to think about the audience and whether the navigation is intuitive.
● As they organise the information on the page, they can use headings, bullets and hyperlinks.

Differentiation
● Support: Less confident learners may need support to access the app creation software and add simple navigation. They could use a writing frame to structure information.
● Challenge: More confident learners can use the app creation software to prototype an app. They can add information and consider how it is appropriate for the audience.

Review
● Bring the class together and ask the children to think about the user experience when they observed their partner testing the app. Could they understand how another person would use the app and find their way around? Did it help them to improve their design?

Curriculum objectives
● To select, use and combine a variety of software (including internet services) on a range of digital devices to design and create a range of programs, systems and content that accomplish given goals, including collecting, analysing, evaluating and presenting data and information.

Lesson objectives
● To know that there are accessible features within apps and why they are important.
● To identify users who may need accessibility features.
● To explain how the accessibility features enable the person to use the app.
● Discuss how the accessibility features could be similar or different for users in the UK and Africa.

Expected outcomes
● Can explain why accessibility is important for an app.
● Can identify users who may need accessibility features.

Resources
Photocopiable page 'Accessibility' from the CD-ROM

Who's using your app?

The children consider how their app may need to contain accessibility features. Accessibility features are built into computer operating systems, web browsers and mobile device operating systems. For a user who is visually impaired, the screen can be adjusted to have higher contrasting colours or a voiceover.

Introduction
● Begin the lesson by thinking about how different people have different tastes, for example, in clothes or music.
● Place four signs in each corner of the room ('Like', 'Dislike', 'Strongly like', 'Strongly dislike').
● Ask the children to stand in the middle of the room. Say the name of a pop group and then 'go'. They must move to the sign that they feel applies to themselves. From each corner, select one child to explain why they like, dislike, strongly like or strongly dislike that pop group.
● Repeat the game, asking the children to suggest the topic (football teams, TV programmes, films, hobbies, types of clothing, for example).
● Bring the class together and explain that they all have personal tastes so a designer needs to carefully consider their audience.
● Explain that people have different physical needs too. For example, wheelchair users need the school to be adapted to allow them to move around, making areas accessible.
● When using computers, mobile phones and tablets, there are accessibility features that can be applied. So, as a designer, making apps accessible is much more important than personal tastes – it can enable someone to be able to use the app.

Whole-class work
● Demonstrate the accessibility features for the class computer or, if a tablet such as an iPad is available, show the section in the settings with the accessibility features (Settings > General > Accessibility). It can be seen that the text size, contrast, colours can be changed, the user can zoom in, have a voice speaking the text, add subtitles and so on.

Paired work
● Using photocopiable page 'Accessibility' from the CD-ROM, the children experiment with the accessibility features on their computers.
● They record who would use the features and discuss how such features enable that person to use the computer or device.
● They incorporate accessibility features into their app on Africa.

Differentiation
● Support: Less confident learners may need support to apply the accessibility features and to understand who might need those features. They could focus on visually impaired people and how the features enable them to access the technology.
● Challenge: More confident learners will be able to apply accessibility features to their computer or device. They should be able to name a type of user who could benefit from the feature and why.

Review
● Bring the class together and ask three children which accessibility features might enhance their Africa app.
● Would the accessibility features in Africa be the same as those in the UK?

Curriculum objectives
● To select, use and combine a variety of software (including internet services) on a range of digital devices to design and create a range of programs, systems and content that accomplish given goals, including collecting, analysing, evaluating and presenting data and information.

Lesson objectives
● To know that apps can collect data.
● To identify how apps can collect data.

Expected outcomes
● Can identify how data may be collected within an app.

Resources
Photocopiable page 'For and against sharing my data' from the CD-ROM; interactive 'For and against sharing personal data' on the CD-ROM

Collecting data

This lesson focuses on collecting data using apps. It will look at collecting data through forms and about being clear how that data is used.

Introduction
● Remind the children of the online survey tools they have used, such as 'Socrative' (www.socrative.com/). Other tools can be used, such as Google Forms (part of Google Apps for Education www.google.com/google-d-s/createforms.html) or Survey Monkey (https://www.surveymonkey.com/).

Whole-class work
● Before the lesson, create a Socrative account and log in as a teacher (www.socrative.com/). Select 'Manage quizzes', then 'Import quiz' and enter the code 'SOC-3827651'. The quiz is now in the your list of quizzes.
● Select the quiz and ask the children to use the 'Student login' and the teacher's room number.
● Run the quiz with the children and when complete, ensure that the report is emailed or downloaded.
● Open the report.
● Display the results of the data and then choose some of the answers to display on signs, such as 'My name is...', 'My favourite pop group is...', 'My favourite interest is...'. Ask children if they are happy about the information being displayed.
● Explain to the children that they need to carefully consider how they share their data and with whom.

Paired work
● Pairs look at the app software to see whether it is possible to collect data in a form. For example, Appshed has form buttons and input boxes. The children can design their forms on the app screens. (At this stage, this is only adding the form components and not adding the programming behind them to collect the data. Following the tutorials on the app tools' websites will allow the children to learn how to add this feature. This will require additional time in the lesson.)

Whole-class work
● Bring the class together and explain that mobile devices and apps can collect data in less obvious ways, for example internet searches and map location data.
● Discuss the advantages and disadvantages of collecting data from a mobile device, using interactive activity 'For and against sharing personal data' on the CD-ROM and recording the argument using photocopiable page 'For and against sharing my data' from the CD-ROM.

Differentiation
● Support: Less confident learners may need support to find reasons for and against mobile devices sharing data. They could think of a scenario where a person loses their phone and a scenario where a person's password is hacked, so their phone is not secure.
● Challenge: More confident learners will be able to consider the advantages and disadvantages of apps collecting data. They present arguments for and against the issue for a partner in the class and record their decisions.

Review
● Bring the class together and ask four pairs to feed back on their discussion.
● To conclude the lesson, introduce the 'Data Protection Act' and share a simple definition (http://simple.wikipedia.org/wiki/Data_Protection_Act).

Curriculum objectives
● To select, use and combine a variety of software (including internet services) on a range of digital devices to design and create a range of programs, systems and content that accomplish given goals, including collecting, analysing, evaluating and presenting data and information.

Lesson objectives
● To be able to give a simple definition of copyright.
● To know that image, text, video, games can be copyrighted.
● To be able to give a simple definition of Creative Commons.
● To be able to search for and locate appropriate Creative Commons images, for a specific purpose.

Expected outcomes
● Can give a simple definition of copyright.
● Can explain that there are different Creative Commons classifications.
● Can search for Creative Commons images.

Resources
Photocopiable page 'Similar games' from the CD-ROM; photocopiable page 'Creative Commons' from the CD-ROM; photocopiable page 'Evaluating the apps' from the CD-ROM

Thinking about copyright

The word 'copyright' may be known by the children, but do they know what it means? They will look at a simple definition of copyright. They will move on to searching for Creative Commons images, to use within their app.

Introduction
● Explain that apps can be similar in looks and function. Explain that many apps can be adapted from others.

Paired work
● Open the Google Play app store and ask the children for a game they like to play, for example, 'Temple Run' (https://play.google.com/store).
● There will be many variations of the game, where a developer has taken the essential parts of the game and adapted it, to create a new game. Using photocopiable page 'Similar games' from the CD-ROM, the children research types of games and record the name and details of the games.

Whole-class work
● Ask: *Is it fair to completely copy another developer's app? What if the game was the same, but just the name was changed? What if the main character was changed, for example, in the 'Temple Run' example, the games are very similar and even the game icon may look like the original one?*
● Ask the children whether they have heard the word 'copyright'. Can they give a simple definition of copyright? Allow them time to research online, before bringing the class back together.
● Explain that copyright protects books, films, music, artwork. As soon as something is written down, made or recorded it is owned by the author(s). They can place the copyright symbol © on it, with the date and their name. Then, people need to seek permission if they want to use the work.
● Now, ask whether the children have heard the term 'Creative Commons' before. Ask: *What does Creative Commons mean?*

Paired work
● The children research the term 'Creative Commons' and write a definition on photocopiable 'Creative Commons' from the CD-ROM, where they also record information about their image search.
● Ask them to locate an image that they think they could use in their Africa app. Why do they think they would be allowed to use it?

Whole-class work
● Using a search engine, search for 'Table Mountain'. Select images.
● Select 'Advanced search' and scroll down the 'Usage' section. Select 'Free to use and share' and then the 'Advanced search' button.
● The results will be the 'non-commercial use' images, where a person can use the images, but not to sell or make money from them.
● The children will see that there are also images that can be modified; for example, they could cut or crop an image and use it in their app.

Paired work
● The children look at the images they have used in their Africa app and check the content to ensure that they have the appropriate permission to use them.
● They test their apps before sharing them with their partners.
● Using photocopiable 'Evaluating the apps' from the CD-ROM, the children evaluate each other's apps.

Review
● Ask children to demonstrate their apps. They should describe the feedback they received in the evaluation and explain how they acted upon it.
● Ask: *Why do you think copyright or Creative Commons is needed?*

Lesson objectives
● To invent a new app and sketch the design on paper.
● To locate Creative Commons images for the app.
● To the test app and describe if the interface is easy to use for a Year 4 child.
● To discuss the needs of mobile phone users in Africa compared with the UK.

Expected outcomes
● Can compare mobile phone apps and recognise common features.
● Can search for Creative Commons images.
● Can explain what 'user experience' means.

Resources
Photocopiable page 'My Year 4 app design' from the CD-ROM; photocopiable page 'My Year 4 app wireframe' from the CD-ROM; photocopiable page 'My Year 4 app evaluation' from the CD-ROM

Africa: Assess and review

This lesson focuses on rapidly prototyping an app for Year 4 children. The children will create a paper prototype of the app, before using app creation tools to make a product. Using online searches, they will select images for the app. They review and evaluate the process and give feedback to their peers.

Introduction
● Remind the children that they have looked at apps that contain images, text, music and videos.
● To review the learning from the lessons, the children will invent a new app for a Year 4 child.
● Ideally, they will interview a Year 4 child to find out the kind of apps that they would use. For example, it might be a times tables app or facts about Greek myths. The children consider the content, appropriate reading level text and appropriate images for nine-year-old children.

Independent work
● Allow the children time to explore the app stores and look at the features of the apps. Let them compare the features, in order to inform their designs.
● Using photocopiable page 'My Year 4 app design' from the CD-ROM, the children sketch the app design.

Paired work
● Children swap designs and describe the purpose and features of their app. The partner gives feedback, which includes one idea for improvement.

Independent work
● Children use photocopiable page 'My Year 4 app wireframe' from the CD-ROM to draw the user interface for the app and record the feedback.
● Using an app creation tool, they now construct the home screen.
● Searching for images for the app, they should identify Creative Commons images, which they have permission to use.

Paired work
● Using photocopiable page 'My Year 4 app evaluation' from the CD-ROM, the children evaluate their partner's apps. They consider the user interface, the text and images used.
● The children act on the feedback and improve their designs.

Differentiation
● Support: Less confident learners may need support to invent a new app for the Year 4 children. They could use a 'name the flag' app, to help learn about the flags of different countries or a simple fact-based app, containing images of a favourite subject.
● Challenge: More confident learners will be able to plan, design and prototype their apps. They should be able to give kind, specific and helpful feedback to a partner. They can then act upon feedback, to improve their designs.

Review
● Bring the class together and ask five children to display their apps.
● If possible, the children could share their apps with the Year 4 children (for example, invite the Year 4 children into the lesson and the Year 6 children try to 'sell' their idea to them).
● Remind the children that they have been designing for a purpose and considering user experience.
● Ask: *Can you explain what 'user experience' means? Would Year 4 African children have different needs to Year 4 children in the UK?*

Common features of apps

■ Draw three app screens you know on this mobile home app page.

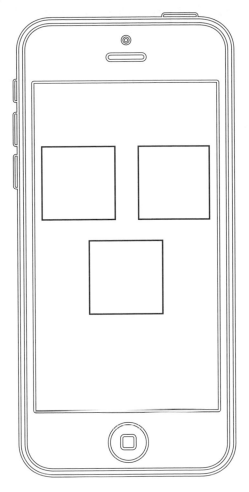

■ What features do these apps have in common?

_____

_____

■ What do these apps do?

1. _____

2. _____

3. _____

I can recognise the common features of apps.

How did you do?

App interface

- Choose one app and look at the different screens.
- Sketch the screens or items that pop up on a screen below. Then label them, for example 'The home screen'.

I can identify the different screens in an app.

How did you do?

My new app

- Design a new app for a Year 6 child.

What would it look like?

_____

_____

What would it do?

_____

_____

Why is it needed?

_____

_____

- Sketch the home screen below and label the features.

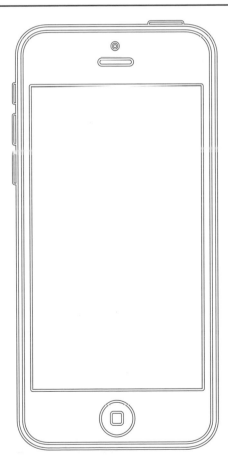

I can sketch a home screen for my new app.

How did you do?

Empathise – the interview

■ Interview your partner. What are his/her needs for an app?

4 mins

_____

_____

_____

_____

■ Interview your partner again, digging a little deeper into their thoughts.

3 mins

_____

_____

_____

_____

I can listen to a person and try to empathise with their ideas.

How did you do?

■ SCHOLASTIC
www.scholastic.co.uk

Define – what is the aim?

■ From your interview, what can you infer about your partner's feelings and motivations?

_____ needs a way to _____
(partner's name)

_____

_____

_____

Because _____

_____

_____

_____

_____

I can listen to a person and summarise my findings.

How did you do?

Name: _____ Date: _____

Ideate – my app sketches

■ Sketch at least four ways to meet your user's needs.

5 mins

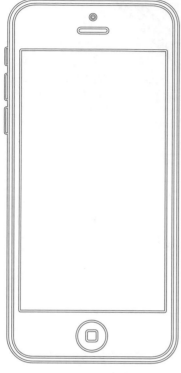  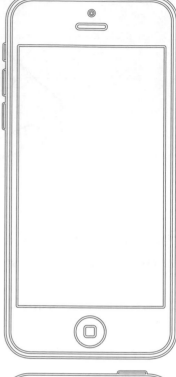

I can rapidly sketch my ideas for an app.

How did you do?

PHOTOCOPIABLE

New app design

- Show the sketches of your ideas for a new app to your partner.
- Summarise their feedback.

_____

_____

_____

_____

- Sketch the home screen of your new app.

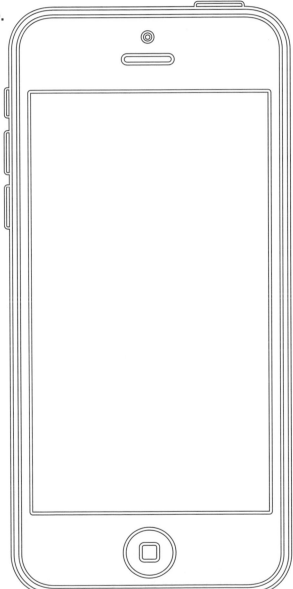

I can act upon feedback and create a new app design.

How did you do?

Evacuees

Using themes of evacuation, propaganda and war poetry based on the story *Carrie's War* by Nina Bawden, the children learn how to effectively use search engines and understand how search results are selected. They know that search engines use 'web crawler programs' and consider the algorithms that rank the results of a search. They demonstrate responsible use of technologies and know a range of ways to report concerns.

Expected prior learning
- The children will have practically used search techniques to locate information.
- They should be clear explaining why they consider information to be reliable or potentially biased.
- They should have an understanding of how search results are ranked and filtered to narrow a search.
- They can repurpose images and information to create posters.

Chapter at a glance

Subject area
• Communication

National Curriculum objective
• To use search technologies effectively, appreciate how results are selected and ranked, and be discerning in evaluating digital content. • To use technology safely, respectfully and responsibly; recognise acceptable/unacceptable behaviour; identify a range of ways to report concerns about content and contact.

Week	Lesson objectives	Summary of activities	Expected outcomes
1	• To locate appropriate images using a search engine and 'Safe Search' filter. • To perform an advanced search to narrow the selection of images found. • To explain whom to contact if they have concerns about the content found during a search.	• Children are introduced to the theme of evacuees in the Second World War. • They read *Carrie's War* by Nina Bawden. • They use 'Safe Search' to filter images of evacuees. • They create a wartime poster for a railway station.	• Can show how to perform a search using the 'Safe Search' filter. • Can explain, if they have concerns about content found during a search, whom they should contact.
2	• To explain how web pages are delivered. • To name different web browsers. • To form analogies of sending and receiving information for web browsers, with war time codes.	• Children continue to read *Carrie's War*. • They discuss how web pages are delivered to a computer. • They think about how information online is sent in packets and form analogies with sending codes in wartime.	• Can explain what happens when a user requests a web page in a browser. • Can name different web browsers.
3	• To know that search results are delivered in different orders, based on rankings. • To describe that algorithms control the ranking of search results. • To use code breaking algorithms to decipher codes.	• Children investigate the Blitz and its effect on their local area. • They describe an algorithm to control the ranking of search results. • They use code breaking algorithms to decipher codes.	• Can evaluate how search results are ranked. • Can decipher codes using an algorithm.
4	• To be discerning in evaluating digital content, by looking at the web address extension (for example .com, .ac.uk) and identifying the organisations they represent. • To use analogies to consider misinformation during wartime, with misinformation from websites.	• Children carry out research to find out why there were evacuees. • They evaluate the content of websites. • They consider how misinformation could occur on websites and make analogies with the war and misinformation.	• Can name common web address extensions (for example .com, .co.uk, .ac.uk) and explain the types of organisations they represent. • Can evaluate web pages for reliability.

Week	Lesson objectives	Summary of activities	Expected outcomes
5	• To evaluate websites for bias using given criteria. • To evaluate websites for bias using Web 2.0 tools. • To tag websites for bookmarking information. • To know that adverts appear on web pages. • To define a cookie. • To know that cookies are used on web pages to direct information to the user.	• Children find out about propaganda during wartime and bias. • They use a word cloud to identify bias. • They bookmark websites. • They are made aware of advertising in the form of pop-ups. • They define a cookie.	• Can evaluate websites for bias using Web 2.0 tools. • Can tag websites for bookmarking. • Can identify advertising links on search websites and how cookies can be used.
6	• To describe and name a URL shortener. • To know that URL shorteners can reduce errors when entering addresses. • To know how to report unacceptable behaviour and how to recognise it.	• Children read a wartime poem, 'Naming of Parts' by Henry Reed. • They use URL shorteners. • They prepare a short sketch and video it. • They revise what to do if they come across unacceptable behaviour online.	• Can explain how to use a URL shortener and why they can reduce errors when entering addresses. • Can recognise unacceptable behaviour and how to report it.
Assess and review	• Assess and review the half term's work.	• Children use 'Safe Search' to research information on wartime propaganda. • They produce an information poster to warn people about keeping information safe. • They are reminded of whom to contact if they have concerns about content online.	• Assess and review.

Overview of progression

● The children make judgements about digital content when evaluating and repurposing it for a given audience. They create propaganda posters, recognising the audience when designing and creating digital content.

● They understand the potential of information technology for collaboration when computers are networked. They develop their understanding of web searches, how 'web-crawler' programs gather information and how the results are ranked.

● The children use criteria to evaluate the quality of solutions and can identify improvements.

Creative context

● The lessons link closely to the English curriculum, through asking questions to improve their understanding of what they have read, drawing inferences and justifying these with evidence.

● They retrieve, record and present information from non-fiction and can use research skills to investigate information, providing reasoned justifications for their views.

● Linking with English, the children prepare poems to read aloud and to perform, showing understanding through intonation, tone and volume so that the meaning is clear to an audience.

● There are many links with the history curriculum, through studying the Second World War and focusing on the evacuees and propaganda from Germany and Britain.

● Linking to geography through the story, through the description of the Welsh landscape, the setting for *Carrie's War*.

Background knowledge

● The children will have previously learned about computer networks and web searches. They have used Boolean terms and the 'Advanced search' tools, to search the World Wide Web to retrieve information.

● They will have repurposed images for different audiences.

● They will have visited websites using URL or web addresses and understood the need for accuracy.

Curriculum objectives
● To use search technologies effectively, appreciate how results are selected and ranked, and be discerning in evaluating digital content.
● To use technology safely, respectfully and responsibly; recognise acceptable/ unacceptable behaviour; identify a range of ways to report concerns about content and contact.

Lesson objectives
● To locate appropriate images using a search engine and 'Safe Search' filter.
● To perform an advanced search to narrow the selection of images found.
● To explain whom to contact if they have concerns about the content found during a search.

Expected outcomes
● Can show how to perform a search using the 'Safe Search' filter.
● Can explain, if they have concerns about content found during a search, whom they should contact.

Resources
Interactive activity 'How relevant?' on the CD-ROM; *Carrie's War* by Nina Bawden

The evacuees

To begin the topic, the children find out about the Second World War and evacuees. They search for images and are reminded of the 'Safe Search' filter and how to narrow their searches. They produce an information poster for evacuees, displaying the images they have found.

Introduction
● Begin the lesson by showing a film clip of evacuees in the Second World War. There are clips of this type available on YouTube (check suitability).
● Read the opening of *Carrie's War* by Nina Bawden and discuss the two openings and the two times that the story is set in.
● Ask the children to describe how technology has changed from the 1940s to 1970s to the modern day.

Whole-class work
● Explain to the children that they are going to search for images of the evacuees using the 'Safe Search' filter.
● Explain that behind the filter is an algorithm, which checks each image and decides whether it is suitable, based on criteria.
● Remind the children that the images have been viewed by a 'web-crawler' program, which searches the World Wide Web and indexes the content.
● Using interactive activity 'How relevant?' on the CD-ROM, display the images. Ask the children to rank them, with the image they think is most relevant to the topic of evacuees at the top, and the one that is least relevant at the bottom.
● Can they give an example of the criteria ranking the images? For example, a picture of children with suitcases and gas masks on it ranks above a picture of children at a station because it is more directly related to the subject.

Paired work
● In pairs, the children use the interactive activity to decide on their own ranking and create the criteria.
● The children search for at least nine images and rank them using the 'diamond nine' structure using a single slide from presentation software.

Whole-class work
● Bring the class together and ask three children to share their examples of the criteria they used to sort the images.
● Explain to the children that they will create an evacuation information poster to be placed in a train station during the Second World War.
● To begin the activity, they will need examples of evacuation posters. Can the children suggest search words that could be used to find these posters?

Paired work
● The children perform an advanced search to locate images of evacuation posters and images that they may use to construct their own posters.
● The posters will need to explain what the evacuee children need to bring with them, how to behave and what will happen on the route.

Differentiation
● Support: Less confident learners may need support to copy the style of posters.
● Challenge: More confident learners will be able to search and locate appropriate images for their evacuation posters. They should look at examples and recreate the style of writing and layout of the posters.

Review
● Display five children's posters. Can the children identify the similarities between the new and old posters?
● How could they adapt the posters to be safety posters, which remind children about going on a journey on the World Wide Web?

Curriculum objectives
● To use search technologies effectively, appreciate how results are selected and ranked, and be discerning in evaluating digital content.
● To use technology safely, respectfully and responsibly; recognise acceptable/ unacceptable behaviour; identify a range of ways to report concerns about content and contact.

Lesson objectives
● To explain how web pages are delivered.
● To name different web browsers.
● To form analogies of sending and receiving information for web browsers, with war time codes.

Expected outcomes
● Can explain what happens when a user requests a web page in a browser.
● Can name different web browsers.

Resources
Photocopiable page 161 'Wartime messages'; photocopiable page 162 'Carrie's code'; photocopiable page 163 'Codebreaking at Bletchley Park'; interactive activity 'Sending and receiving messages' on the CD-ROM; *Carrie's War* by Nina Bawden

Codebreaking

The children think about sending and receiving messages and form an analogy with computers sending and receiving data. They create coded messages and research into codebreaking during the Second World War.

Introduction
● Introduce the lesson by recapping on the story so far in *Carrie's War* (in Chapter 1). Ask the children to summarise what has happened in the form of a short message in the style of a Twitter tweet in 140 characters.
● Ask how else they could send a message? For example, they could email it or use a mobile phone to send a text message.

Paired work
● Pairs research online to find out how messages were sent during the Second World War. For example, were pigeons really used? Were radios used and could the messages be intercepted?
● Using photocopiable page 161 'Wartime messages', they record their research in the form of three cartoons.

Whole-class work
● Bring the class together and ask for three examples of how messages were sent during the Second World War.
● Ask the class about how the web pages are delivered to a computer. They have previously learned about data being sent as ones and zeros in small packets, via a network. When the data arrives at the computer, it can be reconstructed, using a protocol, in the web browser.
● Make the analogy with the children about sending and receiving messages being similar to the computers sending and receiving data. The data is split into short messages or packets, sent and then decoded by the receiving computer, using the protocol.
● Demonstrate sending messages and sending data, using interactive activity 'Sending and receiving messages'.
● Together they create a coded message, by using *Carrie's War* and referencing words in the story. For example, they find a word they want to use in the book, which could be, for example, on page 21, 3 lines down and 4 words across. So, instead of writing the word, they write '21.3.4'.

Paired work
● In pairs, the children write a message, encode it using the book, then swap with a partner and decode it (using photocopiable page 162 'Carrie's code').

Whole-class work
● Ask the children to define a code.
● Display the Google Cultural Institute website (www.google.com/ culturalinstitute/collection/bletchley-park) and display images about Bletchley Park and the people involved.

Paired work
● Ask the children to research codebreaking at Bletchley Park, using photocopiable page 163 'Codebreaking at Bletchley Park'.
● Ask them to find out about Alan Turing and his part in codebreaking and his contribution to computing (www.bbc.co.uk/history/people/alan_turing).
● Ask them to create resources for a display about wartime codebreaking.

Review
● Bring the class together and share the resources the children have produced.
● Display the website 'Tweetping' (http://tweetping.net/), which shows Twitter messages being sent around the world, in real time. Can they see how many are being sent, all as ones and zeros in packets of data?

Curriculum objectives
● To use search technologies effectively, appreciate how results are selected and ranked, and be discerning in evaluating digital content.
● To use technology safely, respectfully and responsibly; recognise acceptable/ unacceptable behaviour; identify a range of ways to report concerns about content and contact.

Lesson objectives
● To know that search results are delivered in different orders, based on rankings.
● To describe that algorithms control the ranking of search results.
● To use codebreaking algorithms to decipher codes.

Expected outcomes
● Can evaluate how search results are ranked.
● Can decipher codes using an algorithm.

Resources
Photocopiable page 164 'Substitution cipher'; photocopiable page 165 'The Blitz near us'; interactive activity 'Caesar cipher' on the CD-ROM; *Carrie's War* by Nina Bawden

The Blitz

Focusing on web searches, the children research the Blitz. They see how the results are ranked and read about how the algorithms order them. They look at substitution codes and deciphering simple messages.

Introduction
● Continue to read *Carrie's War* and ask the children to identify the words that describe the wartime scenes.
● Using photocopiable page 164 'Substitution cipher', children write a message and change the letters for the code letters in the key. They swap sheets and decode their partner's message.
● They then create their own cipher, by changing the letters of the code.

Whole-class work
● Searching online, the children investigate the Blitz.
● Collect together ten search words. Display them for the class.
● Using Safe Search type 'Blitz war' into the search box.
● The children should know from previous years that search results are delivered in a particular order, based on a ranking.
● Remind them that the Google search engine sorts the results of a search on the basis of algorithms.
● Display the infographic on Google searches (http://static.googleusercontent. com/media/www.google.com/en//insidesearch/howsearchworks/assets/ searchInfographic.pdf).

Paired work
● In pairs, the children scroll through the Google search story (www.google. co.uk/insidesearch/howsearchworks/thestory/).
● They can watch the YouTube video on 'How Google improves its search algorithm' (https://www.youtube.com/watch?v=J5RZOU6vK4Q).
● In pairs they write a definition of an algorithm to control the page ranking of search results.

Whole-class work
● Ask children to for their definition of an algorithm to rank search results.
● Return to the search for 'Blitz war', follow the first result and allow the children to see the home page. Now show the second result's home page. Do they think the results are relevant to their search?
● Using photocopiable page 165 'The Blitz near us', they research the period of the Blitz related to their local area. Ask: *Were our local cities heavily bombed? Which search words will you use?*
● Bring the class together and collect ten facts from the children.
● Display the facts on the screen. Ask: *Can you rank the facts, in order of most important to least important? What criteria are you using?*

Differentiation
● Support: Less confident learners may need support to locate three facts about the Blitz.
● Challenge: More confident learners will be able to search and locate, at least, ten facts about their local area and the Blitz, explaining the reasons for their ranking.

Review
● Display the coded message 'jt ju uif foe pg uif mfttpo' and tell the children that it says 'is it the end of the lesson'. Can they crack the code?
● Write the two pieces of text, one above the other. Can they spot a pattern? (the coded words are one letter after the original text, i.e. i = j, t = u).
● Tell them this substitution code is known as a 'Caesar cipher').
● Using interactive activity 'Caesar cipher' on the CD-ROM, allow the children to see how the message changes, as the key changes.

■SCHOLASTIC

Curriculum objectives
● To use search technologies effectively, appreciate how results are selected and ranked, and be discerning in evaluating digital content.
● To use technology safely, respectfully and responsibly; recognise acceptable/unacceptable behaviour; identify a range of ways to report concerns about content and contact.

Lesson objectives
● To be discerning in evaluating digital content, by looking at the web address extension (for example .com, .ac.uk) and identifying the organisations they represent.
● To use analogies to consider misinformation during wartime, with misinformation from websites.

Expected outcomes
● Can name common web address extensions (for example .com, .co.uk, .ac. uk) and explain the types of organisations they represent.
● Can evaluate web pages for reliability.

Resources
Photocopiable page 166 'Evacuees'; *Carrie's War* by Nina Bawden

Misinformation

The children consider the reliability of websites, as they search for information on the evacuees. They consider 'misinformation' during the war, where untrue information was used to convince the enemy of a false situation. This is linked to looking at websites and deciding if the information is true.

Introduction
● Ask: *Why were children evacuated during the war?*
● Allow the children time to discuss then record their notes and the web addresses they locate, using photocopiable page 166 'Evacuees'.

Whole-class work
● Recapping on last week's work; did the children find that the results were ranked appropriately? Were the websites reported in the search results relevant to the search words? Did they narrow their search using Boolean operators ('+' or '−') or the advanced search features?
● They have also previously learned about evaluating website content, by identifying the organisations behind the sites. Ask the children to look at the list of websites and the web address extensions, such as, '.com' or '.co.uk'.
● Ask them to put the websites in order of reliability. Why have they decided on that order?

Paired work
● A presentation tool called 'Prezi' (http://prezi.com/) enables the children to add images and text to share with the class. It uses a zooming and panning style to move from one item to another.
● Children construct a short presentation on the evacuees using Prezi.

Whole-class work
● Bring the class together and ask one pair to present their Prezi, including brief descriptions of the slide content.
● Explain that, during the war, false information was sent out to trick the enemy. This 'misinformation' could be used to pretend that the army was going to attack at a certain time and place, when actually, they were planning to do it differently.
● Ask the children to consider how misinformation could occur in websites. For example, during the war, a country could say it had plenty of food, whereas actually they may have little. A website could claim that they had lots of items in stock to make people think they were a very successful company.

Paired work
● In pairs, the children add an extra slide. They can choose where to place it in the presentation, though it must look authentic.
● Once complete, they swap presentations to spot the fake information.

Differentiation
● Support: Less confident learners may need support to choose appropriate search words and help read the content to decide whether it sounds true.
● Challenge: More confident learners will be able to research information about evacuees and explain whether the source is reliable, by discussing whether the address extension and content look authoritative.

Review
● Bring the class together and choose three presentations to display. Can the children identify the false information? Why is it important to question material on the web?
● Read to the end of *Carrie's War* and discuss the plot. Was what Carrie did so very bad? Did she cause the fire? Was she basing her understanding of what happened on false information?

Keep calm and carry on

Looking at propaganda and bias, the children research into wartime posters. Using word cloud generators, they look at text to identify bias. Finally, they use bookmarks to remember useful websites and discuss cookies.

Introduction
● Ask the children: *Do you know the meaning of the word 'propaganda'?* Display a propaganda poster from the Second World War.
● The poster is biased to convince the reader of a particular point of view, whether it is to show how strong the enemy is or to doubt the truth about their own side.

Independent work
● One British poster used to strengthen belief in the war effort, was the 'Keep Calm and Carry On' poster. They followed a simple format of an instructional phrase and have been copied recently to apply to different situations.
● Allow the children to create a new 'Keep Calm' poster using an online creator (www.keepcalm-o-matic.co.uk/).
● Using photocopiable page 167 'Propaganda poster', they sketch a design for a new style of poster. This could then be produced using digital software.

Whole-class work
● Thinking about propaganda during the war and how it was biased, the children analyse websites for bias, using a word cloud for example, Wordle (www.wordle.net/) or Tagxedo (www.tagxedo.com/).
● Copy and paste the text from a website, such as a BBC News report. The words appearing most often appear larger in the word cloud.

Paired work
● Children look at the text from a German booklet describing the life of Hitler (www.calvin.edu/academic/cas/gpa/pimpfhitler.htm). They paste the text into the word cloud generator and look at the type of words used.

Whole-class work
● Explain that the children have been using many websites and that it takes time to find important information. Ask: *How could you find the website again?*
● Bookmarking websites means that useful websites can be found easily.
● Demonstrate how to add a bookmark. It can be added to a list of current bookmarks or a new folder. They must carefully consider the 'tags' or categories that they place the bookmarks into.

Paired work
● The children locate websites that focus on wartime propaganda and add bookmarks to a 'Wartime propaganda' folder.
● Ask children to notice if adverts to other services appear beside the articles.

Review
● Bring the children's attention to adverts that appear on web pages. Ask the children whether they know how the advert knows what to display?
● Explain that the websites contain cookies, which are small pieces of data, sent from a website and held in the web browser. Every time a user visits the website, data is sent to the website's server. They can be used to inform the website owner of a user purchasing an item and placing it in the shopping cart. However, it can also be used for marketing, knowing which items they have searched for previously.
● When the children are visiting websites, they will often see a small pop-up bar, saying that the site uses cookies and has an accept button.
● Let the children discuss cookies and form a definition. Make sure that they understand that cookies are used on websites, to direct information to a user.

Curriculum objectives
● To use search technologies effectively, appreciate how results are selected and ranked, and be discerning in evaluating digital content.
● To use technology safely, respectfully and responsibly; recognise acceptable/ unacceptable behaviour; identify a range of ways to report concerns about content and contact.

Lesson objectives
● To describe and name a URL shortener.
● To know that URL shorteners can reduce errors when entering addresses.
● To know how to report unacceptable behaviour and how to recognise it.

Expected outcomes
● Can explain how to use a URL shortener and why they can reduce errors when entering addresses.
● Can recognise unacceptable behaviour and how to report it.

Resources
Photocopiable page 'Naming of Parts' from the CD-ROM

URL shorteners

Reading a poem from the Second World War, the children think about using the correct terms for objects and web tools. They use URL shorteners to make it easier to share website addresses. They prepare a video performance of the poem and upload it to a website.

Introduction
● Introduce the lesson by reading the Second World War poem 'The Naming of Parts' by Henry Reed.
● The poem describes a sergeant telling new soldiers about their rifle.
● Let the children read the poem aloud to each other and use online searches to find definitions of any words with which they are unfamiliar.

Independent work
● Using photocopiable page 'Naming of Parts' from the CD-ROM, the children choose an item that they know well to describe the parts.

Whole-class work
● Explain that when typing in a web address, a simple one, for example, the BBC (www.bbc.co.uk/) should be easy to type correctly. However, a YouTube clip may have a seemingly random set of letter, numbers and symbols.
● To help minimise errors, a URL shortener can be used. For example, Bitly (https://bitly.com/) will take a long web address and shorten it to a new one beginning with 'bit.ly' (for example, http://bit.ly/1jybjdD).

Paired work
● The children search for an example of the 'Naming of Parts' online and then use a URL shortener to direct people to the poem's web address. They can then give the new, shortened address to their partner, who can type it in and see whether they arrive at the correct web address.
● In pairs, the children can rehearse a dramatised reading of the poem, one playing the part of the sergeant and the other the soldier. When they are ready, they could record a video of their performance. Alternatively, they could record an audio track version.
● The video could be uploaded to a video sharing website, such as Vimeo or YouTube (ensuring that the settings are kept private). They could also upload to a Google Drive or One Drive account. The main aim is to place it on a cloud or network server, in order to share the address with the class.
● Once uploaded, they can take the web address or URL and paste it into a URL shortener, to share with the class.

Review
● Bring the class together and display examples of the videos of the performances of the poem. The children can share their shortened URL addresses to enable the videos to be seen.
● Ask them to describe the purpose of a URL shortener. Why do they think it could be useful?
● Do they know any other ways of sharing links? For example, QR codes (quick reference codes or 2D bar codes) allow a photograph of the QR code to be scanned and then link to a URL.
● Demonstrate pasting a URL into a QR code generator (www.qrstuff.com/). If a phone or tablet is available, which has a QR code reader app, point it at the QR code that has been generated and see whether it takes the user to the correct website.
● Remind the children that if they encounter videos online that make them feel uncomfortable, they should tell someone they trust and report unacceptable behaviour.

Curriculum objectives
● To use search technologies effectively, appreciate how results are selected and ranked, and be discerning in evaluating digital content.
● To use technology safely, respectfully and responsibly; recognise acceptable/ unacceptable behaviour; identify a range of ways to report concerns about content and contact.

Lesson objectives
● To locate appropriate images using a search engine and 'Safe Search' filter.
● To perform an advanced search to narrow the selection of images found.
● To explain whom to contact if they have concerns about the content found during a search.

Expected outcomes
● Can show how to perform a search using the 'Safe Search' filter.
● Can explain if they have concerns about content found during a search, whom they should contact.

Resources
Photocopiable page 'My Propaganda' from the CD-ROM; photocopiable page 'Poster evaluation' from the CD-ROM; photocopiable page 'Code wheel' from the CD-ROM; photocopiable page 'Code wheel instructions' from the CD-ROM

Evacuees: Assess and review

In this lesson children consider the safe search and advanced search features. They remember that if they find content they find upsetting, they know whom to contact.

Introduction

● Ask: *Which is the best TV programme?* Choose two children with opposing views, to explain why they think their favourite is better than the other child's.
● Ask: *Are you showing signs of bias? What sort of words are you using?*
● In pairs, the children choose a topic where they have different opinions. They each sketch a poster, promoting their view, using photocopiable page 'My propaganda' from the CD-ROM.
● Bring the class together and select four pairs of children to present their sketch and reasons for supporting or opposing their topic.
● Ask: *What does propaganda mean?*
● Display example posters from the Second World War, about keeping information safe. For example, National Archives (www.nationalarchives.gov. uk/documents/education/propaganda.pdf).
● Explain that the children will be creating their own posters about keeping their own information safe.

Independent work

● Using the 'Safe Search' filter, the children research images of wartime propaganda, in order to recognise the style of the posters.
● They then create an information poster to warn people to be careful with their own personal information. They perform an advanced search to locate appropriate images.
● Ask: *Can you identify which search words you will use? How can you narrow a search? What happens if you find images that upset you?*
● The poster should include who to contact if they have concerns about the content found during a search.

Whole-class work

● Bring the class together and ask five children to share their poster.
● They evaluate the poster using the evaluation list on photocopiable page 'Poster evaluation' from the CD-ROM.
● Remind the children to explain who to contact if they have concerns about the content found online.

Paired work

● To remind the children about sending data and codes, they can make a code wheel, to create a substitution code.
● Using photocopiable pages 'Code wheel' and 'Code wheel instructions' from the CD-ROM, they encode messages.

Differentiation
● Support: Less confident learners may need support to choose appropriate search words for their image search. They may need help to create a message for their poster.
● Challenge: More confident learners will be able to research images of wartime propaganda-style posters. They can then create a new poster with a clear message about keeping personal data safe.

Review

● Bring the class together and recap on the learning from the previous lessons.
● Ask: *What happens when a computer requests a website? How does the data travel from one computer to another? How can an image search be narrowed? Why should you use a 'Safe Search'?*

Wartime messages

■ Draw three cartoons below to show three ways messages were sent during the Second World War.

I can draw cartoons to explain how messages were sent during the Second World War.

How did you do?

Carrie's code

■ Use the story of *Carrie's War* to write a coded message. For example, find a word that you want to use, then note its page, line and position in the book.

■ Use the edition of the book on the Scholastic Shop website.

■ On the website, you can preview some pages from the book. From the *Carrie's War* page, select the book to look inside (http://shop.scholastic.co.uk/products/999).

■ Turn to page 21 and read the text. The code will start with the page number, the line number and then count the number of words across from the left.

For example 'bad trouble go home' would be:

Bad	trouble	Go	home
21.10.2	21.11.2	21.26.1	21.9.9

because the word 'bad' can be found on page 21, line 10, second word across.

■ Write your own message and change it into code.
■ Swap with a partner and decode their secret message.

I can create a secret coded message, using words from a book.

How did you do?

PHOTOCOPIABLE   ■SCHOLASTIC www.scholastic.co.uk

Name: _____ Date: _____

Codebreaking at Bletchley Park

1. Why was Bletchley Park so significant in the Second World War?

_____

_____

_____

2. Who worked there?

_____

_____

_____

3. Who was Alan Turing?

_____

_____

4. What was Alan Turing's contribution to codebreaking?

_____

_____

5. What was the Enigma machine?

_____

_____

6. What was Alan Turing's contribution to computing?

_____

_____

_____

I can research the history of Bletchley Park during the Second World War.
I can explain the significance of Alan Turing to computing. How did you do?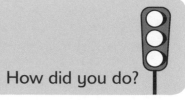

Substitution cipher

■ Using the code key decipher the coded message below.

a	b	c	d	e	f	g	h	i	j	k	l	m
g	d	n	h	c	q	s	o	e	t	m	a	r

n	o	p	q	r	s	t	u	v	w	x	y	z
w	l	b	u	x	i	z	v	f	y	j	p	k

Write the message on the top row:

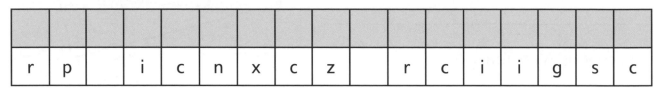

r	p		i	c	n	x	c	z		r	c	i	i	g	s	c

■ Change these messages into coded ones.

a) meet me at the railway station

_____

b) I have the secret files

_____

c) time to go

_____

■ Now, write your own messages, code them and swap with a partner to decode them.

_____

_____

_____

I can create a secret message using a substitution cipher code key.

How did you do?

PHOTOCOPIABLE

■SCHOLASTIC
www.scholastic.co.uk

The Blitz near us

- Find out about how your local area was affected during the time of the Blitz. Which search words will you use?

- Write your facts below.

1. _____

2. _____

3. _____

4. _____

5. _____

6. _____

7. _____

8. _____

9. _____

10. _____

I can research online to find information about the war and my local area.

How did you do?

Evacuees

Research question: Why were children evacuated during the war?
- ■ Research online and record your notes below.
- ■ Record the search words you use and the addresses of the websites you find.

Website name	Search words used to find the site	Web address	Notes about it

I can research online to find out information about evacuees.

How did you do?

Propaganda poster

■ Follow the style of a propaganda poster to sketch a new design below.

■ Make sure that the image is big and bold, the text is bold, the message is clear and is a short phrase or rhyme.

I can sketch a new propaganda poster, in the style of British war-time posters.

How did you do?

Victorians

In this chapter, the children are challenged to create a Victorians-based maze game using Snap!, a programming language similar to Scratch. Snap! can be used in the browser at http://snap.berkeley.edu/run. It can run on many digital devices, including tablets and allows children to build their own coding blocks, developing and extending their understanding of key computational and programming concepts such as decomposition, algorithms, logical reasoning, variables, multiple selection and procedures.

Expected prior learning

● The children are now familiar with Scratch from previous chapters and the knowledge, skills and understanding they have developed will now be applied to a similar, though slightly more challenging programming language. For this chapter, it is also assumed the children have some familiarity with maze games and the topic of the Victorians.

Chapter at a glance

Subject area
• Algorithms and programming

National Curriculum objective
• To design, write and debug programs that accomplish specific goals, including controlling or simulating physical systems; solve problems by decomposing them into smaller parts. To use sequence and repetition in programs; work with variables and various forms of input and output. To use logical reasoning to explain how some simple algorithms work and to detect and correct errors in algorithms and programs.

Week	Lesson objectives	Summary of activities	Expected outcomes
1	• To evaluate video and online games, using given criteria. • To discuss 'good' gameplay and modify evaluation criteria. • To describe the importance of a story to a game. • To identify common feature of game genres.	• Children share their knowledge of games. • They evaluate existing games. • They discuss game genre. • They learn about game play and backstory. • They review video games and identify backstory features.	• Can evaluate video and online games to identify the 'good' gameplay features. • Can describe the importance of a story to a game.
2	• To use commercial video game examples to identify the main features of the plot. • To plan and create a storyboard for a new game. • To design a flowchart to describe the gameplay. • To identify the assets they need to create for their game. • To create sprites, backgrounds and sounds (their assets) for their animation as needed.	• Children work in pairs to plan their own game using storyboards and flowcharts. • They identify game assets. • They begin to create game assets.	• Can create a storyboard and flowchart for their game. • Can plan and create the assets needed for their maze game.
3	• To decompose their game into smaller programmable parts. • To plan simply on paper the code for each part of their game. • To write their code for each part of their game. • To test and debug their code as they write.	• Children complete their game assets. • They plan programming for a game. • They begin to program a game using paired programming.	• Can use logical thinking to decompose their maze game into smaller parts. • Can design and write programs to create their game.
4	• To write their code for each part of their game. • To plan and implement the use of sequences of two-way selection and post-test loops to create efficient programs. • To work collaboratively to debug their code.	• The children continue to program their game. • They add in two-way selection and post-test loops as appropriate. • They learn how to create their own blocks in Snap!	• Can use simple post-test loops and two-way selection where appropriate. • Can work collaboratively to test and debug their programs.

Week	Lesson objectives	Summary of activities	Expected outcomes
5	• To use multiple variables to add scores, timers, lives and so on as appropriate. • To test and debug their code as they write it. • To work collaboratively to debug their code.	• Children add variables to their game. • They test and debug the game.	• Can use multiple variables where appropriate to create an effective game. • Can work collaboratively to test and debug their programs.
6	• To give and receive constructive feedback. • To refine their game after receiving feedback from players and document the changes made. • To discuss how they would change their approach if undertaking a similar task in the future.	• Children act as a testing panel for others' games, reviewing and giving feedback. • They make adjustments based on feedback. • They evaluate their own game and their approach.	• Can refine their game based on others' feedback. • Can evaluate their own work and approach to the task.
Assess and review	• Assess and review the half term's work.	• Children create a poster presentation of their game. • They present their game to the rest of the class.	• Assess and review.

Overview of progression

● Throughout the lessons, the children build on their knowledge and understanding of programming and of the creative process. They begin by considering the role of gameplay and backstory in existing video or online games before applying their knowledge and understanding to the design and creation of their own Victorian-themed game. They work with Snap! for the first time, learning how to make their own blocks and applying their knowledge of procedures to a new programming language.

● Throughout the chapter, they deepen and extend their understanding of the creative design process, carefully planning their work before creating, reviewing, improving and evaluating their game. In doing so, they further develop the skills of decomposition, problem solving and debugging.

Creative context

● The lessons have links to the mathematics curriculum as the children are required to decompose and solve problems using logical thinking. They also need to use numeracy in their game as they program their characters to move and use variables to add scores, timers and health.

● These lessons also draw upon the children's written and verbal English as they plan, create, evaluate and present their game to their peers.

● The lessons also have links to the art curriculum as the children use the inbuilt paint tools to draw their own sprites and backgrounds

● Understanding of history is extended through the topic of the Victorians.

Background knowledge

● From the work they have already completed in earlier years, the children will be able to complete a simple maze game in Scratch. They have used variables, broadcast blocks, If statements and repetition previously and this chapter extends and applies their knowledge, skills and understanding of programming to a different language.

● It is important that you are a relatively confident user of Scratch for this project, perhaps having completed the maze game project in Year 5. You should make yourself familiar with the Snap! interface, which is very similar to Scratch, and how to define a new block. This tutorial may be helpful www.youtube.com/watch?v=Bbl2fh3igQ4

● To save work on Snap!, a simple sign up is required. It may be useful to do this prior to starting the lessons with the children.

● The Snap! reference guide at http://snap.berkeley.edu/SnapManual.pdf may be helpful if you have very confident learners you wish to extend beyond the scope of this chapter.

Curriculum objectives
● To design, write and debug programs that accomplish specific goals, including controlling or simulating physical systems; solve problems by decomposing them into smaller parts. To use sequence and repetition in programs; work with variables and various forms of input and output. To use logical reasoning to explain how some simple algorithms work and to detect and correct errors in algorithms and programs.

Lesson objectives
● To evaluate video and online games, using given criteria.
● To discuss 'good' gameplay and modify evaluation criteria.
● To describe the importance of a story to a game.
● To identify common features of game genres.

Expected outcomes
● Can evaluate video and online games to identify the 'good' gameplay features.
● Can describe the importance of a story to a game.

Resources
Media resource 'Gameplay, genre and backstory' on the CD-ROM; photocopiable page 177 'Analysing games'; selection of suitable games for the children to analyse, for example, Pacman, Space Invaders, Pong – all of which can be found online by searching; headphones

Analysing computer games

In this lesson, the children share and develop their knowledge of video games, examining aspects such as gameplay and backstory in order to better understand the features of games. They explore different games to find commonalities and present their findings to the class.

Introduction
● Invite the children to share different games they know and have played.
● The games they share will inevitably fall under different types or genres, such as maze games, pinball, platform, shooter, action and so on.
● Group the games on the board and explain that these different types of games are called game 'genres'.
● Explain that over the next few lessons they will be creating another game, this time using a language called Snap! and working in more detail on the gameplay and backstory of their game.
● Write these terms on the board and ask the children to share what they think they might mean.
● Explain that gameplay is how players interact with the game – for example, what are the rules of the game, what is the plot, what can a player do, what can be modified by the player and so on. Backstory is the background of the plot and the characters. What has happened and what is happening?

Whole-class work
● As a class, look at an online version of the game Space Invaders. Invite volunteers to play the game and ask half the class to consider what the backstory is and the other half to consider the gameplay.
● Discuss their opinions as a class and address any misunderstandings. If needed, recap the meaning of genre, backstory and gameplay using media resource 'Gameplay, genre and backstory' on the CD-ROM.
● Explain that they will now be looking at a game, identifying the genre and considering the backstory and gameplay.

Small group/paired work
● Give out photocopiable page 177 'Analysing games' and assign pairs of children one of the online games you have identified as suitable.
● Children should work through the activity in pairs, playing their game and then answering the questions on the photocopiable sheet.

Whole-class work
● Ask volunteers to talk the rest of the class through their game and the answers to their questions.
● As they talk, it would be helpful to display the game on the board so they can explain their answers.
● Invite others who also played that game to expand on the answers given.
● Lead a discussion to consider what makes effective gameplay and backstory based on their investigations.

Paired/whole-class work
● Ask the class to come up with their 'golden rules' for good gameplay. Ask each pair to write one golden rule, which can be stuck to the board. Ask the children to sort the notes into order of importance.
● Explain that they will be using these rules during the next lesson to help them to plan their own game.

Review
● Ask the children to share what they have learned this lesson.
● Check their understanding of genre, gameplay and backstory. You could use a game you have not used as an example, for instance, Minecraft. Ask: *What genre would Minecraft be? What is the backstory? What is the gameplay?*

Curriculum objectives

● To design, write and debug programs that accomplish specific goals, including controlling or simulating physical systems; solve problems by decomposing them into smaller parts. To use sequence and repetition in programs; work with variables and various forms of input and output. To use logical reasoning to explain how some simple algorithms work and to detect and correct errors in algorithms and programs.

Lesson objectives

● To use commercial video game examples to identify the main features of the plot.
● To plan and create a storyboard for a new game.
● To design a flowchart to describe the gameplay.
● To identify the assets they need to create for their game.
● To create sprites, backgrounds and sounds (their assets) for their animation as needed.

Expected outcomes

● Can create a storyboard and flowchart for their game.
● Can plan and create the assets needed for their maze game.

Resources

Plain paper; photocopiable page 178 'Game plan'; photocopiable page 179 'Game flowchart'; media resource 'Example game flowchart' on the CD-ROM; Snap! website: http://snap.berkeley.edu/run (prior to the lesson, ensure that the children have usernames and passwords for Snap! so they can save their work)

Planning their game

This week, the children use their understanding of genre, gameplay and backstory to plan their own game, using a simple plan and flowchart. They will also plan and design their characters and other assets and may begin to create these using Snap!

Introduction

● Explain that this week they will be designing and planning their own game, considering the genre, gameplay, backstory and characters. Note: you can decide whether you wish to allow the children free choice over genre, or ask them to complete a maze game, as described in this chapter.

Whole-class work

● Explain that they will be creating a game based on the 'Victorians' topic. Invite some ideas about the types of game that could be created; for example a maze game in which a chimney sweep has to find the chimney, or they have to escape from a factory or workhouse.

Independent/paired work

● Give out plain paper and ask the children to brainstorm possible ideas for their game in pairs.
● Once the pairs have identified possible ideas, ask them to join with another pair to help each other to choose and improve their idea.
● You should highlight the need for them to consider time and software restrictions, so their plans are achievable.

Paired work

● Pairs should sketch out their game idea using photocopiable page 178 'Game plan'.

Whole-class work

● Show media resource 'Example game flowchart' on the CD-ROM on the board and explain that this allows us to see what will happen in the game.

Paired work

● Give out and go through photocopiable page 179 'Game flowchart' and ask the children to complete it to show how the players will play the game.
● Some children may finish this relatively quickly and be ready to get started with collecting the assets for their game.
● Show them the Snap! interface, which should already be very familiar to them and then they can begin to create their assets. They can import assets from elsewhere if needed, although creating them using the drawing tools should be encouraged.
● Ensure that the children know how to save their work in Snap! with their usernames and passwords.

Differentiation
● Support: Encourage less confident learners to work with a simple maze game, as they should already be familiar with completing one from Year 5.
● Challenge: More confident learners will be able to plan and design a highly effective game that has strong gameplay and backstory. Encourage them to think carefully about additional elements that players would find helpful and useful, for example adding a choice of character and different levels that increase in difficulty.

Review

● Review the children's work from the lesson by inviting volunteers to share their ideas and game plans with the group.
● Ask each pair to write a list of what they need to do in the next lesson.
● Review progress by looking at the children's planning.

Curriculum objectives
● To design, write and debug programs that accomplish specific goals, including controlling or simulating physical systems; solve problems by decomposing them into smaller parts. To use sequence and repetition in programs; work with variables and various forms of input and output. To use logical reasoning to explain how some simple algorithms work and to detect and correct errors in algorithms and programs.

Lesson objectives
● To decompose their game into smaller programmable parts.
● To plan simply on paper the code for each part of their game.
● To write their code for each part of their game.
● To test and debug their code as they write.

Expected outcomes
● Can use logical thinking to decompose their maze game into smaller parts.
● Can design and write programs to create their game.

Resources
Completed planning resources from previous lessons; Photocopiable page 180 'Game code'; Snap! website: http://snap.berkeley.edu/run

Writing game code

This week the children plan the code for their game. First, they match up Scratch blocks to the correct action and then break down the writing of their game code into smaller parts (decomposition). They work through their code, matching desired actions to Scratch scripts. This helps them to program their game systematically and with fewer errors.

Introduction
● Recap with the children their work from last week and ask them to revisit their action points.
● Explain that in this lesson they will be completing the creation of their assets and planning and writing the code for their game.

Whole-class work
● Give out photocopiable page 180 'Game code' and talk through the example with the children, discussing why it is helpful to plan the code in this way. (It makes programming quicker/helps with the debugging process and so on.)
● Discuss that they may need to try out some code in Snap! as they are planning. This is to be encouraged.
● Ask the children to complete their own game code plan once they have finished creating their assets.

Paired work
● Encourage the children to use their time wisely – perhaps one of them can complete the game code plan while the other finishes the asset creation and then they could swap and 'debug' each others' work.
● Once they think they have completed their game code, they should partner with another pair to check and debug their code, spotting errors and helping each other to work out what will or will not work.
● They can then begin to program their code into Snap!, using their game code and flowchart as reference for what they need to do.

Whole-class work
● Ensure that the children all know how to name and save their work.
● If there are any common issues that arise from the task above, it may be worth spending time as a class going over them with groups of children or as a class.

Differentiation
● Support: Less confident learners can focus on creating simple assets and writing code for the main aspects of the game, for example getting their character to move using the arrow keys. They may benefit from peer or adult help in breaking down what needs to be achieved into smaller, achievable parts and working through these systematically.
● Challenge: More confident learners can plan and write more complex code with confidence and independence. Encourage them to work out how they can achieve outcomes by trial and error and help others to overcome problems with their code

Review
● Invite any children who are having difficulties with a piece of code to share it and 'debug' it as a class.
● As a class, discuss the pros and cons of planning code on paper first before starting to program.
● Review the children's progress with reference to their game code and the quality of the work they have completed during the lesson.

Curriculum objectives

● To design, write and debug programs that accomplish specific goals, including controlling or simulating physical systems; solve problems by decomposing them into smaller parts. To use sequence and repetition in programs; work with variables and various forms of input and output. To use logical reasoning to explain how some simple algorithms work and to detect and correct errors in algorithms and programs.

Lesson objectives

● To write their code for each part of their game.
● To plan and implement the use of sequences of two-way selection and post-test loops to create efficient programs.
● To work collaboratively to debug their code.

Expected outcomes

● Can use simple post-test loops and two-way selection where appropriate.
● Can work collaboratively to test and debug their programs.

Resources

Completed planning from previous lessons; prior to the lesson, ensure that you are familiar with how to make a block in Snap! – this tutorial may be helpful: www.youtube.com/watch?v=Bbl2fh3igQ4

Build your own blocks

This week, the children continue to program their game, writing their code and adding in more complex elements, such as multiple variables, nested If statements and post-test loops. They also learn how to build their own blocks in Snap!, developing and extending the knowledge of procedures that were first introduced to in Autumn 2 using Alice 2.4. As they work through the lesson, the children continue to work collaboratively to debug their work.

Introduction

● Explain that this week you will be looking at creating procedures in Snap!
● Ask them to share what they can remember about procedures from the work they completed in Autumn 2 in Alice 2.4.
● Ensure that they understand that procedures allow us to create sub-programs, or extra commands that they can use in their game, for example if the characters can all 'jump', then we can create a 'jump' command as a procedure and then use that single command whenever needed instead of having to write the whole jump script over and over again.
● Lead a discussion around why this is important. Ensure that they understand that, in the same way as two-way selection and repetition, using procedures helps to create efficient code, which runs quickly and uses up less space.

Paired work

● Ask the children to identify where they could use a procedure in their own code (avoid looking at variables as this will be covered in the next lesson).
● Ask a few volunteers to share their ideas with the class.

Whole-class work

● Show the children how they can 'build their own block' in Snap! In 'Variables' select 'Make block'. Next, name your block and click OK to bring up the block editor. Add the required code then click OK to save the block. The new block will now appear within 'Variables'. You may find you need to go through post-test loops and two-way selection again with some or all of the children.

Paired work

● The children can highlight where they can use a procedure on their 'Game code' plan and should create their own procedures as they continue to complete the code for their game during the remainder of the lesson.
● Ask the children to add comments to their work, in the same way as they have previously with Scratch, to highlight where they have created their own procedures and why.
● They should continue to work collaboratively to debug their code when they experience errors.
● You may find that common issues arise and you can work with small groups to explain them if this is the case.

> ### Differentiation
> ● Support: Less confident learners may need additional adult or peer support when programming their game and making a block. You may feel that they should focus on creating their game rather than making additional blocks, although creating a simple block, such as the example shown, can be encouraged.
> ● Challenge: Encourage more confident learners to add more complex elements to their game, ensuring that their code is as efficient as possible by using post-test loops, multiple selection and additional procedures where possible.

Review

● Ask the children to share what procedures they have created by making their own blocks and explain their reasoning behind using these.
● Review the children's progress with them during the lesson and ensure that they know what they need to accomplish next lesson to complete their game.

Curriculum objectives

● To design, write and debug programs that accomplish specific goals, including controlling or simulating physical systems; solve problems by decomposing them into smaller parts. To use sequence and repetition in programs; work with variables and various forms of input and output. To use logical reasoning to explain how some simple algorithms work and to detect and correct errors in algorithms and programs.

Lesson objectives

● To use multiple variables to add scores, timers, lives and so on as appropriate.
● To test and debug their code as they write it.
● To work collaboratively to debug their code.

Expected outcomes

● Can use multiple variables where appropriate to create an effective game.
● Can work collaboratively to test and debug their programs.

Resources

Completed planning from previous lessons; photocopiable page 181 'Variables and procedures'

Adding scoring, timers and lives

This week, the children are reminded of the use of using multiple variables, such as scores, lives, and timers in their game. They are also introduced to using a variable for health. They combine the use of variables with their knowledge and understanding of procedures, to create procedures for their variables as appropriate in their game, and continue to work on finishing their game, collaboratively testing and debugging their code.

Introduction

● Remind the children that in the last lesson they were continuing to program their game and created their own procedures. Lead a brief discussion to recap how and why procedures are used and how to make blocks in Snap!
● Explain that this week they will be working with their game variables – you will be showing them how to create a variable for health, if appropriate to their game, and they will be creating procedures for their own variables.

Whole-class work

● As a class, work through how to create a health variable. By now, the children should be able to work this out with a little guidance. First, make a variable called 'health'. The screenshots show how health can be set and reduced every time the player jumps.
● As a class, talk through the code and how it is working (every time the space key is pressed, the procedure 'jump' is called and health is changed by −5. When health reaches 0, 'game over' is broadcast. Ask: *How many jumps can be used in the game? Is this good gameplay?*

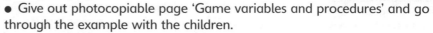

● Give out photocopiable page 'Game variables and procedures' and go through the example with the children.
● Explain that you are now going to show them how a procedure can be used to increase health, for example when the character comes into contact with different energy-boosting items. This is a good time to use a procedure as we can call on it whenever we want an object (sprite) to be able to give an energy-boost to the character. The screenshots below show a possible script for the procedure and different ways that it could be cued.

Paired work

● Ask the children to plan their own variables on photocopiable page 181 'Variables and procedures' and identify where it would be useful to create procedures.

● For the remainder of the lesson, the children should program their variables into their game, as usual working collaboratively to debug any errors.

Differentiation

● Support: Less confident learners may need additional support in understanding how variables work and planning and programming their own variables. You could encourage them to stick to one variable if necessary and you may feel that they do not need to create any further procedures if they found this challenging last lesson.
● Challenge: More confident learners can plan and use multiple variables and procedures with confidence. Encourage them to help others debug their work.

Review

● Ask volunteers to share how they are using variables in their work and highlight where they have created procedures that include their variables.

Curriculum objectives

● To design, write and debug programs that accomplish specific goals, including controlling or simulating physical systems; solve problems by decomposing them into smaller parts. To use sequence and repetition in programs; work with variables and various forms of input and output. To use logical reasoning to explain how some simple algorithms work and to detect and correct errors in algorithms and programs.

Lesson objectives

● To give and receive constructive feedback.
● To refine their game after receiving feedback from players and document the changes made.
● To discuss how they would change their approach if undertaking a similar task in the future.

Expected outcomes

● Can refine their game based on others' feedback.
● Can evaluate their own work and approach to the task.

Resources

Photocopiable page 182 'Game testing'; prior to the lesson load up the games on computers and create a 'testing list' to assign children to the game they will test; photocopiable page 183 'Game evaluation'

Sharing and evaluating games

In this lesson, the children will play each others' games in order to act as game testers and give and receive constructive feedback. They will then improve their games according to the feedback and evaluate both their game and their own approach to the task.

Introduction

● Explain to the children that they are working for a game company and have been asked to test the latest games that have been delivered. Their task is to give independent feedback on the game to the creators so they can improve it.
● Discuss briefly why getting a game tested and receiving feedback on it is an important part of the design process.
● Distribute photocopiable page 182 'Game testing' to the children and assign them to a game as per the testing list you have created.
● Go through the photocopiable sheet and ensure that all children understand the requirements of the task.

Paired work

● Ask the children to play the game to which they have been assigned and complete their photocopiable sheet.

Whole-class work

● Prior to giving out the correct sheets to the game creators, discuss how, as game creators, they can use the feedback to help them to improve their game. Ask: *Why is it important to improve the game after feedback? What if you don't agree with the feedback?* And so on.

Paired work

● The children should read through the feedback given and spend some time making amendments to their game as per the recommendations given.
● They can then complete photocopiable page 183 'Game evaluation'.

> ### Differentiation
> ● Support: Encourage less confident learners to give simple, clear and helpful feedback. They may need support in making the changes suggested by their testers. They may also need additional adult help in completing the evaluation sheet, particularly the questions regarding their approach.
> ● Challenge: Challenge more confident learners to give highly detailed, specific feedback in their testing to improve the quality of the game for the player. They should be encouraged to write thoughtful evaluations of their work and their approach.

Review

● Bring the children together and select some of the games to show and play (saving their work in a shared area will be helpful for this as will be noting which children have created games that will be interesting to show). Ask the children to talk through their games as they are played, discussing how feedback helped them to improve their game further, and what they would do differently if they had to do the task on another occasion.
● Try to find time to show all the games, or at least discuss their game with each child, which will help with assessment of the chapter's work.
● Undertake assessment of children's understanding from their game, their game testing, evaluations and their review discussion with you.

Curriculum objectives
● To design, write and debug programs that accomplish specific goals, including controlling or simulating physical systems; solve problems by decomposing them into smaller parts. To use sequence and repetition in programs; work with variables and various forms of input and output. To use logical reasoning to explain how some simple algorithms work and to detect and correct errors in algorithms and programs.

Lesson objectives
● To understand what is required in a poster presentation of their game.
● To present their game to a panel.
● To demonstrate their knowledge and understanding of the importance of gameplay and backstory when creating a game.
● To explain how they have programmed their game and used variables, procedures, multiple selection and repetition.

Expected outcomes
● Can demonstrate their understanding of designing, planning and creating a game using Snap! to others.
● Can present and explain their work to an audience.

Resources
A variety of poster creation materials such as A3 poster paper, glue, scissors, coloured pens

Victorians: Assess and review

In this lesson, the children will create a poster presentation of their game to present to the rest of the class. They will summarise and explain their game, detailing the backstory and gameplay and demonstrating how they have programmed their game and the steps they have taken to make their code efficient.

Introduction
● Discuss with the children what they have learned during this chapter. You could do this as a think-pair-share activity if you wish.
● Explain that for this assessment task they will be creating a poster presentation of their game to present to the rest of the class.

Whole-class work
● Discuss with them what might be included in a poster presentation (game name, backstory, gameplay, how it was created and so on).
● You could make a list of their ideas on the board.
● Lead a brief discussion around what makes an effective poster (ample white space, images with brief explanatory text).
● Ensure that they understand they may need to print out parts of their code and that they know how to do this (right-click and choose script pic, then save and print).
● Explain that they can present their game in any way they wish and encourage creativity. They can also expand upon their ideas as they present their work to the rest of the group.

Paired work
● Ask the children to select the materials they need and complete their poster presentation of their game, ensuring that they meet the requirements on the checklist.

Whole-class work
● Each pair should present their poster to the class, who should be encouraged to ask questions about the game.

Differentiation
● Support: Less confident learners may benefit from additional adult support and can be encouraged to complete a simple but effective poster.
● Challenge: Encourage more confident learners to cover more than the essentials given in the checklist, for example focusing more closely on why they included certain elements and how they could improve their game further.

Review
● The presentation of the posters is an ideal opportunity for you to assess the children's work and their understanding of the game creation process.
● The children's posters could be used as a classroom display.

Analysing games

■ Play the game and answer the following questions.

Game _____

Genre of the game (maze, platform, action and so on)

_____

Gameplay (how do the players interact with the game?)

_____

_____

_____

Backstory (what is the story behind the game?)

_____

_____

_____

I can analyse a game.

How did you do?

Game plan

■ Complete the game plan below.

Name of game _____

Genre of game _____

What is the backstory of your game? Who are the characters? What has happened to them and what are they trying to do?

_____

_____

_____

Describe the gameplay of your game. What will players have to do? What controls will they use? What options will players have?

_____

_____

_____

Plan your start screen and two other key scenes in your game below.

_____

_____

_____

_____

_____

I can plan the gameplay and backstory of a game.

How did you do?

Variables and procedures

■ Use the table below to plan the variables you will use in your game. The first box shows an example.

Variable/ procedure	What needs to happen
Health procedure – boost health	Set health to 20 at start of game When jump, health reduces by 5 When health at 0, game over message broadcast, which stops game When pick up item of food, health increases by 5

I can plan the variables and identify procedures needed for my game.

How did you do?

Game testing

Game to be tested _____

■ Play the game and answer the questions below:

Is the game working as it should?

_____

_____

What is the backstory of the game?

_____

_____

Describe the gameplay.

_____

_____

_____

What did you like best about the game?

_____

_____

_____

What could the creator do to improve the game?

_____

_____

_____

I can be a game tester.
I can give feedback to a game's creator to help them to make
their game better.
How did you do?

PHOTOCOPIABLE

■SCHOLASTIC
www.scholastic.co.uk

Game evaluation

■ Use the questions below to help you to evaluate your game and how you approached the task.

What are you most pleased with in your finished game and why?

_____

_____

_____

What would you like to improve about your finished game and why?

_____

_____

_____

What did you do well in your approach to creating your game (Did you use your time well? Did you work well on a particular area of the game?)

_____

_____

_____

What could you improve about your approach to creating your game? (Think about any mistakes you made along the way.)

_____

_____

_____

I can evaluate my work.
I can evaluate how I approached a task.

How did you do?

Final project

This chapter engages the children in choosing a real-world problem and creating a website, a game or an app. They learn about the layout of web pages and look at the structure of the HTML (hypertext mark-up language) behind the web pages. They observe how web pages are structured and use web tools to edit and 'remix' them. Using web tools, they edit the HTML of web pages, to learn about the functions of the HTML tags.

The children learn about Dr Barnardo and his charitable work in Victorian Britain. They select and research a real-world problem, before they plan, design and build a website, a game or an app. They discuss the social and ethical issues raised by the role of computers in the world.

Finally, the children present their projects through a 'World Fair' exhibition and invite other children, teachers, parents and school governors to visit and ask them questions.

Expected prior learning

- The children will be able to use logical reasoning to explain how some simple algorithms work and to detect and correct errors in algorithms and programs. They will be able to create flowcharts to represent the instructions.
- They will know how to select, use and combine a variety of software, to create websites, games and apps.
- They will know how to use search technologies effectively and be discerning in evaluating digital content.
- The children will be able to use criteria to evaluate the quality of solutions, and know how to identify improvements and make refinements to the solutions.

Chapter at a glance

Subject area

- Algorithms and programming; Data and information; Communication and e-safety

National Curriculum objective

- To design, write and debug programs that accomplish specific goals, including controlling or simulating physical systems; solve problems by decomposing them into smaller parts.
- To use sequence, selection, and repetition in programs; work with variables and various forms of input and output.
- To use logical reasoning to explain how some simple algorithms work and to detect and correct errors in algorithms and program.
- To select, use and combine a variety of software (including internet services) on a range of digital devices to design and create a range of programs, systems and content that accomplish given goals, including collecting, analysing, evaluating and presenting data and information.
- To use search technologies effectively, appreciate how results are selected and ranked, and be discerning in evaluating digital content.
- To use technology safely, respectfully and responsibly; recognise acceptable/unacceptable behaviour; identify a range of ways to report concerns about content and contact.

Week	Lesson objectives	Summary of activities	Expected outcomes
1	• To modify a web page using the Mozilla X-Ray goggles tool. • To observe the HTML language for text and images in a web page. • To modify a web page using the Mozilla Thimble tool. • To explain how a HTML web page is structured.	• Children describe the main features of a web page and identify which features suggest authenticity. • They look at HTML page source. • They modify web pages with the Mozilla X-Ray Goggles and Thimble tools. • They explain how a HTML web page is structured.	• Can modify a web page using web tools. • Can modify the web page by changing the HTML. • Can explain how a HTML web page is structured.
2	• To modify a web page using the Mozilla Thimble tool, to alter the HTML. • To create a web page using the Mozilla Thimble tool. • To modify and improve a design, based on user feedback.	• Children look at the Mozilla Webmaker website. • They use Mozilla Thimble to alter HTML. • They create a web page. • They capture feedback from other children and act upon it.	• Can use HTML to modify a web page. • Can combine software tools, to create a web page using HTML. • Can improve design by responding to user feedback.

Week	Lesson objectives	Summary of activities	Expected outcomes
3	• To identify a real-world problem which is relevant to the child. • To research a real-world problem using a search engine and appropriate search words. • To evaluate the information located using a search engine, using self-authored criteria.	• Children look at the work of Barnardo's. • They identify a real-world problem to create a website, app or game. • They make notes from research and use them to present to the class. • They evaluate the information located, using self-authored criteria.	• Can research and plan a project for a relevant, real-world problem. • Can search the web, using appropriate search words. • Can evaluate the information found.
4	• To plan and design a website, using flowcharts and wireframes. • To self-review a plan, before asking for feedback from others. • To combine software tools to create a website. • To decompose larger problems into smaller parts. • To know and explain why accessibility features are important.	• Children analyse a flowchart and create their own flowcharts. • They plan and design a website, using wireframes. • They self-review the plan and then ask others for feedback. • They use flowcharts to describe the error–checking process. • They explain why accessibility features are important.	• Can plan a website, using flowcharts and wireframes. • Can combine software tools, to create a website. • Can explain why accessibility features are important.
5	• Using relevant examples, to discuss the social and ethical issues raised by the role of computers in the world. • To consider the role in social and ethical issues focused on the app, game or website produced.	• Children look at examples of social and ethical issues relating to computers and consider these in relation to the website, app or game being produced.	• Can discuss social and ethical issues raised by the role of computers in the world.
6	• To review the knowledge, skills and understanding of computing that they have developed over the key stage. • To discuss career paths in computing.	• Children share the websites, apps and games that they have created for a real-world problem. • They think about career paths in computing.	• Can discuss career paths in computing.
Assess and review	• Assess and review of the half term's work.	• Children look at a web page source to read the HTML language. • They modify a web page using the Mozilla Thimble tool. • They explain how a HTML web page is structured.	• Assess and review.

Overview of progression

● When creating their websites, children recognise the audience when designing and producing digital content.
● They develop their knowledge of web pages and the HTML code behind them, so that they can describe the structure and recognise common tags.
● The children discuss social and ethical issues raised by the role of computers in the world.
● To prepare for working life beyond school, they discuss career paths for those studying computing.

Creative context

● The lessons link closely to the English curriculum, as the children discuss the social and ethical issues raised by the role of computers in the world. They use comparative language and create a discursive argument for a specific purpose. They build on their own and others' ideas and challenge views, courteously.
● Linking to maths, they use flowcharts to sequence instructions and describe decisions. They solve problems by collecting, selecting, processing, presenting and interpreting data, where appropriate, drawing conclusions and identifying further questions to ask.
● Linking to history, they learn about the Victorian era and Dr Barnardo's work with the poor.

Background knowledge

● The children develop their prior learning of search technologies.
● They will have used many websites before and should be able to describe how the pages are laid out, for example horizontal menu bars or side menu bars need to be used consistently.
● They will know of many examples where computers are used in the world, but may not have thought about the social and ethical issues surrounding them.

Curriculum objectives
● To design, write and debug programs that accomplish specific goals, including controlling or simulating physical systems; solve problems by decomposing them into smaller parts.
● To select, use and combine a variety of software (including internet services) on a range of digital devices to design and create a range of programs, systems and content that accomplish given goals, including collecting, analysing, evaluating and presenting data and information.
● To use search technologies effectively, appreciate how results are selected and ranked, and be discerning in evaluating digital content.
● To use technology safely, respectfully and responsibly.

Lesson objectives
● To modify a web page using the Mozilla X-Ray goggles tool.
● To observe the HTML language for text and images in a web page.
● To modify a web page using the Mozilla Thimble tool.
● To explain how a HTML web page is structured.

Expected outcomes
● Can modify a web page using web tools.
● Can modify the web page by changing the HTML.
● Can explain how a HTML web page is structured.

Resources
Photocopiable page 193 'Website layout'

Looking at websites

The children look at a website and try to identify the layout of the elements, for example the logo and menu. They look at older versions of the site to see how it has evolved. Using a web tool, they look at the HTML (hypertext mark-up language) behind the elements and experiment with changing them. They view the HTML source behind a web page to see the structure of the HTML.

Introduction
● Introduce the lesson by displaying the CBBC website. Can they describe the main features, for example, a logo, menu bar, hyperlinks to other pages, text, images, videos and so on.
● Ask: *Has the CBBC website always looked like this?* Using the 'Internet Archive Wayback Machine' (http://archive.org/web/), they can see how the site has evolved over time.
● Demonstrate the changes in the CBBC website, by typing the web address into the Wayback Machine. The old websites have been captured by web-crawler programs, which stored a copy or 'cached' the content of the website at that time.
● Allow the children time to search through the site. Then they choose a website they know. Has the structure of the web page changed?
● Using photocopiable page 193 'Website layout', ask the children to sketch the layout of four websites. Where are the logo, menu, main text and images on each home page? Are they consistently in the same position?

Whole-class work
● Display the BBC News website and ask the children to identify the features that make it look authentic. It could be the language used – it sounds authoritative. It could be the links – linking to other official or trustworthy websites. It could be that the children 'sense' that the content looks real.
● To consider the code behind the website, the page source can be displayed, to view the HTML language. HTML is 'hypertext mark-up language' and is the text-based language that creates the websites.
● From the web browser menu, find the 'view source' item (for example, in Google Chrome, from the 'View' menu, select 'Developer' then 'View source'). The source code for the page will be displayed. This may look a little complicated, so there are tools to help the children make sense of it.
● One of the tools is 'X-ray goggles', which allows the user to see the code behind objects.
● Open the X-Ray Goggles website (https://goggles.webmaker.org/en-US). Ensure that the browser is either Firefox, Chrome or Safari.
● Press the yellow button, to see behind the objects.
● To view another website, drag the yellow button from the web page onto the Bookmarks bar. On any other website you can then press the button on the Bookmarks bar to activate the goggles.
● By selecting a text object, the user can type in new words and then select 'Save' to change the web page (it does not change the original page).

Paired work
● Allow the children time to explore different websites and use X-Ray goggles to see the HTML code behind the elements. They can change the text on web pages and even copy the links to other images, to replace images on a page.

Review
● Bring the class together and share examples of the modified web pages.
● Display Mozilla Thimble (https://thimble.webmaker.org/), another web tool to create and edit web pages. On the example Thimble page, highlight the structure of the page (!<doctype html> at the top then <html>) and the HTML tags, for example, <head>, <body> and <p>.

Curriculum objectives

Curriculum objectives
● To design, write and debug programs that accomplish specific goals, including controlling or simulating physical systems; solve problems by decomposing them into smaller parts.
● To select, use and combine a variety of software (including internet services) on a range of digital devices to design and create a range of programs, systems and content that accomplish given goals, including collecting, analysing, evaluating and presenting data and information.
● To use search technologies effectively, appreciate how results are selected and ranked, and be discerning in evaluating digital content.
● To use technology safely, respectfully and responsibly; recognise acceptable/ unacceptable behaviour; identify a range of ways to report concerns about content and contact.

Lesson objectives
● To modify a web page using the Mozilla Thimble tool, to alter the HTML.
● To create a web page using the Mozilla Thimble tool.
● To modify and improve a design, based on user feedback.

Expected outcomes
● Can use HTML to modify a web page.
● Can combine software tools, to create a web page using HTML.
● Can improve design by responding to user feedback.

Resources
Photocopiable page 194 'Meme evaluation'; photocopiable page 195 'Keep Calm evaluation'

Writing HTML

The children adapt example web pages, before creating their own. The Thimble tool enables them to change the HTML code easily and see a live preview on the same page. They offer feedback and act upon it.

Introduction
● Display the Mozilla Webmaker website (https://webmaker.org/). The organisation, Mozilla, have created many resources to help people learn about the web.

Whole-class work
● Open the Mozilla Thimble tool, 'Meme-Maker' (https://thimble.webmaker. org/project/20795/remix). Explain that a meme is an idea that spreads across the web, usually where an amusing incident or image appeared.
● Looking at the Thimble Meme-Maker example, highlight to the children the first line of the code <!doctype html> – this begins every page.
● Then the next HTML tag is <html>. Can they see where that tag ends? Similar to brackets around words, HTML tags have opening and closing tags. The closing one looks like </html> and is at the bottom of the page.
● Ask the children to identify other tags and the corresponding closing tags, for example, <head> and </head>, <body> and </body> or <p> and </p>.

Paired work
● In pairs, the children follow the instructions in the code, of the Thimble 'Meme-Maker'. The instructions are found in bold black type.
● They can evaluate their meme, using photocopiable page 194 'Meme evaluation'. They swap and evaluate their partner's meme.
● From the feedback, they should make improvements.

Whole-class work
● Share examples of the memes. Ask children to explain how they acted on the feedback they received.
● Display another Mozilla Thimble example 'Keep Calm and Carry On' (https://thimble.webmaker.org/project/21939/remix). Highlight the features of the HTML code. Ask: *Can you see the <!doctype html> tag? What other tags do you know and can you see them?*

Paired work
● The children edit the Thimble 'Keep Calm and Carry On', to change the background colour, words and image, to make a poster for the school hall.
● Using photocopiable page 195 'Keep Calm evaluation', they evaluate their poster and their partner's poster, before acting upon the feedback.

Whole-class work
● Display the blank Thimble page (https://thimble.webmaker.org/).
● Highlight where the text 'Make something amazing with the web' is displayed on the screen and where it corresponds to in the HTML code.
● Explain that they can create their own web page, using this template.

Paired work
● Let the children choose a topic for their web page. In pairs, they write their own code or copy and paste code from other Thimble examples.
● Once complete, they view another pair's website and offer feedback. Then give time for them to act upon feedback they receive.

Review
● Bring the class together and share examples of the children's web pages. Can they explain how they acted upon the feedback received?
● Ask the children to name HTML tags and explain their function.

Curriculum objectives
● To design, write and debug programs that accomplish specific goals, including controlling or simulating physical systems; solve problems by decomposing them into smaller parts use sequence, selection, and repetition in programs; work with variables and various forms of input and output.
● To use logical reasoning to explain how some simple algorithms work and to detect and correct errors in algorithms and program.
● To select, use and combine a variety of software (including internet services) on a range of digital devices to design and create a range of programs, systems and content that accomplish given goals, including collecting, analysing, evaluating and presenting data and information.
● To use technology safely, respectfully and responsibly; recognise acceptable/unacceptable behaviour; identify a range of ways to report concerns about content and contact.

Lesson objectives
● To identify a real-world problem which is relevant to the child.
● To research a real-world problem using a search engine and appropriate search words.
● To evaluate the information located using a search engine, using self-authored criteria.

Expected outcomes
● Can research and plan a project for a relevant, real-world problem.
● Can search the web, using appropriate search words.
● Can evaluate the information found.

Resources
Photocopiable page 196 'Barnardo's charity work'; photocopiable page 197 'Our evaluation criteria'; photocopiable page 198 'The problem'; *Street Child* by Berlie Doherty

Creating a website, game or app about a real-world problem

The children learn about poor children in Victorian Britain and research the Barnardo's charity, past and present. They consider real-world problems and select one as a focus for their project. They decide whether they are going to create a website, a game or an app.

Introduction
● The children need to choose a real-world problem as a focus for their project.
● The children have been learning about making web pages. In previous topics, they have created games and apps. For their project, they can choose to create a website, a game or an app.
● For stimulus, read from *Street Child* by Berlie Docherty. It is about poor children in Victorian London. Read an account of Dr Barnardo and his work (www.barnardos.org.uk/barnardo_s_history.pdf).
● Look at information about the modern work of Barnardo's and the issues faced by children (www.barnardos.org.uk/barnardo_s_children_v2.pdf).

Independent work
● The children research the work of the Barnardo's charity. They use a 3-5-7 strategy (described below) to gather information and prioritise the results.
● Using photocopiable page 196 'Barnardo's charity work', they record notes from their web research. Then they select three facts.

Paired work
● The children form pairs and compare notes. They each have three facts and now need to select only five of them. This means discarding one fact.

Group work
● Now the children form a small group of four, by two pairs joining together. They now need to reduce their ten facts to seven facts. Once sorted, they create a short presentation about the facts they have chosen.
● Using photocopiable page 197 'Our evaluation criteria', they construct their own criteria to evaluate the reliability of the information located.

Whole-class work
● Bring the class together and ask each small group to present their facts.
● They should include an evaluation of the reliability of the information.

Group work
● The children now choose a real-world problem for their project. Then they decide whether they will create a web page, a game or an app.
● Working in groups, they discuss real-world problems, which could be local, national or international. They could concern the individual child or be a class problem.
● Allow the children time to discuss the real-world problem they would like to focus upon. The group may decide to all focus on the same problem or they could choose four individual problems. The purpose of discussing in groups is to gain initial feedback on their ideas.
● Using photocopiable page 198 'The problem', they summarise the problem they have chosen, who it affects and how they are going to help (by creating a website, game or app).

Review
● Bring the class together and ask each individual child to name their project's focus, why it is important to them and decide whether they going to create a website, a game or an app.

Curriculum objectives
● To design, write and debug programs that accomplish specific goals, including controlling or simulating physical systems; solve problems by decomposing them into smaller parts use sequence, selection, and repetition in programs; work with variables and various forms of input and output.
● To use logical reasoning to explain how some simple algorithms work and to detect and correct errors in algorithms and program.
● To use search technologies effectively, appreciate how results are selected and ranked, and be discerning in evaluating digital content.

Lesson objectives
● To plan and design a website, using flowcharts and wireframes.
● To self-review a plan, before asking for feedback from others.
● To combine software tools to create a website.
● To decompose larger problems into smaller parts.
● To know and explain why accessibility features are important.

Expected outcomes
● Can plan a website, using flowcharts and wireframes.
● Can combine software tools, to create a website.
● Can explain why accessibility features are important.

Resources
Interactive 'Hokey Cokey flowchart' on the CD-ROM; interactive 'Wireframes' on the CD-ROM; photocopiable page 199 'Musical flowchart'; photocopiable page 'Web page wireframe template' from the CD-ROM; photocopiable page 'Mobile phone wireframe template' from the CD-ROM; photocopiable page 'Game storyboard template' from the CD-ROM; photocopiable page 'Evaluation' from the CD-ROM; photocopiable page 'Error–checking flowchart' from the CD-ROM

Planning a website

The children consider simple action songs and create instructions for them, using flowchart symbols. They continue their projects, planning their website, game or app, using wireframes. They self-review, give and receive feedback and act upon it. They explain why accessibility features are important.

Introduction
● Introduce the lesson by playing the 'Hokey Cokey' music and the children forming a circle to do the dance.
● Explain that they are following an algorithm, a precise set of instructions, in order to do the dance.
● Display interactive 'Hokey Cokey flowchart' to show the flowchart for the song. It also has the symbols for the flowcharts and their meanings.
● Using photocopiable page 199 'Musical flowchart', they look at the instructions for the 'Hokey Cokey' and add the next steps.

Paired work
● The children look at the 'Hokey Cokey' flowchart and develop it to include 'decisions'. For example, 'Is your right leg in? Yes, then take your right leg out. No, then put your right leg in'. They see how the instructions can become quite complicated. Remind them that computers need very precise instructions.
● They select their own music song and create their own flowcharts.

Whole-class work
● Bring the class together and ask three pairs of children to perform their song, while displaying the flowchart to show the instructions.
● Remind the children about their projects, which they selected in the previous lesson, and that they are going to create a website, game or app.
● A 'wireframe' is an outline, used for planning the look of a product. Display a website 'wireframe' using interactive activity 'Wireframes' on the CD-ROM.
● This outline of a website can be used to plan their own website (there is also an app wireframe and a game storyboard).

Independent work
● The children plan and design their website, game or app using wireframes (in photocopiable pages 'Web page wireframe template', 'Mobile phone wireframe template' and 'Game storyboard template' from the CD-ROM).
● Once the children have sketched their designs, they can self-review them, using photocopiable 'Evaluation' from the CD-ROM.
● They can construct a checklist to reduce errors, using photocopiable page 'Error–checking flowchart' from the CD-ROM. They can add steps to the flowchart, to ensure that any mistakes are corrected.

Paired work
● The children ask a partner for feedback and evaluate their partner's design.
● They need to act on the feedback. This could mean that they take the advice about improving the project. However, it could equally mean that they listen and consider the feedback, before deciding not to follow the advice. They must be able to justify why they are not changing, based on the feedback.

Review
● Bring the class together and ask three children to display their wireframes, to describe the self-review process, the evaluation process and then how they acted upon the feedback.
● Remind the children about the 'accessibility features' that they have encountered in previous lessons. Have they included references to those features in their designs? Why is it important to include accessibility features?

Curriculum objectives

● To design, write and debug programs that accomplish specific goals, including controlling or simulating physical systems; solve problems by decomposing them into smaller parts use sequence, selection, and repetition in programs; work with variables and various forms of input and output.
● To use logical reasoning to explain how some simple algorithms work and to detect and correct errors in algorithms and program.
● To select, use and combine a variety of software (including internet services) on a range of digital devices to design and create a range of programs, systems and content that accomplish given goals, including collecting, analysing, evaluating and presenting data and information.
● To use search technologies effectively, appreciate how results are selected and ranked, and be discerning in evaluating digital content.
● To use technology safely, respectfully and responsibly; recognise acceptable/unacceptable behaviour; identify a range of ways to report concerns about content and contact.

Lesson objectives

● Using relevant examples, to discuss the social and ethical issues raised by the role of computers in the world.
● To consider the role in social and ethical issues focused on the app, game or website produced.

Expected outcomes

● Can discuss social and ethical issues raised by the role of computers in the world.

Resources

Photocopiable page 'Social and ethical issues' from the CD-ROM

Social and ethical issues

This week the children are provided with an introduction to social and ethical issues surrounding computers in our lives. They continue with their projects, using software to create a website, game or app. They also consider the social and ethical situations of different scenarios and discuss their views. They apply their learning to their own projects, identifying whether there are issues concerning their ideas.

Introduction

● To begin the lesson, ask three children to describe their projects and to display their wireframe designs. Ask: *Can you describe the audience for your project? What is going to be your next step?*

Independent work

● The children need time to continue with their project, to use software to create a website, app or game for a real-world problem. Therefore, you could extend this lesson to include more time for this development.

Whole-class work

● Ask the children to stand in the middle of the room. They are going to be a human scale, with the left side of the room being 'strongly disagree' and the right side of the room being 'strongly agree'.
● Introduce examples of the social and ethical issues of computers in the world (use photocopiable page 'Social and ethical issues' from the CD-ROM). Then the children arrange themselves in a line across the room, placing themselves in order of their strengths of opinion. They need to explain their opinion to the person on each side, to check that they are standing in the correct place. Once the scenario has been discussed along the line, choose three children to explain the reasons for their position.

Group work

● Using photocopiable page 'Social and ethical issues' from the CD-ROM, the groups re-read the scenarios and record the outcomes of their conversation.
● In the group, they should state the purpose of their project and apply the thoughts on social and ethical issues of computers in the world to their website, game or app. Can the group identify any issues? How should they address them?

Differentiation

● Support: Less confident learners may need support to form an opinion about the scenarios. They may need scaffolding by being provided with phrases such as, 'I agree with... because...' or 'I disagree with... because...'
● Challenge: More confident learners will be able to give a justified opinion of their thoughts about the scenarios. They should identify potential social and ethical issues arising from their project.

Review

● Bring the class together and ask each group to nominate one project that they have discussed. Ask: *Did you identify any social or ethical issues with it? How do you suggest the issues could be addressed?*

Curriculum objectives

● To design, write and debug programs that accomplish specific goals, including controlling or simulating physical systems; solve problems by decomposing them into smaller parts use sequence, selection, and repetition in programs; work with variables and various forms of input and output.
● To use logical reasoning to explain how some simple algorithms work and to detect and correct errors in algorithms and program.
● To select, use and combine a variety of software (including internet services) on a range of digital devices to design and create a range of programs, systems and content that accomplish given goals, including collecting, analysing, evaluating and presenting data and information.
● To use search technologies effectively, appreciate how results are selected and ranked, and be discerning in evaluating digital content.
● To use technology safely, respectfully and responsibly; recognise acceptable/ unacceptable behaviour; identify a range of ways to report concerns about content and contact.

Lesson objectives

● To review the knowledge, skills and understanding of computing that they have developed over the key stage.
● To discuss career paths in computing

Expected outcomes

● Can discuss career paths in computing.

Resources

Photocopiable page 'Career paths in computing' from the CD-ROM

World Fair

Concluding the projects, the children share their websites, games or apps in a 'World Fair' style. They present their work on a table as a 'stall' at the fair. Other children or parents can be invited to view and ask questions, giving them an audience. Finally, the children discuss career paths in computing.

Introduction

● The children will prepare a 'World Fair' to display their projects. Ideally, the classroom or hall will be set up with a table for each child of pair of children.
● On the table, they will be 'selling' the concept of their project. So, they could have printed images or text to describe the real-world issues and a banner showing the name of their project. They could display a short video highlighting the issues. For example, if their game is to raise awareness of famine in Africa, they could locate and share a video showing the situation. They then could have their game ready on the computer, for others to play.
● Give the children time to prepare their table or 'stall'. They could decorate it with objects relating to their project.
● Another idea for displaying a game is a 'cardboard arcade', where the computer screen is encased in a cardboard box and decorated to look like an arcade game.
● To make the experience more interactive, accessories, such as, MaKeyMaKey (www.makeymakey.com/) can be used as an input device, allowing the children to create a game controller for their game.
● Give the children time to produce their stalls, before inviting other children, parents, teachers or school governors to ask questions about the projects.

Whole-class work

● After the fair, bring the children together to consider all of the many skills they used to create their projects and how they applied their knowledge. This could be specific software skills or making judgments based on online research.
● Using a Padlet sticky note wall (http://padlet.com/), ask the children to think of three things they have learned about computing over the key stage.
● As the notes are submitted, try to sort them into categories.
● Ask the children whether they would like to continue in computing in the future. Could they imagine following a career in computing?
● The British Computing Society (BCS) has advice on career paths (www.bcs. org/category/7874).

Paired work

● Using photocopiable page 'Career paths in computing' from the CD-ROM, the children can see examples of the current careers in computing. They research online to find out more about the roles.

Differentiation

● Support: Less confident learners may need support to create prompt cards to explain their project. They could use the Mozilla Web Literacy Map (https://webmaker.org/ literacy) to discuss the skills they have developed.
● Challenge: More confident learners will be able to present their projects, explaining how they developed it from the original concept to the finished product. They should identify the knowledge and skills they have developed throughout the key stage and why these are important.

Review

● Bring the class together and ask about careers in computing. Do they imagine there will be new jobs in the future that are not invented now? Do they think everyone will need computers in the future?
● Ask three children to name a current career in computing that they have researched. What does it involve and do they think it is an area they would enjoy and be able to do?

Curriculum objectives
● To design, write and debug programs that accomplish specific goals, including controlling or simulating physical systems; solve problems by decomposing them into smaller parts use sequence, selection, and repetition in programs; work with variables and various forms of input and output.
● To use logical reasoning to explain how some simple algorithms work and to detect and correct errors in algorithms and program.
● To select, use and combine a variety of software (including internet services) on a range of digital devices to design and create a range of programs, systems and content that accomplish given goals, including collecting, analysing, evaluating and presenting data and information.
● To use search technologies effectively, appreciate how results are selected and ranked, and be discerning in evaluating digital content.
● To use technology safely, respectfully and responsibly; recognise acceptable/ unacceptable behaviour; identify a range of ways to report concerns about content and contact.

Lesson objectives
● To observe the HTML language for text and images in a web page.
● To modify a web page using the Mozilla Thimble tool, to alter the HTML.
● To explain how a HTML web page is structured.

Expected outcomes
● Can modify the web page by changing the HTML.
● Can explain how a HTML web page is structured.

Resources
Photocopiable page 'Postcard planning' from the CD-ROM; interactive activity 'Labelling HTML code' on the CD-ROM

Final project: Assess and review

The children study the code in a web page and change it to create a new product. The web page contains a postcard, with an image on one side and text on the other. They must summarise their project and display it on the postcard, by modifying the HTML code.

Introduction
● Explain that the children are going to send a postcard to you. It will contain a short message and an image, which summarises their project.
● Remind them of the Mozilla Thimble tool to edit the HTML code (https:// thimble.webmaker.org/) and using the Mozilla Firefox browser.
● Display the Thimble project 'Postcard' (https://thimble.webmaker.org/ project/1291/remix).
● Explain that they are going to summarise their project in one image and also in a short description.
● For review, ask the children to name different HTML tags and to describe their functions.

Independent work
● Using photocopiable page 'Postcard planning' from the CD-ROM, the children create a rapid paper prototype of their postcard. Set a timer, to allow ten minutes for them to sketch four postcards and decide upon the five main points they will include in the text.

Paired work
● In pairs, they share their prototypes and gain feedback from their partner. Once they have listened carefully, they should choose one of their sketches to develop and also act upon the feedback on their five headings.

Independent work
● Using the Thimble project 'Postcard', the children develop their summaries.
● On completion, they self-review their work, asking whether the image is clear and the text is suitable for an adult.

Whole-class work
● Use interactive activity 'Labelling HTML code' on the CD-ROM to remind the children of the structure of a web page.
● A further resource to support the learning is a HTML summary from Mozilla (https://mozteach.makes.org/thimble/html-cheatsheet).
● Ask the children to name a favourite website. Visit the page and find the 'View source' menu item (in Firefox, Tools > Web Developer > Page Source). They can select all of the HTML code and copy it into the clipboard.
● Opening a blank Thimble project (https://thimble.webmaker.org/), they can now paste the HTML code into the left-hand box. A preview should be shown in the right-hand box.
● The website may not look exactly like the original, as they often have 'styles' applied to the basic HTML. The children may have seen 'CSS' mentioned in their projects. This stands for 'cascading style sheets' and it is a way of quickly adjusting the look and behaviour of a page.
● Ask them to look at the HTML language. Can they explain how the HTML web page is structured? Can they locate the HTML tags for <head>, <body> and paragraphs <p>?

Review
● Bring the class together and display interactive activity 'Labelling HTML code' on the CD-ROM. Ask the children whether the websites they looked at were structured in the same way?
● Conclude the lesson by displaying examples of the postcard project summaries.

Name: _____   Date: _____

Website layout

- Visit four websites and sketch the layouts of the home page below.
- Use simple shapes to represent the logo, menus, banners, images and text.

Do they all follow the same layout?

Meme evaluation

- Explain what an internet meme is.

_____

_____

- Evaluate your partner's meme and give them feedback.

Does the meme still have a similar image to the original?

_____

Does the meme have clear simple text?

_____

Does the text follow the pattern of the original text?

_____

Are the words appropriate for a Year 6 child?

_____

Is it funny?

_____

- Write down the words you will use to feedback to your partner.
Are they kind, specific and helpful?

_____

_____

_____

I can explain what an internet meme is and evaluate it, for a given audience.

How did you do?

'Keep Calm' evaluation

- Evaluate your partner's 'Keep Calm and Carry On' poster.

Do the words follow the style of the original poster?

_____

Does the image look appropriate for the wartime period?

_____

Do the words fit onto the poster?

_____

Is the background colour suitable for the audience?

_____

Does the slogan use appropriate words for the audience?

_____

- Listen to your partner's feedback on your 'Keep Calm and Carry On' poster.
- Write below how you are going to act upon their feedback.

_____

_____

_____

_____

_____

_____

_____

I can evaluate a poster for a given audience and respond to feedback.

How did you do?

Barnardo's charity work

- Who was Dr Barnardo? Research online to find out facts about him and about his legacy.
- Write your notes below, then choose three important facts.

My chosen three facts are:

1. _____

2. _____

3. _____

I can research online about Dr Barnardo and select important facts.

How did you do?

Our evaluation criteria

■ Can you create evaluation criteria for the facts you have collected? Use the headings below to help create the criteria.

Authority
(Does the person or organisation have the correct background, qualifications or knowledge?)

_____

_____

Purpose
(What is the purpose behind the website? Are they trying to share an idea, a belief, sell something? Does it have adverts on the site?)

_____

_____

Time
(Has it been updated recently?)

_____

_____

Content
(Does it sound biased? Does the text seem to be accurate?)

_____

_____

Navigation
(Do all of the links work? Which other sites does it link to?)

_____

_____

I can create evaluation criteria and apply them.

How did you do?

The problem

■ Complete the details about your problem below.

The problem is:

_____

_____

_____

The people it affects are:

_____

_____

_____

I am going to help by creating: (a website, game or app).

_____

_____

_____

I can identify a real-world problem and select how I am going to address it.

How did you do?

PHOTOCOPIABLE ■SCHOLASTIC
www.scholastic.co.uk

Musical flowchart

Do you know the 'Hokey Cokey'?

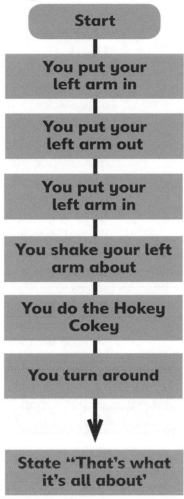

Start

You put your left arm in

You put your left arm out

You put your left arm in

You shake your left arm about

You do the Hokey Cokey

You turn around

State "That's what it's all about'

Rewrite the flowchart to include decisions (two-way selection) on another sheet. Use the flowchart beginning below to get you started.

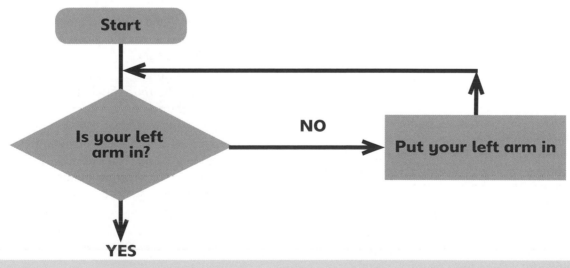

Start

Is your left arm in?

NO → **Put your left arm in**

YES

I can create a flowchart for a song.

How did you do?

Year 5 Autumn 1: King Arthur

Overview

- In the lessons, the children have been creating shapes using software and precise instructions. Using the King Arthur theme, they now think about the shapes of the Round Table, the crown, shields and swords. They think about variables and precise instructions.

Resources

- Hopscotch app (by Hopscotch Technologies)

Lesson activities

- Using the Hopscotch app, the children think about how instructions can be given. For example, King Arthur was a king who gave orders. They give instructions to their partner to draw shapes. However, the first person must try to be precise. If they said, 'Draw me a crown', would their partner know what shape it would be? How many points should it have on top? Would it have jewels or be plain?
- The partner then attempts to program the onscreen character to draw the shape. Once complete, they show it to the person who requested it – does it look like they imagined?

- The following are items the children could draw: a crown, a sword, a shield or even the Round Table with decorations.

Using the Hopscotch app on the iPad

1. Open the Hopscotch app and select the 'Community' tab at the bottom of the screen. Look at examples created by other users.

2. Select the 'Projects' tab and then 'New project'.

3. From the 'Add an object' menu, select the Monkey and 'Start'.

4. Select the drop-down menu to read 'When play button is tapped'.

5. Drag the block 'Move with trail distance' under the first instruction. Press play and see a horizontal line being drawn.

6. Press the 'X' and return to the programming screen.

7. Beginning with using the 'Rotate', 'Move with trail' and 'Repeat' blocks, the children can experiment with drawing the objects.

Year 5 Autumn 2: *The Railway Children (1)*

Overview

- In the lessons, the children have been learning about computer networks, including the internet as a global network. They have been thinking about the rail networks and how they can travel from one station to another. However, if a station was blocked, could they find another way around?

Resources

- London Transport map (https://www.tfl.gov.uk/cdn/static/cms/documents/standard-tube-map.pdf)
- London Underground app (free) (by Zuti Visual IT Ltd)

Lesson activities

- Using an image of the London Transport map, the children choose two stations and try to plan a route between them. They challenge their partner to find an alternative route.
- Using the London Underground app, they use the software to see if it follows the same route.
- Now they introduce a blockage into the network, so they need to re-plan their route.
- They test out the app again to find the new route.
- The app has other features, which allow the children to find the quickest route – this is not obvious from the map, as it is not drawn to scale and some stations may be nearer or further apart in real life.

Using the London Underground free app on the iPad

1. Open the London Underground app.

2. Select the 'Route' tab at the bottom of the screen.

3. Select 'Set start' and choose the name of a station.

4. Select 'Set end' and choose the name of the terminating station. Press the green arrow on the top right-hand side to begin.

5. A journey description will appear. Select the new green arrow and the map should be displayed with the route highlighted.

6. There are variables, which can be changed when first choosing the route, such as, 'Quickest route' or 'Fewest changes' and 'Transfer time'. Allow the children to try out the different options and see the effects on the route suggested.

Year 5 Autumn 2: *The Railway Children (2)*

Overview

● To continue the children's thinking about networks, they can use a mind-mapping tool to create a map of a network. They can then see how the data packets could flow around the network.

Resources

● Popplet (by Notion)

Lesson activities

● Using a mind-mapping app, the children construct a computer network. They could imagine the school network, with a computer in each classroom. How could the computers connect to the internet? Is there a school server? Where is it located?

● Working in pairs or small groups, the children could carry out a 'site survey' to locate the computers, the wired network points and the wireless access points. The network diagram would be constructed using the mind-mapping app to show the connections.

Using the Popplet app on the iPad

1. Open the Popplet app and select 'Make new popplet'.

2. Choose a name, for example, 'School network'.

3. On the rectangle on the screen, tap in its middle to add text. This could be to represent a room in the school, where the server is kept.

4. While the rectangle is selected, tap on one of the small circles and a new rectangle will appear. Add the details of the next classroom and the computers. Continue to map the classrooms nearby or even the whole school.

5. By holding on one of the small circles (instead of tapping), a link can be joined to another rectangle (if more than one connection is required).

Year 5 Spring 1: China and India

Overview

● In the lessons, the children have been using Wikipedia for research. The Simple English Wikipedia pages allow a book to be created and downloaded. When using a computer, the format chosen was a simple pdf. However, using a tablet, they can create an electronic book and take advantage of the note-taking tools for books.

Resources

● Safari web browser (by Apple)
● Simple English Wikipedia (available online http://simple.wikipedia.org/)

Lesson activities

● When searching online, the children will use a web browser. On tablets such as the iPad, Safari is the default browser, although others can be loaded – Google Chrome, for example. The children can compare the features of the browsers and also, explore the accessibility features.

● They have been using Wikipedia to research about China and India. The Simple English Wikipedia website contains information in a simpler language level of English than the full Wikipedia site.

● The children have used the 'Book creator' feature of the Simple English Wikipedia website, but they exported the final book as a plain pdf document. When using a tablet, it is possible to download the document as an electronic book.

● Using the tablet's own ebook reader software, the children can use the note-taking tools to explore the text and highlight the more important parts.

Using Simple English Wikipedia and the iBooks app on the iPad

1. Open the Safari web browser. Into the address box, type 'simple.wikipedia.org'.

2. Once the Simple English Wikipedia home page has been displayed, enter a search word into it, for example, 'Gandhi'.

3. Once the page has been displayed, look at the menu on the left-hand side, select 'Print/export > Make a book'.

4. Select 'Start book creator' and, when returned to the Gandhi page, select 'Add this page to your book'.

5. Now either select hyperlinks from the page or type in new search words. Add three pages to the book.

6. Select 'Show book' and add a title and subtitle, for example, 'Gandhi' and the child's name could be the subtitle.

7. On the right-hand side, under the 'Download' menu, select 'e-book (EPUB)' and then the 'Download' button.

8. After a short wait, while the book is rendering (being made), a new title 'Rendering finished' appears at the top of the screen.

9. Select 'Download the file', on the next page select 'Open in "Books".

10. The book will open in the iBooks app. Select some text (by pressing and holding) and the tools, such as 'Highlight' and 'Note', are available to enable the children to annotate the text.

Year 5 Spring 2: *Kensuke's Kingdom*

Overview

● In the lessons, the children have been collecting information using online surveys and questionnaires. They have used the Socrative tool online. This tool is also available on tablet computers and the camera can be used to add to the questioning experience. A spreadsheet is another way the children can gather data and plot graphs quickly.

Resources

● Socrative app (by Socrative) available as a teacher app and a student app.
● Numbers (by Apple)

Lesson activities

● The Socrative tool can be accessed via the website (www.socrative.com/) and there are also tablet apps available. The children have used the tool in the lessons to create quizzes to ask each other questions about the *Kensuke's Kingdom* story.
● When creating a new quiz, they can add an image, downloaded from the World Wide Web or taken using a camera. An advantage of the tablet computers is that they contain a camera, which means an image can be captured and quickly and easily inserted into the quiz.

● A spreadsheet is another tool that can be used to collect data and then plot graphs (for example, Numbers by Apple or Excel by Microsoft).
● Now they have created a way of displaying a piece of work and getting feedback from their peers.

Using the Socrative app on the iPad

1. Open the Socrative app named 'Teacher'.

2. Login with the user's email address and password.

3. Select 'Manage quizzes' then 'Create a quiz' and enter a quiz name. The children could use this tool for feedback on a story they have written, for example.

4. Select 'Multiple choice' and enter the text for the question as 'The opening paragraph of my story grabs the reader's attention? Select 'A' for Strongly agree, 'B' for agree, 'C' for neither agree nor disagree, 'D' for disagree or 'E' for strongly disagree.

5. Select 'Add image' and press the 'Choose file' button. They can then take a photo of their opening paragraph.

6. Select 'Short answer' and enter the text 'How could I improve the opening paragraph?'

7. Save the quiz.

Year 5 Summer 1: Greek mythology (1)

Overview

● Using the Greek mythology theme, the children can use software to create a maze game. In order to learn about good game play, they can play lots of maze games on tablet computers. Some maze games allow the children to edit and develop a maze too.
● Other ways of simulating collisions between objects (similar to a character and a wall in a maze) could be using the Hopscotch app. It looks similar to the Scratch software and enables the character to be guided around the screen and respond when it 'bumps' into another character.

Resources

● 3D Mazes: Play, Create & Share app (by Andre Muis)
● Hopscotch app (by Hopscotch Technologies)

Lesson activities

● Using a maze game or app enables the children to think about the game player's experience.
● In the lessons, give the children time to deconstruct other people's games. This helps them to identify that the challenge is set at an appropriate level. For example, if the game was too difficult, then the player would give up; if too easy, the player may not enjoy the game.

● Using an app, such as Maze, they can view example games created by other players, test them out and then create their own game.
● A programing app, such as Hopscotch, could be used to simulate collisions between objects, like the player and an obstacle or a reward. For example, they can use the command 'When Monkey collides with...', and then an event can occur.

Using the 3D mazes app on the iPad

1. Open the Maze app and select the 'Mazes' button at the bottom of the screen. Select 'Highest rated' and try out several mazes.

2. Select the 'Create' button at the bottom of the screen.

3. Choose a size for the maze and continue.

4. Scroll the yellow bar to the right, to give the maze a name.

5. Scroll the yellow bar to the left, to begin to create the maze. Tap on a wall to change it or select a square to add a location type, such as a 'Start' and 'End' position.

6. Save the maze, then select 'Mazes'. On the main page, select 'Yours' at the top of the screen. Now try out the new maze that has been created.

Year 5 Summer 1: Greek mythology (2)

Overview
- In the lessons, the children have been learning about programming by giving precise instructions. There are a growing number of apps, which allow them to practise problem solving and being precise. An example is, A.L.E.X. for the iPad, where a robot is controlled to perform challenges, and it also enables the user to create levels.

Resources
- Light-bot (online Flash version http://light-bot. com/ or Light-bot Hour of Code is a free app)
- A.L.E.X. app (by AwesomeApps.com)

Lesson activities
- The children have previously used Light-bot, so another app such as, A.L.E.X. allows them to compare the game play.
- Similar to the maze games, give them time to explore and play games to experience whether the level of challenge is appropriate. The games often coach them through easier levels, slowly increasing the challenge and introducing new features.

Using the A.L.E.X. app on the iPad
1. Open the A.L.E.X. app and select 'Play'. Allow the children time to play through the basic levels.

2. At the end of a level, select 'Menu' and then 'Create'.

3. Choose 'Level 1', then 'Create'.

4. Using the floor pieces, make a challenge for another Year 5 child to solve.

5. Once complete and tested, the children can swap iPads and see if they can complete the level.

Year 5 Summer 2: The Arctic and the Antarctic

Overview
- Shackleton had great adventures and the children have been thinking about the places he visited and his routes. There are many apps designed for health and fitness that track a person's route and their speed. The children can explore how their movements can be tracked and think about the security of the data.

Resources
- Runmeter app by Abvio (requires internet or phone signal access)

Lesson activities
- Ask the children whether they know where they have been that day? Do they know how many steps they have taken or how fast they were going?
- Explain that there are many health and fitness apps that track a person's route, using GPS (global positioning system). This data can be used to help inform the user or motivate them towards a goal, for example 10,000 steps a day or a target number of calories burned.
- However, if the phone or tablet can collect this data, could it be used for the wrong purposes? For example, could a company track the movements of their workers without them knowing? Would this be ethical?

- Before the lesson, search online using the words 'app', 'sending' and 'data' and see the many articles where people express concern about mobile devices sharing information about their lives without permission. If an appropriate article can be shared, show an example to the children.

Using the Runmeter GPS app on the iPad
1. Open the app (this app requires access to the internet).

2. On the screen, the user can see a map of their location. Press the 'Start' button and then begin walking or running.

3. As you move, the app displays the run time, distance, pace and estimates the number of calories burned.

4. Modern athletes intently study data like this, in order to improve their training schedules and performance.

5. Selecting 'Graphs' from the menu from the left shows the data as a graph and includes an 'Elevation' graph.

6. Ask the children how Shackleton might have used data in his expeditions?

Year 6 Autumn 1: Great Journeys

Overview

- In the lessons, the children have been collaborating and sharing online. They have used Web 2.0 tools to create interactive resources, such as, Padlet sticky note walls (http://padlet.com/) and collaborated using Etherpad (http://etherpad.wikimedia.org/). Another tool is Thinglink, which is a web-based tool for adding links to an image.

Resources

- Thinglink app (by Thinglink). Available as an app and through the website http://thinglink.com

Lesson activities

- Using the Thinglink website or app, the children add links to an image. These may simply be text comments, hyperlinks to other websites or links to YouTube videos. These links help to annotate the image, making it much more interactive.
- There is an opportunity to use Thinglink as an assessment tool, where the children could demonstrate their knowledge about a subject.
- With the focus on Great Journeys, the children could annotate a map with information about the places or the events that occurred on routes of the journeys.

Using the Thinglink app on the iPad

1. Open the Thinglink app and select an image, from the camera roll (this could be a screenshot of a map).

2. The app prompts the user to add a link (a small circle with red and white concentric circles, indicates a link). It asks whether they want to 'Add text' or 'Add media'.

3. Drag the link circle to the appropriate place on the image and select 'Add text'. Details of the explorer's journey can be typed in.

4. The text added can be plain text or a URL link to another web page or a Twitter name. Select 'Done' and the circle remains, but the text is hidden.

5. Now tap on another place on the image and select 'Add media'.

6. The user is prompted to add media, with the instructions 'Take a video', 'Choose from gallery' or 'Add from YouTube'. They can add the media, such as recording a video about the explorer, by speaking directly into the camera.

7. Once finished, select 'Next' and add a title.

8. On the bottom right-hand side, ensure that the button 'Unlist on Thinkglink.com' is switched to 'On'.

9. Then select 'Save' to keep the image.

Year 6 Autumn 2: Fantasy Worlds (1)

Overview

- In the lessons, the children have been programming using the Alice software. They control an onscreen character, using their knowledge from their previous experiences of programming.
- On the tablet computers, there are several apps that allow a character to be moved by giving instructions. These apps include A.L.E.X. (by AwesomeApps.com), Hopscotch (by Hopscotch Technologies) or Snap! byob (http://snap.berkeley.edu/). In this example, they use Just2code, which contains a turtle graphics tool and a visual programming tool, similar to Scratch.

Resources

- A.L.E.X. app (by AwesomeApps.com)

Lesson activities

- The children have experienced using different programming tools, using blocks of instructions, to control the objects onscreen.
- They can apply their learning to other apps or programs. This will help to prepare them for programming in 'text-based' or 'syntax' languages, so they can apply their previous learning to a new situation.

Using the A.L.E.X. app on the iPad

1. Open the A.L.E.X app.

2. Slect Play and then choose a level (you can only choose levels you have completed already, so if this is your first go you will have to choose level 1).

3. Allow the children to complete a few levels. Ask the children: *How does this app compare with the Move the Turtle app you have used previously?*

4. Ask the children to compare their experiences of using Hopscotch, Scratch and the A.L.E.X app.

5. Can the children explain which versions of the software or apps they prefer or find easier to use?

Year 6 Autumn 2: Fantasy Worlds (2)

Overview

● Game-making software is useful for the children to create games. However, they need to play games to find out 'What makes a good game?' The process of breaking larger problems into smaller ones is called 'decomposition'.

● By playing games, they can recognise the elements that they enjoy, those that they find enjoyable and those that they find frustrating.

● There are games that have been specifically designed to teach programming through play.

Resources

● Hakitzu Elite: Robot Hackers app (by Kuato Games)

Lesson activities

● The Hakitzu Elite app aims to teach a text-based, programming language through its game play. The children control the robot in the game, by adding instructions, in the format of the Javascript programming language.

● The children play the game and, as each challenge arrives, they are led through modifying the code to progress.

● Ensure that they have time to play the game and also time to debrief, explaining to a partner or teacher what happened in the game.

● Learning Javascript will prepare the children for the transition to other languages such as Python. This is the language used with the Raspberry Pi computer.

Using the Hakitzu Elite app on the iPad

● Open the Hakitzu Elite app.

● The children will need to create a user login. They can choose to add a photo or skip a step.

● The app opens into 'Hakitzu Elite: Boot Camp Training' and they follow the instructions to learn the commands.

● They will see that the app is similar to programming apps in the way it move squares, but this time is using a text-based (syntax) language.

Year 6 Spring 1: Africa

Overview

● In the lessons, the children have been creating apps and using data. They have been thinking about the needs and user-experiences of the children using the apps.

● They have been introduced to the concept that different operating systems have accessibility features. Therefore, looking at the iPad's controls, they can try out the features and consider how they make it accessible.

Resources

● Accessibility features of iOS (https://www.apple.com/uk/accessibility/ios/)

Lesson activities

● Using the accessibility features on a tablet computer enables the children to customise their user experiences. They can adjust the text by changing the font or font size. They can enable the text to be read to them or even dictated into a word-processor.

● The children will also see that there are categories of 'Vision', 'Hearing', 'Physical & motor' and 'Learning'. This should raise questions with the children about the different users and their individual needs.

Using the accessibilty features on the iPad

1. Open the 'Settings' and select 'General' and then 'Accessibility'.

2. Under the heading 'Vision' the children can adjust the font size, to make it bolder and larger.

3. They can experiment with 'Invert colors' to see the pages with a black background and bright colours.

4. By selecting 'Speak selection', the iPad can read the text and highlight the words.

5. Further down the page, there is the 'Learning' section. Using 'Guided access', they can lock the user into a single app. Can they think why this feature may be useful?

Year 6 Spring 2: Evacuees (1)

Overview

● In the lessons, the children have been learning about e-safety and about the Second World War. Using the book, *Carrie's War*, they have been learning about the evacuee children and their experiences.

● The children will research into the lives of the evacuee children and empathise with them, by creating an animation and using a script to explain their experiences.

Resources

● Morfo app (by SunSpark Labs). Free to try, then a payment to enable the animated video to be saved.

Lesson activities

● The children research the lives of evacuee children online. They look for images of the faces of the children (specifically for an image of a child looking straight ahead, directly at the camera).

● Using the Morfo app, they add the image to an animation. Once the face has been fitted in the app, they plan the script, which they will use to describe the experiences of the children during the war.

Using the Morfo app on the iPad

1. Research online to find images of evacuee children (ideally, the face will be looking straight ahead, to enable the app to fit the template to the face).

2. Open the Morfo app.

3. Select 'Create' then 'Touch here to choose a photo'.

4. Choose the photo, then 'Done'.

5. Pinch and stretch the white outline, to fit it onto the photo face, then 'Done'.

6. Move the eyes, nose and mouth to fit, by dragging, pinching and stretching, then 'Finish'.

7. A voice recording can be added by selecting 'Record', then 'Start'. Record the voice of an evacuee child, sharing their experiences, during the war.

8. Play back the recording to see the face talk.

Year 6 Spring 2: Evacuees (2)

Overview

● In the lessons, the children are learning about e-safety and about the Second World War. During the wartime, street signs were removed, so people had to recognise places from memory.

● Augmented reality apps use the camera to recognise markers or images and then overlay information on top of them. For example, if an augmented reality app recognised a picture of an Apple logo, it could display a picture or video of an iPad. The apps can be used to add information to a scene.

Resources

● Aurasma (by Aurasma)

Lesson activities

● The children choose a topic about the Second World War to focus upon, for example, evacuees or the Blitz.

● They locate an image to represent the topic and research information about it.

● They record a short 30-second video to show their understanding of the topic.

● Using the Aurasma app, they add the video to be 'triggered' or played by the app.

● The children try out their apps, to see the videos being played, when the camera sees the image.

Using the Aurasma app on the iPad

1. Open the Aurasma app.

2. The children can create a username and password to log in.

3. The app may go straight to the 'Camera mode' to look for trigger images or 'Auras'. Select the 'Menu' at the bottom of the page.

4. A selection of examples will be displayed, for example, famous brand logos or magazine covers. Let the children see the types of images used.

5. From the bottom of the screen, select '+' and go into the 'Create' mode.

6. In the library, they will see a selection of pre-set overlays that they can choose from.

7. Select 'Device' and then '+' at the top to create a new aura. Select 'From camera' and the children can record a short video. Alternatively, select 'Photo roll' to choose from the camera roll.

8. They then photograph the trigger image, which their new overlay will appear upon.

9. Once added and given a name, the Aura will be created. Now when the camera sees the aura, it should show the overlay on top.

Year 6 Summer 1: Victorians

Overview

- In the lessons, the children have been learning about the Victorians and programming a game.
- They need to examine other games to evaluate what makes a good game.
- You can find history-themed apps, which use game play to educate the player about the Victorians.

Resources

- Full Steam Ahead app (by SS Great Britain Trust)

Lesson activities

- Using a Victorian-themed game app, the children learn through play. For example, the Full Steam Ahead app focuses on Brunel's ship, the SS Great Britain, to learn about his rail and engineering achievements.
- The children need time to explore the game, to design their ship's hull and then to test its shape.
- They need to understand how the scoring system works and also, where variables and two-way selection are part of the game.

Using the Full Steam Ahead app on the iPad

1. Open the Full Steam Ahead app.

2. Select 'New game' and 'Sink or swim'.

3. The children can design the shape of the ship's hull and see if it would be sea-worthy.

4. Can they improve on their score (by changing the variables of the ship's hull shape)?

5. They can then attempt the following tests and identify the variables (scores, materials, stability, time and so on).

6. Once they have completed each level, ask: *Which level did you enjoy the most and why? Was it the easiest or most challenging level? Did you understand what they needed to do? What were the variables?*

Year 6 Summer 2: Final project

Overview

- In the lessons, the children have been learning about controlling onscreen objects in a game. They need to experience different platforms to see how similar commands and instructions can be represented.
- The children can control an onscreen object using instructions.

Resources

- Gamespress app (by UntitledD)

Lesson activities

- By using game creation apps, the children consider the characters and then control them. They need to think about the properties of the characters and hence the rules, which dictate how they behave and interact.
- The 'behaviours' of the characters can be constructed through a series of modules (which can be pre-set or linked together), for example, 'Joystick controlled' or 'Tilt controlled'.
- The children need to carefully consider their plans for the game, so that when they add the components and commands, these behave as intended.

Using the Gamepress app on the iPad

1. Open the Gamepress app.

2. Users can skip the login, though setting up an account will allow them to continue with their game in another session.

3. Following the tutorial, the children are introduced to adding a character and controlling it with pre-programmed modules.

4. Once the tutorial has been completed, they can create their own game, by experimenting with new characters, backgrounds and events.

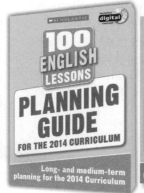
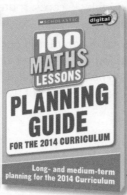
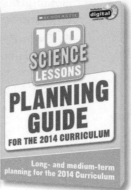

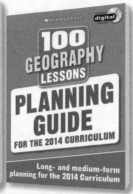
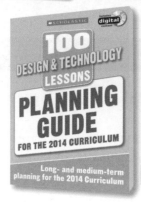

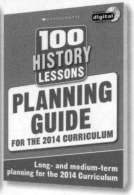